Aisling Corcoran

Aisling Corcoran
1 Maune place
Windmill Road
Cork

ECDL
The
Complete
Coursebook

GW00382991

ECDL
The Complete Coursebook

Brendan Munnelly

with:
John Fleming
Peter Hillary
Paul Holden
Siobhán Ní Chúlacháin

Gill & Macmillan

Gill & Macmillan Ltd
Goldenbridge
Dublin 8
with associated companies throughout the world
www.gillmacmillan.ie

© Rédacteurs Software Documentation Limited 1999

0 7171 2960 8

Print origination by Rédacteurs Software Documentation Limited

Printed by ColourBooks Ltd, Dublin

The paper used in this book is made from the wood pulp of managed forests. For every tree felled, at least one tree is planted, thereby renewing natural resources.

All rights reserved.

No part of this publication may be reproduced, copied or transmitted in any form or by any means without written permission of the publishers or else under the terms of any licence permitting limited copying issued by the Irish Copyright Licensing Agency, Writers' Centre, Parnell Square, Dublin 1.

Screen images reproduced by permission of Microsoft Corporation.
All trademarks in this book are acknowledged as the property of their respective owners.

A catalogue record is available for this book from the British Library.

Rédacteurs Software Documentation Limited is at www.redact.ie

Brendan Munnelly is at www.munnelly.com

Dedicated to
Robert, Andrew
and
Catherine Munnelly

Preface

Visit our Website

For sample exercises and solutions, updates to the ECDL syllabus and more, link to:

www.gillmacmillan.ie/ecdl

The European Computer Driving Licence (ECDL) is an internationally-recognised qualification in end-user computer skills. It is designed to give employers and job-seekers a standard against which they can measure competence – not in theory, but in practice. Its seven Modules cover the areas most frequently required in today's business environment.

In addition to its application in business, the ECDL has a social and cultural purpose. With the proliferation of computers into every aspect of modern life, there is a danger that society will break down into two groups – those who have access to computer power, and those who do not: the information 'haves', and the information 'have nots'. The seven modules of the ECDL are not difficult, but they equip anyone who passes them to participate actively and fully in the Information Society.

This book covers the entire ECDL syllabus. The ECDL is not product-specific – you can use any hardware or software to perform the tasks in the examinations. All the examples in this book are based on PCs (rather than Apple Macintoshes), and on Microsoft software, as follows:

- Microsoft Windows 95/98

- Microsoft Word 97

- Microsoft Excel 97

- Microsoft Access 97

- Microsoft PowerPoint 97

- Microsoft Internet Explorer 3.0 or higher
  or Netscape Navigator 3.0 or higher

If you use other hardware or software, you can use the principles discussed in this book, but the details of operation will differ.

Welcome to the world of computers!

Contents

Module 3: Word Processing   67

Section 3.1: Your First Letter in Word   68

Section 3.2: Formatting, Positioning and Copying Text 79

Section 3.3: Long Documents, Little Details 93

Section 3.4: Tables, Tabs and Graphics   *111*

Section 4.2: Arithmetic With Excel   *152*

Section 4.3: Formatting, Aligning and Moving Data   *164*

Section 4.4: More About Numbers, Text and Calculations — 178

Module 7: Information Network Services   271

Section 7.5: File-sharing and the World Wide Web — 301

Section 7.6: Browsing, Downloading and Searching — 312

Basic Concepts of Information Technology

Learning about computers for the first time is rather like learning about a foreign country. A land where words like *megabyte* and *peripheral* are part of the everyday conversation. The only crop grown and harvested is something called *data*. And it is important not only to be faster than your neighbour, but smaller too!

But you need to learn about this country. It was once an out-of-the-way place that attracted only handfuls of scientists to its shores. Now there is no more popular destination.

Like all good tourist guides, this Module introduces you gently to the more commonly-spoken words of the computer dialect. It points out the major landmarks (the hard disk, memory and processor are all places you need to take in). And it steers you away from the pitfalls that most offend native computer speakers – such as confusing an *operating system* with an *application program*.

Have a pleasant trip. And good luck!

Section 1.1: A Short History of Computing

From earliest times, people have counted things, measured things, kept records of things, and told other people about things. The 'things' could have been the number of sheep in a flock, the weight of a child, the size of a field, the length of time since the last drought, or the intensity of an earthquake.

From earliest times, people used tools and techniques to help them count more reliably, measure more accurately, record more indelibly, transmit more clearly. Think of measuring tapes, slide rules, sextants. Think of weighing scales, clocks, Newgrange. You get the idea.

The computer is simply the latest in this long line of calculating and recording machines. That's all it is. Everything we see computers doing today – and we see them doing a lot – they are doing because they can calculate and they can store the results of their calculations.

However, this principle is masked by an awesome practical fact: what they do may be simple, but they do an incredible amount of it, incredibly fast, and incredibly reliably. The speed of computers today is measured in millions of operations per second. The operations may be simple, but they can be combined in all sorts of ways to yield a vast array of useful functions.

This has almost all come about within the last thirty or forty years: that is the entire history of commercial computers. Before that, computers were used only in very specialist applications, such as military code-breaking.

In the 1960s, a commercial computer occupied a large air-conditioned room; it needed a team of specialists to operate it; it consumed vast amounts of electricity; and it frequently broke down.

All that changed with the advent of microelectronics and the so-called 'chip'. Chips enabled computers to be miniaturised: what previously took up a full room could fit into a small box. And as they got smaller, computers became faster; they could store more information; they consumed less power; and they became easier to operate.

To give you some idea of the speed of advance, the first personal computers (PCs) were launched in 1979, with a clock speed (don't worry about it – it's just how we measure the speed of computers) of about 5 MHz. Today, if you go out to buy a new PC, it is unlikely that you will be offered anything less than 400 MHz or even 500 MHz – eighty or one hundred times as fast. Similar progress has been made in the other main measure of computer power – storage capacity.

You don't need to know how this has been achieved, and you don't need to know all the details. However, you should be aware of the speed of progress and the main ways in which it is measured, so that if you go out to buy a computer, you will at least know what questions to ask, and will understand the answers.

Every year, computers are becoming smaller, faster, cheaper, more reliable, easier to use. This means that they are being used in all sorts of situations where it would previously have been impossible to use them: not only in business and government, but also in education, entertainment, health care, sport, art and design. You see computers in homes, clubs, and restaurants; you *don't* see them (but they are there) in car engines, in bank automatic teller machines, in supermarket checkouts, in washing machines, in telephone systems, in video recorders. You are probably wearing one at this moment, on your wrist, buried inside your watch.

You're surrounded.

But you're *not* under threat: computers are machines, tools. They are designed by people to meet people's needs; they are operated by people. People turn them on. People turn them off.

People like you.

The ECDL is designed to take the fear out of computing, to give you the knowledge and the skills you need to use this technology. With this book, you will learn about the most common PC applications. You won't learn everything: it is not necessary to know everything – nobody does. What this book aims to do is to teach you *enough* – enough to perform most of the tasks that most people do most of the time, and to give you enough confidence to tackle the unknown, and to learn from experience.

Section 1.2: What Computers Are Used For

Let's take a quick look at some of the ways in which computers are used, and the effects they have on our lives.

Business and Administration

Most offices today are dependent on computers. Computers are used to keep accounts, to send invoices, to maintain records of customers and suppliers, to hold details of stock, to calculate payroll, to write and edit letters, memos and reports, to design sales presentations, to communicate with other companies, to collect market intelligence, to collaborate with others in research activities.

Computers are also used in more complex business processes, such as resource planning, scheduling, route planning, customer relationship management, sales analysis, and simulation.

Computers are particularly useful where there are large volumes of data to be maintained, analysed, stored and filtered, or where complex or repetitive calculations have to be performed.

Industry

In manufacturing industry, the range of applications includes all of the administrative functions mentioned above, and a whole lot more besides. Computers are used to schedule production, to monitor raw material usage and finished product quality, to control machine tools, to design new products, to minimise waste, to determine optimum stock levels.

In the most automated plants, computers are used to collect orders from customers, to issue instructions to build the required products to the customer's specifications, to automatically order the parts and materials from the relevant subsuppliers (having first checked that they can deliver on time), and to schedule the plant and personnel necessary for satisfying the customer's order.

Retailing

In supermarkets, and increasingly in smaller shops, computers are used at the checkout to scan the bar codes on your purchases, and to calculate your bill. In many stores, the information on your purchases is passed immediately to the warehouse, and orders for replacement stock are generated automatically when stock falls below a given point. Instructions can also be generated for the personnel responsible for stacking the shelves, so that the products are always available. This technology enables the supermarket to keep its stock to the minimum necessary to satisfy its customers, instead of having money tied up unnecessarily in stock and storage space.

Home

In the home, computers have found a wide variety of uses – for playing games (most often), for keeping household accounts, for getting information over the Internet (to research ancient history for a homework project or for checking the scores in the Italian football league), for sending e-mail to friends and relatives abroad – the list grows every day, and the only limit is imagination.

Schools

When you hear about young people using computers in schools, you may think they are doing something very technical, like programming, or electronics. They very seldom are.

The main uses for computers in schools are in the traditional subject areas. There is a lot of educational software available that presents school subjects in a structured and entertaining way. Some students respond better to information presented this way, and computers also enable each student to progress at his or her own pace – the computer will repeat lessons as often as necessary, without losing patience!

In addition, the computer opens up the school to the outside world. Students can retrieve information from libraries, universities, government agencies, voluntary bodies, news organisations, and other sources. They can communicate with students in other countries, and co-operate with them on research projects. They can take lessons from world experts without leaving their classroom.

In some science subjects, computers can be used to simulate experiments which are either dangerous or expensive. This enables the students to learn without exposing themselves to the dangers, or without incurring the costs of the materials of equipment involved in the experiment.

Students can also use the computer to write reports, produce school newsletters, and design posters.

Health Care

The administration of hospitals depends more and more on computers. In fact, many of the applications are similar to manufacturing: scheduling expensive and scarce equipment, drawing up rosters, making appointments for patients, etc. In addition, computers are used for monitoring patients' conditions and alerting staff when abnormalities arise. Computers also allow doctors to keep comprehensive patient records, and to conduct research into the effectiveness of different treatments.

Research is also heavily dependent on computing power: most modern drugs are designed with the aid of computers and manufactured under computer control. The Human Genome Project, which promises major breakthroughs in the treatment of genetic disorders, would simply be impossible without very powerful computers.

Computers and communications technology is also being used for delivering health services to remote regions: the patient can connect to a major centre (or a centre of specialist expertise) for diagnosis and, in some cases, for treatment. This development is expected to yield significant cost-savings and better treatment for patients in the coming years.

Everyday Life

You would recognise the computers used in the applications outlined so far. However, computer technology is also used in less visible ways. It is a computer that controls the cycles in your washing machine, a computer that controls the timer in your video recorder, a computer that controls the sequences of the traffic lights, a computer that delivers money through an Automatic Teller Machine, a computer that controls the supply of fuel to your car engine. Almost anywhere you see something happening 'automatically', there is a computer at its heart, monitoring the outside world (i.e. you), and responding to it.

Information Technology and Society

Some people find this proliferation of computers somewhat disturbing. Is there no aspect of our lives that is untouched by computers? Are computers replacing people, creating unemployment? Are all uses of computers good, or are computers being used to manipulate and control us? Are all computer-assisted services, and all computer-manufactured goods better than their predecessors?

These questions don't have clear-cut answers.

From the examples above, you probably agree that the society we live in uses computers a lot, that many of the goods we consume, and many of the services we use would not be available without computers. Like it or not, we *are* living in the Computer Age, or the Information Age, or the Digital Age (take your pick), and our society can justifiably be called an Information Society. In essence this means that value in the society comes from information. In the Age of Agriculture, most of the work, and most of the value, related to food production. In the Industrial Age, it was manufacturing that defined the society: the availability of food was almost taken for granted; proportionately less time and effort went into ensuring the food supply to the individual. Value, wealth and incomes depended more on manufactured goods.

In recent years, the balance has shifted again, this time towards service occupations, office-based occupations, in which information, knowledge, and intelligence play the key role. The emphasis has been transferred from brawn to brain. And in this new economy, computers play a critical, central role.

It is worth asking, however, whether all uses of computers are good. We can see the benefit of using computers, for example, to process bank transactions. Would we be equally happy to let computers decide loan approvals? Routine administration of, say, parking fines could usefully be delegated to computers, but what about putting computer systems in the role of judges in court? In medicine and health care, there are many obvious useful applications, and there are other applications that make many people uncomfortable.

In the world of art, there are also difficulties: does computer-generated 'art' deserve the name? Can a computer write poetry, make paintings, compose music? And should we judge these 'creations' by the same criteria that we judge work made by humans?

As we said, these questions do not have clear-cut answers. But it is worth thinking about them, because they are becoming increasingly relevant to everyday life.

Participation in the Information Society

Computers and related technologies are touching our lives from the time the electronic alarm clock wakes us up to the time we use the remote control to turn off the television at night. We can respond as passive consumers of entertainment and advertising, or by becoming active participants in this society.

Participation means exercising choice: choice about what information we get, when we get it, in what form we get it, and how we use it. It means analysing the information for relevance, salience, accuracy. It means deciding what to keep, and what to discard. It means deciding what to produce: what to publish, to whom you publish it, in what form, and at what time.

The idea of the ECDL – and the idea of this book – is to enable you to use some of the tools necessary for this kind of active participation in the Information Society.

However, you already have the most important tools, and you know how to use them: your natural intelligence, your critical faculties, the ability to judge whether something makes sense or is rubbish. No amount of technology can replace these, and you should never be blinded by technological wizardry so that you doubt these innate talents.

Section 1.3: Down to Business:
What Exactly Is a Computer?

In This Section

In this Section, you will learn what a computer is, what its component parts are, and what they are for. You will learn the difference between hardware and software. You will learn how software is made. You will learn what the most valuable part of a computer system is – the data. And you will learn how to look after the hardware, the software and the data.

New Words

In this Section we will start using some of the dreaded jargon of computing. Most of the new terms or ideas are introduced by placing them in *italics*.

The Trouble with Definitions

It is relatively easy to define a washing machine, or a motor car, or a telephone: these devices may be complicated and technologically advanced, but we can talk about them in terms of what they do. They wash clothes, transport people from A to B, enable people to hold conversations with one another over a distance.

As we saw in the previous section, a computer can be used for almost anything – including controlling the different washing cycles in a washing machine.

In fact, the first part of our definition of a computer recognises this fact: computers are *general purpose* machines.

When you flick the light switch, the light comes on: you could say that the light has obeyed your instruction. Well, computers respond in the same way to instructions: these instructions are called *programs*. And programs are written to make computers behave in specific ways: to act as word processors or to control generating stations. Computers are *programmable*.

We could leave our definition at that, but it will help to add two other ideas: computers can *calculate* and they can *store* the results of their calculations.

Computer
A computer is a general-purpose, programmable device that is capable of calculating and storing results.

One way of thinking about a computer is as a 'black box' that accepts input on one side, processes it in some way, and then produces output on the other side.

The input might be a mathematical problem, the supplier invoices for the month, a search for a good restaurant in Tullamore, or the temperature of a furnace. The output might be the answer to the mathematical problem, the cheques to pay the invoices, the name and address of the restaurant, or the instructions to shut the control valves on the fuel supply.

What goes on inside the black box is called *processing*: the manipulation of the input necessary to produce the output.

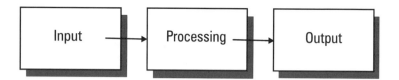

However, the black box is not magic: everything – *everything* – going into a computer is first converted into numbers, and all forms of output – including text on the page, graphics on the screen, music, even telephone conversations – have to be converted into their final form from numbers. In the middle, inside the black box, the numbers are added together in various ways and combinations, under a set of rules called a program. The only magic is the fact that these calculations take place at a rate of millions per second – and, of course, the human ingenuity in the design and the programming.

Computer systems consist of two very different types of elements: *hardware*, which includes all the physical things that you can touch, feel, weigh, and, on rare occasions, kick, and *software*, which is the intangible information component – the instructions, or programs, that tell the hardware how to behave.

Hardware

If you go out to buy a computer, you will immediately be faced with a range of options that even experienced computer people find bewildering. Concentrate on two things: speed and capacity.

Processor

The length of time it takes a computer to perform a task depends on a number of factors. The first of these is the speed of the processor – the chip at the heart of the computer. This is measured in MegaHertz (MHz), and the bigger the number, the faster the processor (the more calculations it can perform per second).

This measure of the computer's performance is so critical, that it is usually included in the name of the computer. So the Dell Dimension R450, for example, includes the Intel Pentium II 450MHz processor.

The processor chip and the electronics that support it are referred to as the *Central Processing Unit* (CPU).

Memory

Our definition of a computer includes the idea of storage: the computer has to be able to store the results of its calculations. In practice, a computer has to store a huge amount of information, and it has a number of different kinds of memory, two of which are regularly cited in the advertisements for computers: RAM and disk space.

Random Access Memory (RAM) is used by the computer as a sort of working area while it is carrying out a given task. (It is often called *working storage*.) Here it holds the list of instructions that it is currently working on, the data on which it is working, and the interim results of its calculations. The 'R' in RAM is its main advantage: it can be accessed randomly, which means that the computer can get at any piece of it directly – it does not have to look through it from the start until it finds the piece of interest. This makes it fast.

In general, the more RAM the better, and a certain minimum is required for many programs. RAM is often called *main memory*.

Memory capacity is measured in *bytes*. One byte consists of eight *bits*. You can think of a bit in electrical terms as a switch: on or off, or in mathematical terms as a single binary number: 0 or 1. Eight of these – a byte – can represent a letter of the alphabet, or a single number. You are likely to be offered a new computer with at least 32 megabytes (32 MB – 32 million bytes) of RAM. (This is twice as much as you would have been offered for the same price last year, and probably half as much as you will be offered this time next year.)

RAM should not be confused with another kind of memory that you may occasionally hear of: ROM (Read Only Memory). This is where the computer stores its low-level programs – the ones that tell it how to behave, how to check its own circuitry, how to treat various kinds of input devices, and so on. ROM differs from RAM in two ways: first, it is not changed after the computer is assembled (you can read it, but not write to it), and second, its contents remain unchanged even when the power is turned off.

(RAM is *volatile* – its contents are erased if the power supply is cut off.)

It is relatively easy to upgrade the memory on your computer by buying additional memory chips. They are inexpensive and easy to install. Depending on what you are using your computer for, additional memory can make a huge difference to its performance. (Don't, however, attempt to install additional memory without expert guidance.)

Disks and Diskettes

After processor speed and amount of RAM, the next major determinant of computer power is the amount of disk space. A disk is a device for storing information. It is very different from RAM, for a number of reasons.

First, disks record information magnetically, in much the same way as music tapes or video tapes. They are not volatile: once the information is recorded, it remains on the disk until it is changed or deleted.

Second, the process of getting information onto a disk or retrieving information from a disk involves mechanical movement. The disk revolves at a constant high speed, and a *read/write head* moves in and out just above the surface of the disk. The read/write head can change the polarisation of tiny magnetic particles on the surface of the disk, and can detect the polarisation of particles. Moving parts eventually wear out and as a result, disks are more likely to malfunction than non-moving RAM.

The moving parts also introduce delays into the processes of reading and writing, whereas reading from RAM is almost instantaneous.

Like memory capacity, disk capacity is measured in *bytes*. Disk capacity is bigger by several orders of magnitude: a new computer today will typically come with a 3 gigabyte disk (3 GB – 3 billion bytes).

Let's consider that slowly. 3,000,000,000 bytes. The 32 volumes of *Encyclopaedia Brittanica* contain approximately 44,000,000 words, or approximately 220,000,000 characters (bytes). A 3 GB disk could hold that text almost fourteen times, yet it only weighs about 1 kilogram, and takes up less space than one of the encyclopaedia's volumes. The amount of information that a disk can hold is the third performance measure that you should consider when buying a computer.

Removable Storage

The disks described above are built in to the computer. They are often called *hard disks*. Another kind of disk is the so-called 'floppy disk' or *diskette*. (Early removable disks were housed in flexible envelopes, which earned them the name 'floppy'; the more recent design, with which you are probably familiar, uses a hard plastic shell with a sliding metal cover.)

The most common type of diskette holds 1.4 MB. This is enough to hold a typical document, for example, so that it can easily be passed from one person to another. You can use a diskette to transfer a document from your office computer to your home computer – simply copy the document to the diskette, and bring it home in your pocket. The entire text of this book (but not the graphics) fits onto a single diskette, with room to spare.

Just as RAM is often referred to as 'working storage' or 'main memory', disks and diskettes are often called 'backing storage', or 'secondary storage'.

CD-ROM

Until quite recently, diskettes were also the principal way of loading programs onto a computer. Nowadays, however, software is most often supplied on CD-ROM (Compact Disk Read Only Memory). Physically, a CD-ROM is indistinguishable from a music CD, and in fact CD readers in computers are almost all capable of playing music CDs.

The move from diskette to CD-ROM as the favoured medium for distributing software has taken place mainly because of the size of modern software systems: they need more storage space. (Part of this is because of added functionality; part is because the programs are more graphic in design, and may include other multimedia elements.) And a CD-ROM can hold as much information as 700 diskettes – about 650 MB.

CD-ROM drives (the part of the computer that reads CD-ROMs) are now offered as standard on all new computers. The only performance measure to watch out for is the speed of the drive, always quoted as a multiple of the normal music CD player speed: nowadays, 24x speed or 32x speed CD-ROM drives are normal.

CD-ROMs are now being overtaken by DVDs (Digital Versatile Disk), which look similar, but have a great deal more storage capacity – up to 3.9 gigabytes or GB.

To record information on a CD, you need a CD Writer. Information is encoded on the surface of CDs as tiny holes, which are detected by a laser beam.

Remember, however, that CDs differ from magnetic disks (hard disks and diskettes), in that the holes burnt into the read/write surface of the CD are permanent: once burnt, they cannot be changed or erased (hence Read Only Memory). Magnetic media, on the other hand, can be changed at will. For this reason, disks will continue to be the favoured media for storing information in normal office applications.

Other Storage Media

We have dealt with the most common storage media, but there are others. Magnetic tape – usually in cassettes not unlike music cassettes – is used for distributing software and for keeping backup copies of large volumes of data. It is less useful in normal everyday use, because it cannot be accessed randomly: the computer has to read it through from the beginning to find the part of interest.

High-capacity removable diskettes are gaining favour for keeping backups and for transferring large files between computers. Some use magnetic technology, some laser technology.

In the Box

All the parts of the computer described above – the processor, the RAM and ROM, the hard disk, the diskette drive, and the CD-ROM drive – are normally housed in a single beige or grey box – usually called the system unit. This can stand vertically on the floor (a *tower*), or horizontally on the desk, usually with the screen on top (a *desktop* unit). A *laptop* or *notebook* computer is a more compact, portable unit, which usually has a flat screen built in to a hinged lid.

Inside the system unit are the power supply and a fan that is designed to keep the whole thing cool – this is responsible for the hum from the computer when you turn it on. There are various other bits of electronics that control the other parts of the system, described below, but in essence, that's the computer.

Out of the Box: Peripherals

Everything else is peripheral – which is why all the other things are called *peripherals*. (Here we're cheating a little: technically, all secondary storage, such as disks, CD-ROMs, etc. are considered to be peripheral as well.)

In most computer systems, the three essential peripherals are the keyboard and mouse (used for input), and the screen (used for output).

Keyboard

A keyboard is a set of typewriter-like keys that enables you, the user, to enter information and instructions into a computer. Keys on a computer keyboard are of three types:

- **Alphanumeric keys**: Letters and numbers
- **Punctuation keys**: Comma, full stop, semicolon, and so on
- **Special keys**: Function keys, control keys, arrow keys, Caps Lock key, and so on

Screen

The screen is the thing that looks like a television. It is also called the *monitor*, because you use it to monitor what is going on in the computer. Most programs are designed in such a way that you appear to enter input directly from the keyboard onto the screen – in fact, you enter it into the processor, and the processor shows you what it has received by displaying it on the screen. Most programs also give you constant feedback on their progress, and display their output on the screen.

Mouse

Many programs present themselves on the screen as Graphical User Interfaces (GUI – pronounced, believe it or not, 'gooey'). A GUI represents programs, files, and functions as pictures on the screen. The GUI includes a pointer that you can move around the screen until it is at the picture that represents what you want to do. You then indicate your intention, and the program responds accordingly.

Well, the mouse is the tool that you use to move the pointer around the screen. The underside of the mouse houses a ball, and movements of the mouse over your desk are detected and converted into movements of the pointer: move the mouse left, the pointer moves left; right, and the pointer moves right; push the mouse away from you, and the pointer moves up the screen; pull it towards you, the pointer moves down. After a very short time it becomes second nature.

Note that the ball only moves (and therefore the pointer only moves) when the underside of the mouse is in contact with the desk, so you can move the pointer a long distance in one direction by making a succession of short moves in that direction with the mouse, each time lifting the mouse so that the return journey does not affect the position of the pointer.

The mouse has two or three buttons on top: these are used to signal to the computer that the pointer is correctly positioned – you have arrived where you want to go. You press one or other button once (called a *click*), or twice in quick succession (called a *double click*).

Other Pointing Devices

Mice are by far the most common pointing devices, but there are others.

Trackballs are like upside-down mice: you move the pointer by manipulating a ball in a special housing with your fingers. They are useful in situations where desk space is limited.

Joysticks and *Games Controllers* fulfil the same function, but are designed specially for games and simulation.

Most portable computers have a device built in to the keyboard for moving the pointer, either in the form of a miniature joystick, or a pressure-sensitive pad that detects movements of your finger.

The mouse (or whatever pointing device you use) makes operation of the computer very easy, and even intuitive, but it is very seldom absolutely necessary: most programs allow you to move the pointer around the screen and choose your options using special keys or combinations of keys on the keyboard. Some users prefer this: it means they can do all their work from the keyboard – they don't have to switch back and forth between the keyboard and the mouse.

Printers

The screen is one way for the computer to show you the results of its work. But few users are satisfied without printed output of some kind, and so most computers are connected to some sort of printer.

There are several kinds of printer on the market: the two most common are *laser printers* and *inkjet printers*.

Laser printers use a technology similar to that used in photocopying to transfer the image of a page onto paper. The image is 'drawn' under instruction from the computer.

Inkjet printers have a moving 'pen' (the *write head*) that holds an ink cartridge. This moves back and forth over the page and, under computer control, ejects a minute quantity of ink at the precise point where it is required on the page.

Some of the things you should consider when buying a printer are:

Speed of output: Most laser printers can print 8 or 12 pages a minute. This speed may depend on what exactly you are printing: graphics, or text pages with a variety of different fonts, tend to be slower. If you need a faster printer, be prepared to pay a lot more.

Inkjet printers are generally a lot slower than laser printers, but their speed doesn't depend on what you are printing. The quality of the print tends to vary, as they rely on a moving write head.

Colour: If you want colour output, you have to buy a colour printer. It's that simple. Colour laser printers are expensive; colour inkjet printers are only slightly more expensive than black-and-white printers.

Some colour printers use three different inks to produce their output, some four. Some use a combined three- or four-colour cartridge, some a separate cartridge for each colour. Your choice depends on what you are using the printer for. If you are only occasionally using colour output, make sure you have a separate black cartridge: the density of the black printout from a black cartridge is much higher than that from a combination of colours; and if you get a combined four-colour cartridge, you will be throwing out the almost-full colour inks just because you have run out of black.

Cost of Consumables: The initial cost of the printer is only one of the cost factors that you need to consider: ink cartridges (for inkjet printers) and toner cartridges (for laser printers) have to be replaced regularly, and it is worthwhile calculating the cost per page of output before making your final decision.

Other Kinds of Printer

You will occasionally come across a third category of printer: impact printers. These work like a typewriter: they hammer out the required characters onto the page through an ink-impregnated (or carbon-covered) ribbon. There are several kinds, using slightly different techniques for making the marks on the paper: dot matrix printers, daisy wheel printers, line printers. Nowadays their use is confined to specialist applications (printing receipts from cash registers, printing the time of arrival on a ticket in a car park) or high-volume printouts that do not use graphics (tax forms, electricity bills).

Other Peripherals

A wide range of other devices can be connected to your computer for input or output.

Scanner: Works like half a photocopier – it copies a photograph, drawing, or page of text into the computer, where you can use a program to manipulate it. For example, you can include a scanned drawing in a newsletter, or use *Optical Character Recognition* software to decipher the text, and use all or part of it in a word-processing document (without having to re-type it).

Modem: Used to connect your computer to the telephone network, so that you can send e-mail, or use the Internet. Modems can be supplied as external devices, or built-in to the system unit. With most modems, you can enable your computer to function as a fax machine (although, unless you have a scanner, you are limited to sending text-only faxes).

Loudspeakers: Standard equipment on almost all new computers. Used to play music and other sounds.

Multimedia

Computers can manipulate any kind of data that can be converted into numbers. And that includes music, pictures, animated drawings, video, and speech. A range of applications has grown up around this capability, in which text, video, and sound are mixed to deliver instruction, information, or entertainment. These applications are called *multimedia applications*, and a computer that can run them is often called a *multimedia computer*. Most computers nowadays can run these applications, but if this is your main interest, you may want to consider a computer with a larger screen, and more advanced sound generation and video display capabilities.

Cables

We have described a number of different physical units. The peripheral devices are all connected to the system unit by cable, and the system unit is plugged into the electricity socket. On some models, the screen takes its electricity supply from the system unit; in others it plugs directly into the electricity socket.

Cards and Ports

Other hardware-related terms you may come across include:

Card: Inside the system unit, many of the pieces of electronics that control specific functions are located on self-contained *cards*. Examples include the video controller (which sends the signals to the screen), the sound card, the hard disk control card, the (internal) modem. A network card may be installed, which enables your computer to connect to other computers in your organisation.

Port: When you connect a printer, scanner, or other external device to the computer, you plug the cable into a *port* at the back of the system unit. Ports come in two flavours: serial and parallel. Parallel ports are sometimes labelled with a picture of a printer, serial ports with a series of 1s and 0s. It may look confusing, but it is hard to plug something in to the wrong port: the shape and size of the connector is different for each kind.

Looking After Your Hardware

Modern computers are robust and reliable: once they start working, they tend to go on working. But you should remember that they are sensitive instruments, and avoid testing their tolerance.

DO give your computer room to breathe: it has to have access to fresh air so that the fan can keep the electronics cool.

DON'T block the air vents by stacking books or magazines or (worse) draping clothes over the back of the computer.

DO keep the computer dry. Excessive moisture can play havoc with electric circuitry.

DON'T eat or drink while using your computer: crumbs can clog up your keyboard. A spilt cup of coffee can wreck your computer and (probably worse) cause the loss of all your files stored on the computer.

DO keep your computer free of dust: you will notice that it tends to attract dust. Clean the air vents occasionally, and use an anti-static wipe on the screen.

DON'T expose your computer to extremes of temperature.

DO shut down the computer in an orderly fashion, by systematically closing the applications you have opened.

DON'T just switch it off or pull the plug from the socket.

DO keep diskettes away from the screen: the strong magnetic field generated by the screen may erase or change some of the data.

DON'T move the system unit while the computer is in operation – you risk damaging the hard disk drive.

When Something Goes Wrong

You are more likely to be a computer user than a computer engineer. Therefore respect your PC as a delicate instrument – if it seems to be malfunctioning, don't try to fix it. You risk destroying it or electrocuting yourself. Always call a person qualified to deal with the problem.

Software

Software is the intangible side of computing: it is the generic name given to all the programs – the sets of instructions – that determine how the computer behaves.

We distinguish between two kinds of software: *system software* which is concerned with the computer itself – what devices it can control, how it manages files and storage, how it deals with exceptional conditions, and *applications software*, which is concerned with the world outside the computer – the world of business, entertainment, or education.

System Software

The main piece of system software that we are concerned with is the *Operating System* (OS). This is the driving program of the PC: without it, the PC would be virtually unusable. All other programs depend on the OS to communicate with and control the hardware. The OS also controls the timing of different events, to make sure they happen in the correct sequence, and manages access to data, to ensure security and integrity.

When you add a new piece of hardware to your system, you might have to load a special piece of software called a *driver* to enable the operating system to control the hardware.

Older PCs use an operating system call DOS (Disk Operating System). To use DOS, you have to type in commands, such as DIR, COPY, or REN.

More recent computers present their operating system through a Graphical User Interface (GUI). The GUI represents all the computer's resources – the hardware resources, such as disks and printers, the software resources, including both system software and application programs, and the data files on which you can work – as small pictures or symbols called *icons*. You use the mouse to move the pointer to the icon representing the object you want to use, and press (or *click*) the mouse button to signal your wish. This is considerably easier than having to remember a command and typing it accurately.

Application Software

Nobody wants to use a lawnmower or a telephone or a satellite: what they want to do is cut the grass, talk to their friends, or predict the weather. Similarly, you don't really want to use a computer: you want use a computer to do *something else*. That 'something else' is your application, and the program that enables you to do it is called the *application program*.

By the time you have finished this book you will be able to use several application programs: wordprocessing, spreadsheets, electronic mail, and so on.

In the previous section, we looked at various areas of business, administration, education, entertainment, and communication. These are applications.

Some application programs are very common – it is hard to find an office that doesn't use Microsoft Word or Excel or various Internet browsers such as Netscape Navigator or Microsoft Explorer. Many computers are sold with these applications pre-loaded.

Other applications are developed for more specialised tasks. People and organisations purchase these in accordance with their particular needs. An architect might use a sophisticated drawing package to design houses; a submarine builder might purchase a piece of project management software to help keep track of the thousands of components.

How Software Is Made

The development of any software system involves a cycle of research, analysis, development, and testing, involving the following types of people:

Systems Analysts: These study the business processes that the software is intended to support, and produce the design for the software. They decide what the software should do (but not necessarily how it should do it). You can think of the systems analyst as the software architect. Systems analysts are focused on the needs of the users and the application area.

Programmers: These translate the design into a working program. They write instructions that tell the computer what to do in order to accomplish the task for which the system is intended. You can think of the programmer as the software builder. Programmers are focused on the computer, its capabilities and its limitations.

Software Copyright

In general, software is *licensed* rather than sold. When you buy a software package, you don't actually own the software: you gain the right to use it under specified conditions.

In general, software is easy to duplicate, so it is easy for unscrupulous people to make unauthorised copies: don't do it. It's piracy; it's illegal; and it deprives an individual developer or a company of their rightful income, which they need to produce the next version of that piece of software, or the next application that you will want to use.

Don't accept software from dubious sources, whether in person, by mail-order, or over the Internet. You are responsible for the legality of the software that you use.

Some software, called *freeware* is distributed without charge: you find it on disks given away with magazines, or download it from the Internet. Again, you should be clear about the terms of use: in most cases, you can use it, but you may not, for example, sell it for profit, change it in any way, or label it as if it was your own product.

Other software is called *shareware*. It is widely distributed in much the same way as freeware. You can try it out, but if you decide to use it, you are expected to send a licence fee to the developer. In some cases, this is based on honour; in other cases, the shareware version will not function after a time period (typically 30 days), or certain functions are disabled in some way. When you register with the developer and send the licence fee, you are given a fully working copy of the software, or a password to unlock the disabled functions.

Problems with Software

Software – even the smallest piece of application software – is complex. It is difficult to test thoroughly, because it is difficult to imagine every possible input in every possible combination. Sometimes mistakes are made, or unusual circumstances are not adequately catered for by the designers or programmers.

When the software produces incorrect or unexpected results, it is said to have a *bug*. Bugs can range from minor irritations, where, for example, the screen displays are inconsistent, through significant errors, such as incorrect totals on invoices, to total collapse.

When the computer 'freezes' – it ceases to function, refuses to accept any input, won't produce any output – we say that it *hangs*. When this happens, you have to resort to an old trick: press three of the keyboard keys simultaneously – CTRL, ALT, and DEL. Most of the time, this will enable you to shut down the offending program, and continue working on something else.

Very occasionally, a bug will cause the whole system to *crash*, when the only solution is to turn off the power, wait a minute, and then turn it on again. A quicker way to achieve the same end is to press the Reset button on your system unit. Treat this as a last resort, however: you will lose any work since you last saved in all the applications you have open at the time.

Data

We haven't yet dealt in any detail with data. Data is another intangible in a computer system, but it is not generally built by the software developer. It's built by users – people like you.

So to write a letter, you need a keyboard, a screen, and a printer (hardware), and you need a wordprocessing program (software). The letter itself, and the name and address of the recipient, is *data*.

Data is held on a computer system in *files*. Files are organised into *directories* (otherwise known as *folders*).

Files and directories are given *names*, so that you can find them and recognise them when you need them, and, equally important, so that the operating system can find them and work on them when it needs to.

Looking After Your Data

In most computer systems, the data is the most important element. Hardware and software are easily replaced if they break down, or are lost or stolen. Data can represent years of work, and may be irreplaceable. So it makes sense to look after it.

Data can be lost, corrupted, damaged, or abused in a variety of ways, accidentally or deliberately.

Security and Passwords

You can protect your data against theft, corruption, and prying eyes by using a system of *passwords*. Depending on the application, you can use passwords to decide who can see the data and who can change it.

Most applications allow you to choose your own password, and encourage you to change it frequently. Choose a password that is not too obvious – if it is easy to guess, its purpose may be defeated. However, choose a password that is easy to remember: if you forget it, you may not be able to get at your own data, and if you write it down, it may be discovered and used by someone else.

Backups

Files can be lost or destroyed accidentally. The hard disk may develop problems, or the whole office may be destroyed by fire. You can protect yourself against these nightmare scenarios by keeping backup copies of all your data files, on diskette or another removable medium, and storing it safely at home or at another location. That way, even in the worst situation, you can be up and running very quickly after a disaster.

Save Frequently

You should also save your work at regular intervals while you are working. Remember that the computer works on your data in working storage, which is volatile: if there is a power cut, or if someone accidentally unplugs your PC, everything you have done since you last saved will be lost. It is a good discipline to save after every paragraph of text, or after you have done any complex operation.

Viruses

Computer viruses are attempts at sabotage. They are clever but poisonous programs written by malicious software developers and amateur hacks who have nothing better to do. They attack the integrity of your files, and are designed to transfer easily and stealthily from one computer to another. Their effects vary from minor irritation (where a message is displayed on your screen, but no files are damaged), through inconvenience (where one or more files are affected), to total disaster (where the entire hard disk is rendered unusable).

Viruses are spread through e-mail attachments and the exchange of infected diskettes. So: never open an e-mail attachment if you are unsure of its origin, and always use virus scanning software to check any diskette that comes into your organisation from outside.

Prevention is better than cure: make sure that you install reputable anti-virus software on your computer that will automatically scan your disks (hard drive and diskette), and detect and remove any viruses found. Anti-virus software must be kept up to date – new viruses are being concocted all the time, and the software used to detect them needs to be the very latest.

Data Copyright

Remember that computer data carries the same copyright rights and responsibilities as printed works or musical compositions: someone created it, and they own it. If you download information from the Internet, you may not have the right to include it in your own publications without the consent of the author or creator.

Data Protection

We all appear in numerous databases: banks, insurance companies, educational institutions, employers, and governments all hold files full of personal information. Our date of birth, address and marital status, our incomes, credit and educational records, our health, criminal and bill-paying histories are all known by various institutions. This information is sometimes general, sometimes special. It may be sensitive and, in the wrong hands, damaging or dangerous.

Marketing departments are willing to pay large sums of money for name and address databases of specific categories of people – this enables them to target products and services at precise sectors of the population.

It follows that the collection, maintenance, and protection of information is a responsibility that demands great respect. Wrong or misleading information could lead to a person being refused a mortgage, a job, an overseas work visa, or medical insurance. It could ruin their life.

Holding personal information demands sensitivity and respect. This is reflected in the *data protection laws*.

Data Protection Legislation

In Ireland, the Data Protection Act, 1989, entitles every person to request (in writing) any personal information pertaining to him or her which is contained in a computerised database. Such information can be deleted or corrected at the request of the individual concerned. This includes the right to have one's name taken off a mailing list or database.

Data Controllers are also responsible for obtaining and using such personal information in a fair way. The information can only be maintained for specified lawful purposes, and cannot be disclosed for any illegal purpose. Appropriate security measures must be taken to ensure unauthorised persons do not have access to the data and to ensure the safe disposal of the information. Data must be up-to-date and accurate, and must not be kept longer than necessary.

The UK Data Protection Act, 1984, has almost identical provisions.

Networks

Computers can function quite happily on their own, but increasingly they are being connected together. Connecting them together in a *network* enables them to share resources – hardware such as printers and scanners, software such as database or publishing programs, and data such as reports and customer address files.

Once two or more computers are connected, the possibilities begin to multiply. They can exchange files: one person can write an article for the newsletter, another can edit it, a third can lay it out, while a fourth can contribute a drawing or a scanned photograph.

This sharing of files and computer resources is called *workgroup computing*.

Passing files between computers like this is called *data communication*. When it takes place over long distances – between different branches of the same company, or between a company and its customers, for example – it typically uses the telephone network.

Networks also enable users to exchange personal messages with one another: this is the idea behind *e-mail*.

To send someone an e-mail message, you need to have a computer connected to a network, and the recipient has to have a computer connected (directly or indirectly) to the same network. You also need e-mail software, and the unique 'address' of the recipient. That's the minimum.

In practice, this means that both of you have a PC and a modem, a telephone line, and a subscription to an Internet Service Provider (ISP). The ISP maintains a continuous connection to the Internet, and stores on its computer all e-mail that is sent, from anywhere in the world, to your *mailbox*, until you collect it.

This system means that you can send a message to your friend even when their computer is turned off: it is stored for them, by their ISP, until they collect it.

This means that you can carry on an electronic conversation over a period of time, during which neither you or your friend are ever talking at the same time. This is particularly useful if you live in different time zones.

The Internet

Okay, we used the *Internet* word, which is probably one of the main reasons you decided to learn about computers.

The Internet is a worldwide network of interconnected networks. If you connect to the Internet, you can not only send e-mail to other users, you can access a wealth of information stored on computers all around the world. It's a fabulous resource, and can be used for news, entertainment, education, information, sports, current affairs, shopping, and art.

The term *World Wide Web* is used to describe documents made available over the Internet which are in a particular graphic format. The documents can be linked together, irrespective of where they are physically located, and users can follow the links from document to document. This enable you to pursue a research topic from the general to the specific, from detail to 'big picture', from graphic to text, from text to sound. These links are called *hyperlinks*, and documents constructed with hyperlinks are called *hypertext* or *hypermedia*, if sound, graphics, or video are involved.

Section 1.4: Looking After Number One: Health & Safety

Health Warning!

Just as we have accustomed ourselves to using safety belts and childproof locks in cars, we need to adopt safe computing practices.

Problems can arise in a number of areas, but sensible precautions can help you avoid them.

Repetitive Strain Injury

This is the computer user's equivalent of tennis elbow. Persistent typing on a PC keyboard can lead to sore wrists, fingers and arms. Make sure your desk and chair are at a suitable height, and that your keyboard is at a comfortable angle. Don't spend too long at a PC without taking a break.

Eyesight

Extended periods of staring at a PC screen can lead to fatigue and ultimately to eye strain. Avoid locking your eyes in to a fixed screen stare. Look away frequently and focus your eyes on objects on the other side of your room.

Posture

Simple ergonomics are often so obvious that they are overlooked. You should arrange the hardware elements of your PC in such a way as to provide the easiest and most physically comfortable access. Your desk should support your monitor at the correct eye level. Your chair should be comfortable, adjustable, and provide adequate lumbar support.

Using a Computer and Managing Files

Module One was the tourist guide book you read to prepare for your visit to computer land. Module Two is where you get to meet the natives in the flesh.

What exotic creatures they are! The citizens are called files. They reside in houses called folders. And folders are built on areas called drives. (Files inside folders, and folders on top of drives – you have learnt quite a lot already!)

And such obedient citizens too! You can change their names, move them to a different location, alter their appearance, get rid of ones you don't want anymore – you can even create new ones out of nothing.

But remember this: files are delicate. So treat them with care. You do this by saving them regularly and by making copies of them every so often – just in case something bad happens to the originals. It's always the files you like and need most that seem to disappear the quickest. Better to learn this lesson from the book than from real-life in computer land.

Section 2.1: Starting Up, Clicking Around, Shutting Down

In This Section

Are you ready to take your first steps in computing?

This Section guides you through the basics. You will learn the correct ways of starting and shutting down a computer, discover the meaning of the various little pictures on the Windows screen, and find out how to start and close Word, Excel and other software programs that you will meet in later ECDL Modules.

New Activities

At the end of this Section you should be able to:

- Power up and power down a computer
- Use the Start menu to open software applications
- Switch between open applications
- Use the control buttons at the top right of a window
- Move, resize and scroll windows
- Click, double-click, drag and right-click with the mouse.
- Display and choose an option from a pull-down or a pop-up menu
- Work with icons on the Windows desktop.

New Words

At the end of this Section you should be able to explain the following terms:

- Powering up/Booting
- Clicking
- Taskbar
- Restore button
- Maximise button
- Dragging
- Double-clicking

- Cursor
- Menu
- Close button
- Window
- Minimise button
- Pull-down menu
- Pop-up/Shortcut menu

Starting Your Computer

Before you start your computer, check that it is plugged in to the electricity socket. Now, press the button to switch on the computer.

- On some computers, a *single button* switches on both the computer and the computer's screen.

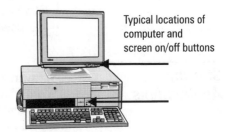

Typical locations of computer and screen on/off buttons

- Other computers have *two buttons*: one for the computer itself and a second for the screen.

Your computer will make some humming noises and some messages will flicker on your screen. Don't worry: this is just your computer warming up and checking that everything is in working order.

The Windows Desktop

The Windows desktop appears – little pictures set against a coloured background. These pictures are called *icons*. Along the bottom of your screen you will see a grey bar, with a button named **Start** in its left corner. This is called the *Taskbar*.

You will learn more about icons and the Taskbar later. You will also discover how you can change the appearance of your Windows desktop to suit your working needs and personal taste.

Right:
A sample Windows desktop.

The little pictures are called icons.

The grey bar along the bottom of the screen is the Taskbar.

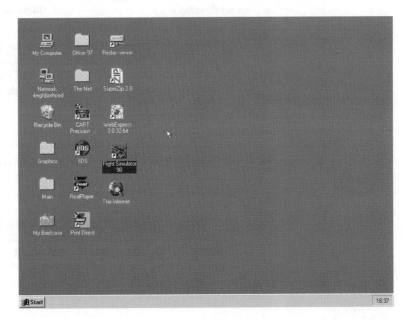

Congratulations. You have now powered up your computer.

Powering up/Booting

*The technical terms for starting a computer and displaying the
Windows desktop on the screen. You don't 'switch on' a computer;
you 'power it up' or 'boot' the computer.*

Starting Applications

Software applications are useful programs such as Microsoft
Word, Excel, Access and PowerPoint that enable you to create
documents, spreadsheets, databases and presentations. You will
learn a lot about these in Modules 3, 4, 5 and 6 of this ECDL
course. Your first step in working with applications is to learn
how to start them.

Using the Mouse

Place your hand over the mouse and move it around your
(physical) desktop. As you do so, notice how the pointer (the
cursor) moves around the Windows desktop.

**To move the cursor up the
screen, move the mouse in the
up direction.**

**To move the cursor down the
screen, move the mouse in the
down direction.**

Cursor

*A special symbol, usually an arrow, that you move around the
computer screen by moving the mouse across your (physical)
desktop.*

The Start Button

Move the cursor down to the bottom-left of your screen so that it
is over the **Start** button. Now, press down the left mouse button
and then release it. You don't need to hold down the button for
more than a second. This is called clicking.

Clicking

*Briefly holding down the left mouse button. By clicking on an item
on the screen, you telling your computer: "I want to select this item".*

Above:
The Windows start-up menu

Your mouse-click causes the **Start** button to display the start-up menu. Move the cursor up over the item called **Programs**. As you do, another menu appears to its right. On this second menu, move the cursor over the item called **Microsoft Word** and click on it. This opens the Microsoft Word application.

Menu

A list of items displayed on the computer screen. You select an item (tell the computer which item you want) by moving the cursor over it, and clicking on it with the mouse.

You can open more than one application at one time. Move the cursor back down over the **Start** button and click on it. Next, move the cursor over the menu item called **Programs**. On the next menu displayed, move the cursor over the item called **Microsoft Excel** and click on it. You have now started a second application.

Right:
The opening screens you see when you start Microsoft Word and Microsoft Excel

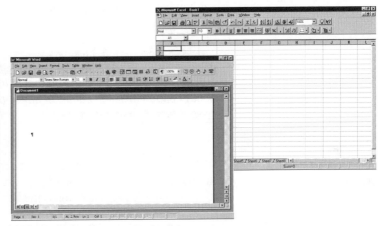

Why stop at two applications? The following Exercise takes you through the steps of starting a third application, Microsoft PowerPoint.

Exercise 2.1: Opening Microsoft PowerPoint

1) Click on the **Start** button.

2) Click **Start | Programs**.

3) Click **Start | Programs | Microsoft PowerPoint**.

Congratulations. You now have three applications open on your screen.

The expression **Start | Programs** is shorthand way of saying 'Open the Start-up menu, and select the option called Programs'. And **Start | Programs | Microsoft PowerPoint** means 'Open the Start-up menu, select the option called Programs. Next, on the Programs menu, choose the option called Microsoft PowerPoint'.

Switching Between Applications

At any one time, you can open lots of applications - but only work with one. How you tell Windows which application you want to work with?

Take a look at the Taskbar at the foot of the screen. Notice how it displays the names of all your open applications.

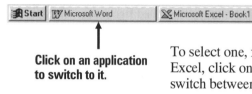

Click on an application to switch to it.

To select one, for example Word, click on Word. Or, to select Excel, click on Excel. You can therefore use the Taskbar to switch between open applications and display a particular one on your screen.

Taskbar
A horizontal bar across the bottom of the screen that displays the Start button, plus the names of any open applications. Click an application's name to display it.

The Control Buttons

Using the Taskbar, switch to the Microsoft PowerPoint. Move the mouse to the very top-right of the screen and click on the button that contains an X. This closes the PowerPoint application.

Close button

Close Button
A button at the top right of an application window that, if selected, closes the application.

Using the Taskbar, switch to Excel. Click on the Restore button near the top right of the Excel screen. This reduces the size of the Excel screen.

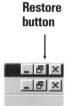

Restore button

Restore button
A button beside the Close button that reduces the size of the application screen area.

Using the Taskbar, switch to Word. Click on Word's Restore button. You should now be able to see both applications on the screen, with the currently selected application (Word) overlapping the other (Excel). Each application appears within its own *window*.

Window

A rectangular area of the Windows desktop that can display a file from an application. All windows, regardless of their content, share a number of common features.

When you click on a Restore button to reduce the size of a window, the Restore button disappears and is replaced by another button, called the Maximise button.

Maximise button

Clicking on this button reverses the effect of Restore: that is, it increases the size of the window so that it again fills the Windows desktop.

Maximise Button

Maximises the size of a previously reduced window so that it fills the Windows desktop.

One button remains: the Minimise button. With Word as the currently selected application, click on its Minimise button to 'shrink' Word so that it appears on the Taskbar and nowhere else. To display Word again, click on its name on the Taskbar.

Minimise button

Minimise Button

Shrinks an application window to remove it from the desktop to the Taskbar only.

The Close, Restore, Maximise and Minimise buttons are on every window. Collectively, they are known as the control buttons.

Moving Windows with the Title Bar

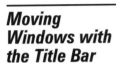

Another feature every window shares is a title bar – the identifying bar that runs across the top of the window. You can move a window to a different position on the desktop as follows:

- Click on the window's title bar – but do not release the mouse button.

- With your finger still on the mouse button, move the mouse to reposition the window.

- When you the window is positioned where you want it, release the mouse button.

X *Microsoft* Excel   ▭ ▢ ✕

Above: **Click on the title bar and drag with the mouse to reposition the window on the desktop.**

This series of actions is called dragging.

Dragging with the Mouse
Moving a selected item on the desktop by clicking on it with the left mouse button and holding down the button.

Using the Close box, close Excel. You now have only the Word application open on your desktop.

Using Menus and Commands

Take a look at the line of words that run just under the title bar of Microsoft Word. Each of these words represents a menu.

Word's menu bar ——►   File   Edit   View   Insert   Format   Tools   Data   Window   Help

Click on the **File** menu to display the commands (actions) available on this menu. Click the **Exit** command to close Word.

Whenever you see an arrow to the right of an option on a menu, selecting that option displays a further sub-menu of choices.

All Windows applications share a number of common menus. Understand their general purpose and you will be able to use most Windows programs.

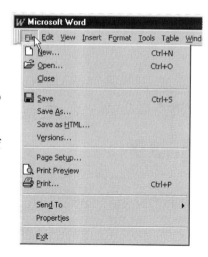

The common menus are:

- **File:** Use the commands on this menu to create a new (blank) file, open an existing file, save the current file, save the current file with a new name (Save as), print the current file, and quit the application.

- **Edit:** Use the commands on this menu to copy and move selected files, or items (such as text or graphics) within files.

- **View:** Use the commands on this menu to display your file in different ways, including a zoomed-in (up close) view or zoomed out (bird's eye) view.

- **Help:** Use the commands on this menu to display information about the application you are using.

Word's File menu is an example of a pull-down menu.

> **Pull-down Menu**
>
> *A list of options that appears when you click on a menu name. The menu name is generally on a menu bar along the top of the window, and the menu appears below that bar, as if you pulled it down.*

Working with Folder Icons

On the Windows desktop, move your cursor over the icon (little picture) named My Computer and click. Notice that the icon is highlighted. Your single-click selected it – but does not perform any action on it.

Now, click anywhere on the desktop to deselect the My Computer icon.

Once more, move the cursor over the My Computer icon. Now, click once and then, very quickly, click a second time on My Computer. This two-click action (called *double-clicking*) opens the My Computer icon so that you can see its contents.

Click on the Close box at the top right of the My Computer window to close it.

My Computer is an example of a desktop *folder* – an icon that represents a number of items grouped together. Except for My Computer, every other folder on your desktop look like a 'real' folder. Here are some examples.

Office 97   The Net   Graphics

Practise opening folders on your desktop by double-clicking on them. Some folders, you may find, will contain sub-folders. (A sub-folder is no different to a folder; it's just a folder that happens to be inside another folder.)

Close any folders you open by using the Close box.

Working with Non-folder Icons

Icons that do not represent folders indicate one of the following types of items:

- **Programs:** Software applications such as Word, Excel and PowerPoint. Double-clicking on an application opens it, just as if you selected the application from the **Start | Programs** menu.

Microsoft Word   Microsoft Excel   Microsoft PowerPoint

- **Files:** These are created by applications. Examples include a Word document, an Excel spreadsheet and a PowerPoint presentation. Double-clicking on a file opens that file, *and* the application in which the file was created.

electric.doc   apogee.xls   KBpres2.ppt

- **Drives:** These indicate physical storage devices on your computer. Double-clicking on a drive displays a list of folders, applications and files on that drive.

3½ Floppy (A:)   [C:]   (E:)   (D:)

Double-clicking with the Mouse

Pressing the left mouse button quickly twice in succession. This tells Windows to perform an action on the selected item.

Right-clicking and Pop-up Menus

In addition to clicking (to select), dragging (to move) and double-clicking (to perform an action), Windows offers a fourth kind of mouse movement: right-clicking.

To right-click something is to click on it once with the *right* mouse button.

Above:
A pop-up menu displayed
by right-clicking on a
Word file

Right-clicking on anything – whether a folder, application or file icon, or even the desktop – displays a pop-up menu. The particular menu options shown depend on the item you right-click.

One option that a right-click always displays is called **Properties**. Select this option from the pop-up menu to view details about the item.

Practise right-clicking on icons and on the desktop background. In each case, click the **Properties** option on the pop-up menu.

Pop Up or Shortcut Menu
A small menu that appears temporarily, typically when you right-click on an item. When you select an option from a pop-up menu, the menu usually disappears.

Changing the Shape and Size of a Window

You can change the shape and size of a window by selecting it and dragging any of its four sides.

To change the width of a window, click on its left or right edge. The cursor changes to a double-headed arrow. Then drag with the mouse. As you drag the window, Windows changes its edges to dashed lines.

To make a window taller or shorter, click on its top or bottom edge. Again, the cursor changes to a double-headed arrow. Drag the edge with the mouse.

To change both window height and width, click in the bottom right corner of the window. The cursor changes to a double-headed, diagonal arrow. Drag the corner with the mouse.

Practise your window resizing skills with the My Computer folder window.

Scrolling a Window

Sometimes a window may not be large enough to display all its contents. In such cases, scroll bars appear on the right edge and/or along the bottom of the window. To view a different part of the window:

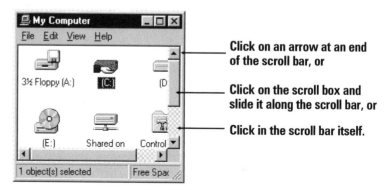

Click on an arrow at an end of the scroll bar, or

Click on the scroll box and slide it along the scroll bar, or

Click in the scroll bar itself.

Shutting Down

The opposite of powering up a computer is powering or shutting it down. *Never* just switch off your computer – you may lose unsaved information and damage your computer's hard disk (thereby losing saved information too!)

To shut down properly, follow these steps:

1) Click the **Start** button.

2) Click **Shut Down**.

3) Select the **Shut Down the Computer** option.

4) Click **Yes** to confirm.

Some computers now automatically switch themselves off. On others, you need to press the on/off button after you see the message: 'It is now safe to turn off your computer'.

Restarting a Computer

Sometimes a computer may 'hang', making it unresponsive to any keyboard or mouse action. In such cases, you have no option but to shut it down, turn it off, and turn it back on again.

Always wait about twenty seconds before you switch back on a computer that you have just switched off.

Section Summary:
So Now You Know

To power up a computer, switch on the system box and, where it has a separate on/off switch, the screen also. Windows starts and displays *icons* on the *desktop*.

Use the *Start | Programs* menu to start software applications such as Word or Excel, and the Taskbar to switch between open applications.

The *control buttons* at the top left of a window enable you to maximise, minimise and close that window.

To *move* a window on the desktop, drag it by its *title bar*. To *resize* a window, drag its edges.

All software applications include a *menu bar* with *pull-down menus,* offering lists of actions that you can perform within that application.

Icons on the desktop represent drives, applications, files and folders.

Clicking an item selects it. *Double-clicking* performs an action on it. And right-clicking displays a small, pop-up menu of relevant options.

Where a window is too small to display all its contents, use the *scroll bar* to view different parts of that window. Always use the *shut down* procedure when switching off your computer.

Section 2.2: Files, Folders and Drives

In This Section

Files, folders and drives – as you will discover in this Section – are the three levels at which information is organised on a computer. You will learn how to create folders and files, copy and move them, rename and delete them, and find out their properties.

And if, through disorganisation, you do mislay a file on your hard disk, this Section shows you how to search for and find it.

New Activities

At the end of this Section you should be able to:

- Distinguish between files, folders and drives
- Use Windows Explorer to view and work with folders and files
- Explain file name extensions and recognise the most common types
- Search for files

New Words

At the end of this Section you should be able to explain the following terms:

- File
- Folder
- Drive
- Recycle Bin
- File name extension
- Wildcard

How Computers Store Information

If you throw all your belongings in a together heap on the floor, you will have a difficult time finding anything. How much easier to sort your valuables beforehand, dividing them neatly between shelves or drawers. When you need to find something, you know exactly where it is.

As with your belongings, so with information stored on a computer. In this Section you will learn about files, folder and drives – the three levels at which information is organised on a computer.

Files

All the information and programs on your computer are stored in individual files. Think of a file as the computer's basic unit of storage.

File
The computer's basic unit of information storage. Everything on a computer is stored in a file of one kind or another.

Folders

A computer may contain many thousands of files. To make it easier for you (and the computer) find and keep track of files, you can group files together in folders. A folder can also contain one or more other folders, thereby forming a tree-like hierarchy.

Right:
A sample hierarchy of folders and files

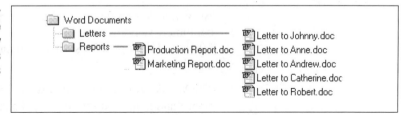

Another advantage of placing files in a folder is that you can work with the files as a group. For example, you can copy or delete all files in a folder in a single operation.

Folder
A group of files. Files grouped into folders are easier to find and work with.

Drives

A drive is a storage device that holds files and folders. Every computer has a hard disk drive (named the C: drive). On some computers, the hard disk is divided into two – a C: drive and a D: drive.

The next available letter after the hard disk is given to the CD-ROM drive. This can be D: or E:, depending on how your hard drive is named. The floppy disk drive is named the A: drive.

Drive
A physical storage device for holding files and folders. Typically, A: is the floppy drive, C: the hard disk, and D: is the CD-ROM drive.

Where is the B: drive? Early personal computers had just two floppy disk drives, A: and B: The advent of hard disks, which were named as C: drives, eliminated the need for a second floppy drive.

Using Windows Explorer

Use this program to view the hierarchy of folders on your computer, and to see all the files and sub-folders in any folder.

To open Windows Explorer, choose **Start | Programs | Windows Explorer**. You will usually find Windows Explorer at the end of the list of programs that you can display from the Start button.

As well as letting you view the files and folders on your computer, Windows Explorer enables you to perform various folder and file operations, such as renaming, copying, moving and deleting.

The Windows Explorer window is divided into left- and right-hand panes (sub-windows). The right pane is one level down the hierarchy from the left pane.

Viewing Your Drives

Disk Drives

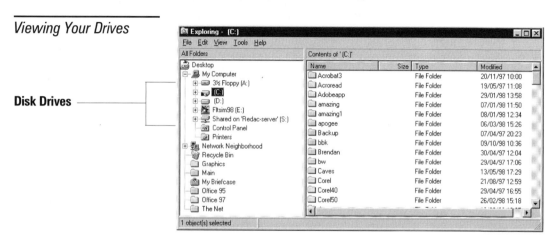

In the left hand pane, you can see the drives on your computer. In this example, the hard disk is divided into two, a C: drive and the D: drive. A CD-ROM named Fltsim98 is currently in the E: drive, and the computer is connected to a shared network drive, S:

Along the bottom of the Windows Explorer window you can see the number of items in the currently open folder (the one shown in the right pane), the disk space occupied by the folder's contents, and the remaining free space on the drive.

Viewing Your Folders and Files

Double-click on any drive to display, in the right-hand pane, the folders and files stored on that drive.

For example, double-click on the C: drive. Then, scroll down the right-hand window until you can see the Windows folder.

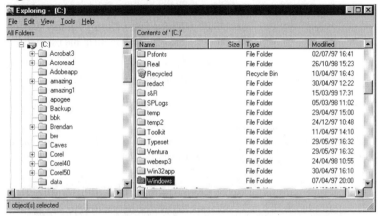

Double-click on this to see what folders and files are stored within it. Folders are listed first. Scroll down through the Windows folder to see what files are within it.

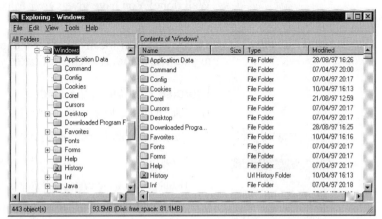

Working With Folders

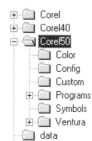

A folder without a plus (+) or a minus (-) sign in front of it is either empty or has only files inside it. To open it, click on the folder.

A folder with a plus (+) symbol has folders inside it, and perhaps files too. To open it, click on the folder name or the + sign.

A minus (-) symbol in front of a folder indicates that the folder is open – its sub-folders and files are currently displayed on the screen. To close an open folder, click on the - sign.

In Exercise 2.2 you will create two new folders on your C: drive.

Exercise 2.2: Creating Two New Folders

1) In the left-pane of the Windows Explorer window, click on the C: drive.

2) Choose **File | New | Folder**. Windows displays a new folder at the bottom of the list in the right-hand pane.

3) Type a name for your new folder. If your initials are KB, for example, call it KB Folder.

4) Repeat steps 1), 2) and 3). Name your second folder (say) KB Folder 2.

Changing a Folder's Name

You can change a folder's name at any stage. Exercise 2.3 shows you how.

Exercise 2.3: Changing a Folder's Name

1) Right-click on one of your new folders to display a pop-up menu.

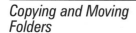

2) Choose **Rename**.

3) Type a new folder name. For example, KB New Folder.

Well done! You have given your folder a new name.

Copying and Moving Folders

To copy a folder means to make a copy of it, and place that copy in a new location. Exercise 2.4 takes you through the steps.

Exercise 2.4: Copying a Folder

1) Click on the folder you renamed in Exercise 2.3 to select it.

2) Choose the **Edit | Copy** command.

3) Scroll down the right-hand pane to locate the folder called Windows.

4) Double-click on the Windows folder to open it.

5) Choose **Edit | Paste** to place a copy of your folder within the Windows folder.

To move a folder means to place it in a new location – and to *remove* it from its original location. Exercise 2.5 shows you how.

Exercise 2.5: Moving a Folder

1) Click on the folder you copied to the Windows folder in Exercise 2.4 to select it.

2) Choose the **Edit | Cut** command.

3) Scroll back up the right-hand pane to locate the folder called System.

4) Double-click on the System folder to open it.

5) Choose **Edit | Paste** to place your folder within the System folder of the Windows folder.

Deleting a Folder

You don't need your folder any more. Here is how to delete an unwanted folder.

Exercise 2.6: Deleting a Folder

1) Right-click the folder that you copied to the System folder within the Windows folder.

2) From the pop-up menu, select the **Delete** command.

3) Click **Yes** to confirm that you want to remove the folder.

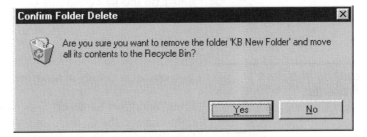

The folder is deleted, as are any files it may have contained.

Restoring a Folder

Where did your deleted folder go? Answer: only as far as the Recycle Bin. Follow these steps to bring your deleted folder back to life.

Exercise 2.7: Restoring a Folder

1) On the Windows desktop, double-click on the Recycle Bin icon

Recycle Bin

2) Double-click the folder to restore it.

Recycle Bin

A storage area where Windows holds deleted folders and file. You can retrieve items from the Bin that you deleted in error, or empty the Recycle Bin to create more disk space.

Looking at a Folder's Properties

To display information about a folder, right-click on it. To view details of your Windows folder, for example, right-click on it to display a pop-up menu.

Next, select the **Properties** option.

You are shown a dialog box similar to the one on the right.

Among other details, this tells you the number of folders and files within the Windows folder.

It also shows the drive where the folder is located (in this case, C:), and the size of the folder (in this case, 445 megabytes).

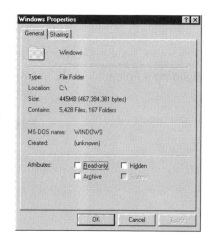

Looking at a Drive's Properties

You can view details of an entire drive in a similar way.

From Windows Explorer, right-click on the C: drive and, from the pop-up menu, select **Properties**. You are now shown a dialog box similar to the one on the right.

You can see how much space is occupied on your hard disk, and how much is still free. You can also use this dialog box to give a name to your hard disk drive.

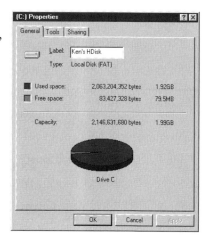

Working With Files

A file, as stated at the beginning of this Section, is the basic unit of information storage on a computer. In the remainder of this Section you will learn how to create, save and name, copy, move and delete a file.

Creating a File

Files are created by application programs. For example, you can create a document in Microsoft Word and a spreadsheet in Microsoft Excel.

The simplest type of file that you can create on a computer is a plain text file. A file of this kind contains just words, numbers and punctuation marks – and no fancy formatting or graphics of any kind.

The Windows application for creating plain text files is called Notepad.

Exercise 2.8: Creating a File

1)   Choose **Start | Programs | Accessories | Notepad**. A blank Notepad window appears on your screen, ready to accept text.

2)   Type the following words: Just testing

You have now created a file and entered content in that file. But your file is not saved on your hard disk. It exists only in the computer's memory. If the computer were to switch off for any reason, your file would be lost.

Naming and Saving a File

The first time that you save a file, Windows asks you to give that file a name. Follow the steps in Exercise 2.9 to discover how.

Exercise 2.9: Naming and Saving a File

1)   Choose **File | Save** to display the Save As dialog box.

2) Double-click **My Computer** to display a list of drives within the dialog box.

3) Double-click the **C:** drive to display a list of folders on your hard disk.

4) Scroll down through this list to locate the folder you renamed in Exercise 2.3. Double-click on this folder.

5) In the File name: box, type a name for your new file. If your initials are KB, for example, name it KB New File. Click **OK**.

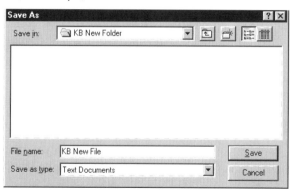

Well done! You have learnt how to name and save a file.

Move the mouse to the top-right of the Notepad window, and click on the Close box to close it.

Changing a File's Name

You can change a file's name at any stage. Exercise 2.10 shows you how.

Exercise 2.10: Changing a File's Name

1) Using Windows Explorer, open the folder containing your new file.

2) Right-click on the file to display a pop-up menu.

3) Choose **Rename**.

4) Type a new file name. For example, KB Renamed File. Do not change or delete the second part of the file name (.txt)

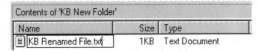

Contents of 'KB New Folder'		
Name	Size	Type
KB Renamed File.txt	1KB	Text Document

You have given your file a new name. Another Exercise completed!

Copying and Moving Files

In Exercise 2.11 you will make a copy of your plain text file, and place that copy in a different folder on your hard disk. Following that, in Exercise 2.12, you will move the file from its current folder to a new one.

Exercise 2.11: Copying a File

1) Click on the file you renamed in Exercise 2.10 to select it.

2) Choose the **Edit | Copy** command.

3) In the left-hand pane, scroll down to locate the folder called Windows.

4) Double-click on the Windows folder to open it. Its contents are now listed in the right-hand folder.

5) Choose **Edit | Paste** to place a copy of your file within the Windows folder.

Exercise 2.12: Moving a File

1) Click on the folder you copied to the Windows folder in Exercise 2.11 to select it.

2) Choose the **Edit | Cut** command.

3) Scroll back up the right-hand pane to locate the folder called System.

4) Double-click on the System folder to open it

5) Choose **Edit | Paste** to place the file within the System folder of the Windows folder.

Deleting a File

When you have been working on your computer for a while, you may find that its hard disk is taken up by files and folders you no longer use or need.

You can delete these files, but be careful not to delete any files your computer needs to run programs! If in doubt, don't delete!

Exercise 2.13 shows you how to delete an unwanted file.

Exercise 2.13: Deleting a File

1) Right-click the file that you copied to the System folder of the Windows folder in Exercise 2.12.

2) From the pop-up menu, select the **Delete** command.

3) Click **Yes** to confirm that you want to remove the file to the Recycle Bin.

Restoring a File

Follow the steps in Exercise 2.14 to restore your deleted file.

Exercise 2.14: Restoring a File

1) On the Windows desktop, double-click on the Recycle Bin icon.

2) Click the file to select it, and then choose **File | Restore**.

Looking at a File's Properties

To display information about a file, right-click on it. To view details of the file called Defrag.exe in the Windows folder, for example, right-click on it to display a pop-up menu.

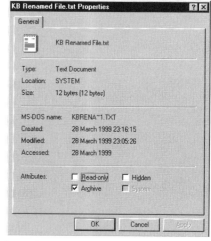

Next, select the **Properties** option to display a dialog box similar to the one on the right.

Among other details, this tells you the file type (text), size (12 bytes), the folder that contains it (System), and the file creation and last modification dates.

File Name Extensions

When you name and save a file within an application (for example, a Word document from within Microsoft Word), Windows attaches a three letter label to that file.

This is called a *file name extension,* and is separated from the remainder of the file name by a full stop. Its purpose is to identify the file type. Here are some common file name extensions:

.doc	Microsoft Word	.txt	Plain text file
.xls	Microsoft Excel	.exl	Program file
.mdb	Microsoft Access	.dll	Program file
.ppt	Microsoft PowerPoint		

File Name Extension

A three-letter addition to a file name that indicates the type of information stored in the file. A full stop separates the extension from the remainder of the file name.

Searching for Folders and Files

To find a folder or file on a drive, choose the **Start | Find | Files or Folders** command. This displays the dialog box below. In the Named: box, type the file name. Next, click **Find Now**.

Wildcard Searches

In file names, an asterisk (*) is called a wild card – it can represent one or several characters. If you cannot remember the full name of the file you want to search for, type the wild card character in place of the missing letter(s).

For instance, report*.doc finds all files that begin with 'report' and have the .doc extension. Examples might be report3.doc, reportnew.doc and report-a.doc.

If you search for *.xls, Windows finds all files on your computer that that have the Microsoft Excel extension name. Try it and see!

Date-based Searches

If you click on the Date Modified tab of the File Find dialog box, you can limit your search to only those files created or changed between certain dates, or during a specified number of days or months.

***Right:
Limiting
your
search
by date***

Name & Location	Date Modified	Advanced

○ All files
● Find all files created or modified:
   ● between `29/12/98` and `29/03/99`
   ○ during the previous `1` month(s)
   ○ during the previous `1` day(s)

Wildcard
The asterisk symbol (*) that can stand for one or a combination of characters when performing a search for a folder or file.

Content-based Searches

If you have absolutely no idea of the name of the file(s) you are looking for, you can search by content.

Click on the Advanced tab of the File Find dialog box and type one or more words you think are contained within the file(s) you are searching for.

Right:
Searching by
file content

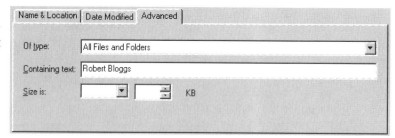

Viewing and Sorting Folders and Files

Windows Explorer offers a number of options that let you control how you view files and folders. To learn more about these, choose **Start | Programs | Windows Explorer**, and, in the left-hand pane, select the Windows folder.

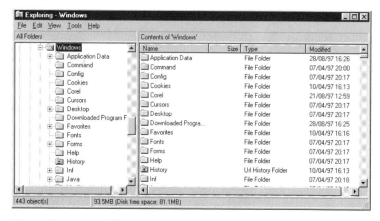

Next, choose the **View** menu to display its options. Here are the main ones:

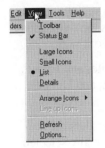

- **Large icons:** Displays folders and files like this:

- **Small icons:** Displays folders and files in columns, with folders at the top of each column and files underneath.

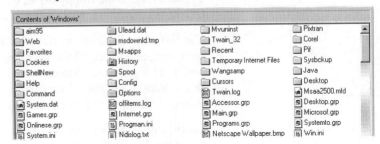

- **List:** Displays folders and files in columns, but lists all your folders before it shows the files.

- **Details**: Lists folders first and then files in a single column, and displays additional information about each item.

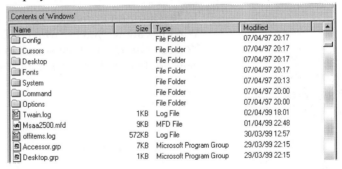

Sorting Folders and Files

When you choose **View | List**, you can change the order in which Windows displays your folders and files.

By default, folders and files are listed alphabetically by name. To view them by size, for example, click on Size in the bar across the top of the pane.

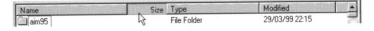

Alternatively, you can sort them by Type or (date) Modified.

Section Summary: So Now You Know

A *file* is the computer's basic unit of information storage. A *folder* is a group of files (and perhaps sub-folders too). Grouping files into folders makes them easier to find and work with.

A *drive* is a physical storage device for holding files and folders. Typically, A: is the floppy drive, C: the hard disk, and D: is the CD-ROM drive.

Use *Windows Explorer* to view the hierarchy of folders on your computer, and to see all the files and sub-folders in any selected folder. This program enables you to *copy*, *move*, *rename* and *delete* folders and files. You can also create folders with Windows Explorer. You create files with software applications.

To display details of a drive, folder or file, right-click on it and select the *Properties* option.

Windows adds a three-letter *file name extension* to every file, to indicate the file type. A full stop (.) separates the extension from the remainder of the file name. Common file name extensions are *.doc* (Word), *.xls* (Excel), *.mdb* (Access) and *.ppt* (PowerPoint).

To *find* a file on a drive, choose the **Start | Find** command. Windows allows you use *wild cards* to represent missing letters. You can also restrict your search to files of a certain date or date range, or that contain a specified keyword(s).

Section 2.3: Mastering Windows

In This Section

Now that you are familiar with Windows basics, you are ready to move on to some of its more advanced features.

You will discover how to take control of your Windows desktop, enabling you to customise it to reflect your working needs and your personal taste. You will also learn how to password-protect your computer, work with floppy disks and other backup media, and print out your files.

New Activities

At the end of this Section you should be able to:

- Personalise your desktop by moving icons and creating folders to hold application and file icons

- Create shortcuts that take you directly to a particular application, file or folder

- Customise your wallpaper and screen saver

- Adjust your computer's date and time settings

- Place a password on your computer, and change it as required

- Install a software application

- Format a floppy disk

- Use the Backup and Restore facility

- Use various print features and options, and explain what a print driver is and why it is necessary

New Words

At the end of this Section you should be able to explain the following terms:

- Shortcut

- Print queue

- Device driver

Managing Your Desktop

You can arrange your desktop to suit your working needs and personal taste.

- To reposition your icons, simply drag them to where you want them.

- You make your desktop look tidier by creating folders and placing application and file icons in them.

  To create a new folder, right-click on the desktop, choose **New | Folder**, type a folder name, and press ENTER. Next, double-click the folder to open it, and drag icons into it, either from the desktop or from other folders.

Creating Shortcuts

You will use some applications more frequently than others. You can save yourself time by creating a shortcut to these programs from your desktop (or from a folder on your desktop). As a result, you won't have to go the **Start | Programs** route every time you want to start that application.

Follow the steps in Exercise 2.15 to create a shortcut for Notepad.

Exercise 2.15: Creating a Shortcut for Notepad

1) Chose **Start | Programs | Windows Explorer**. If the Explorer window occupies the full Windows desktop, click on the Restore button (top-right).

2) Display the application you want to create a shortcut for. You will find Notepad in the Windows folder.

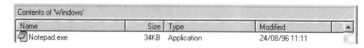

Contents of 'Windows'				
Name	Size	Type	Modified	
Notepad.exe	34KB	Application	24/08/96 11:11	

3) Right-drag Notepad from Windows Explorer onto your desktop, and release the right mouse button.

4) On the pop-up menu displayed, choose Select Create Shortcut(s) Here.

If you don't like your shortcut's default name, right-click on it, choose **Rename**, type a new name, and press the ENTER key. You can also create shortcuts for frequently-used folders and files.

The ENTER key

Shortcut
An user-created icon that, when clicked on, takes you directly to an application, folder or file. It is a fast, convenient alternative to using the Start menu.

Customising Your Screen

You can change the wallpaper (desktop background) and the screensaver (which appears when your computer is left untouched for a short period). Exercise 2.16 shows you how.

Exercise 2.16: Customising Your Screen

Display

1) Choose **Start | Settings | Control Panel**.

2) On the folder displayed, double-click the Display icon.

3) On the various tabs of the displayed dialog box, you can customise your screensaver, background, the appearance of windows, the viewing options.

   To change any of these settings, click on the relevant tab, make the required changes, click **Apply** and then **OK**.

Don't be afraid to experiment with different settings.

Setting the Time and Date

Is your computer set to the correct date and time? If not, the files you create and edit, and e-mails you send, will show misleading dates or times. Exercise 2.17 shows you how to set the date and time on your computer.

Exercise 2.17: Setting Your Computer's Date and Time

Date/Time

1) Choose **Start | Settings | Control Panel**.

2) On the folder displayed, double-click the Date/Time icon.

3) Make the changes you want. Click **Apply** and then **OK**.

A small battery inside your computer ensures that Windows remembers date and time settings, even when your computer is turned off.

Installing New Software

If you want to use an application that is not on your computer, or to upgrade an application to a newer version, you need to have to know how to install software. Windows makes this quite straightforward.

Exercise 2.18: Installing a New Software Application

1) Insert the CD-ROM or floppy disk containing the software into the relevant drive.

2) Choose **Start | Run** and click the **Browse** button. Find the file that begins the software installation – typically, this is called SETUP.EXE or INSTALL.EXE – and double-click this file.

3) One or a series of dialog boxes will appear. Follow the displayed instructions until the installation is complete.

You may have to close down your computer to complete the installation, so it's a good idea to save all your work and close down other applications before installing new software.

Security and Passwords

Passwords are designed to prevent others from reading, changing or deleting your files. Passwords should be at least 6 characters long. Combine letters and numbers in your password, because this makes it harder for others to guess. Rather than choosing a password of banana, for example, choose banana4 or ban7ana.

If you suspect that someone is snooping around your files, you may decide to place a password on your computer, or change your current password. Exercise 2.19 shows you how.

Exercise 2.19: Adding Changing your Password

Passwords

1) Choose **Start | Settings | Control Panel**.

2) On the window displayed, double-click the Passwords icon.

3) Click **Change Windows Password**.

4) Enter your old password (if you had one), your new password, and then retype your new password to confirm it, and then click **OK**.

   Windows displays a dialog box confirming that your password has changed.

If your computer is connected to a network, you may need to enter a password to use the services on that network, such as accessing the files on a file server or printing. Network passwords are covered in ECDL Module 7.

Working With Floppy Disks

You can copy files and folders from your hard disk to a floppy disk to:

- Make a copy of your work that you can give to a colleague or friend.

- Have a second, back-up copy of your work just in case your computer is somehow damaged and the files on it are 'lost'.

Formatting a Diskette

Before you can copy files to a floppy disk, you must format the disk. When Windows formats a floppy disk, it:

- Sets up a 'table of contents' on the disk which it later uses to locate files stored on the disk.

- Checks for any damaged areas, and, when it finds them, marks those areas as off-limits for file storage.

You can buy pre-formatted diskettes. But it is cheaper to buy unformatted ones and to format them yourself.

Exercise 2.20: Formatting a Floppy Disk

1) Insert the floppy you want to format into the disk drive.

2) Chose **Start | Programs | Windows Explorer** and right-click the A: drive icon in the left-hand pane.

3) Choose **Format** and select the following two options on the dialog box displayed.

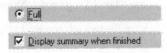

4) When Windows has formatted the disk, click **OK** to display the Format Results dialog box.

6) Click **Close**.

Formatting a disk overwrites any table of contents there may have been previously on the disk, so making it impossible for Windows to find files that were saved on the diskette before it was formatted.

For that reason, don't even think about formatting your computer's hard disk.

You cannot format a disk if there are files open on that disk.

Backing Up and Restoring

You should regularly make second, backup copies of your work on a different storage medium in case your computer is permanently damaged and your files are lost forever.

Typical places for backing files on are:

- Floppy disks (cheap, but with limited storage room)

- High-capacity disks or tapes (expensive, but can hold lots of files)

- Hard disks of other computers (convenient if your computer is connected to a network)

The more frequently you make backups, the more up-to-date they will be in event of your computer failing.

To simplify backup operations, Windows offers a feature called Backup and Restore. Exercise 2.21 takes you through the relevant steps.

Exercise 2.21: Backing Up and Restoring Files

1) Choose **Start | Programs | Accessories | System Tools | Backup**.

2) Click **OK** a number of times until you reach the Backup dialog box.

3) Select the folders and/or files you want to back-up, and the backup storage medium. When finished, click **OK** to start the backup operation.

If, for any reason, the original files are no longer available, follow these steps to copy the backups to your hard disk in place of the originals (this is called 'restoring').

1) Choose **Start | Programs | Accessories | System Tools | Backup**.

2) Click the Restore tab and select the location on your hard disk you want to restore the backup files to.

3) Click **OK** to start the restore operation.

You can take a backup from one computer and restore the files to another.

Printing Files

Now that you can open and work with files, you will want to print copies of your work so you can see it on paper.

Exercise 2.22: Printing a File

1) Open the file – for example, a Word document.

2) Select **File | Print**.

If your printer is connected and set up correctly, your file should print.

The Print Queue

What happens to a file after you choose to print it with the **Print** command? The answer is that it goes to a file called a print queue, and is then taken from the print queue by the selected printer.

The print queue can store a number of files, which the printer then collects in turn as it becomes ready to print them. The time it takes to print a file depends on the number and size of the other print jobs in the print queue.

You can view your print queue to see what print jobs are waiting in it, delete print jobs from the queue, and reorder the sequence in which print jobs are listed.

Print Queue

A list of files (print jobs) that are waiting to be printed. The printer pulls the files off the queue one at a time.

Viewing the Print Queue

What jobs are currently in the print queue? Follow the steps in Exercise 2.23 to find out.

Exercise 2.23: Viewing the Print Queue

1) Choose **Start | Settings | Printers**.

2) Double-click on the icon for the printer you want to look at.

Windows displays a list of all the print jobs in the queue.

Cancelling a Print Job in the Queue

There are many reasons why you may decide to cancel a print – you may discover that the job is not printing correctly. You may realise that you already have a copy of the printout. Or you may simply change your mind about printing the file.

Follow the steps in Exercise 2.24 to cancel a job.

Exercise 2.24: Removing a Job from the Print Queue

1) Choose **Start | Settings | Printers**.

2) Double-click on the icon for the printer you want to look at. Windows displays a list of all the print jobs in the queue.

3) Select the document you want to cancel printing.

4) Choose **Document | Cancel Printing**.

Changing the Order of Jobs in the Print Queue

You can change the current sequence of jobs in the print queue. Here's how.

Exercise 2.25: Reordering the Jobs in a Print Queue

1) Choose **Start | Settings | Printers**.

2) Double-click on the icon for the printer you want to look at. Windows displays a list of all the print jobs in the queue.

3) Select the file you want to move, and drag it to the required place in the queue.

You can't move a file that is already in the process of printing.

Deleting All Documents from the Print Queue

Follow the steps in Exercise 2.26 to remove all pending print jobs from the print queue.

Exercise 2.26: Deleting All Jobs in the Print Queue

1) Choose **Start | Settings | Printers**.

2) Double-click on the icon for the printer you want to look at. Windows displays a list of all the print jobs in the queue.

3) Choose **Printer | Purge Jobs**.

The Print Dialog Box

When you choose the **File | Print** command within an application, you are shown a dialog box that typically offers the following options:

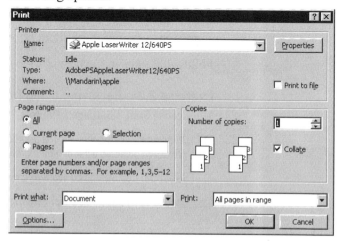

Name

To choose a different printer, click on the arrow on the right of the Name: drop-down list box, and then click on the printer you require.

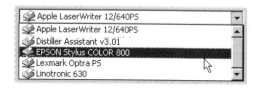

Print Range

You can choose to print all pages, the currently displayed page only or a range of pages.

To print a group of continuous pages, enter the first and last page number of the group, separated by a dash. For example, 2-6 or 12-13.

To print a non-continuous group of pages, enter their individual page numbers, separated by commas. For example, 3,5,9 or 12,17,34. You can combine continuous with non-continuous page selections.

Copies

You can specify how many copies of the file you want to print. For multiple copies, ensure that the Collate checkbox is selected.

The Properties Button

Clicking on the **Properties** button displays some further print choices that will vary with the type of printer selected – colour or back-and-white, inkjet or laser.

All printers offer choices about paper size (A4 is standard) and orientation (Portrait means 'standing up', Landscape means 'on its side').

When you have selected your options, click **OK** to print your file.

Print Preview

Most Windows applications have a **Print Preview** command on their **File** menu that lets you see on screen how the file contents will look when printed on paper.

Installing a Printer

Connecting a new printer to a computer is not just matter of plugging the printer cable into the back of the computer. A printer, like a scanner or other hardware device, has its own small software program – a device driver – that allows it to communicate with Windows. Different models of printers have different drivers.

When you purchase a new printer, it will come with a floppy disk or CD-ROM containing the driver. You install the driver on your computer as you would any other software application.

Device Driver
A small program that controls a hardware device such as a printer. You cannot use the device without first installing the appropriate driver.

Section Summary: So Now You Know

You can *personalise* your Windows desktop by repositioning icons, creating new folders, and placing program and file icons in them. You can create *shortcuts* – icons that take you directly to a particular application, file or folder. You can also customise your *wallpaper* and *screen saver*.

You can adjust the *date and time* setting on your computer so that Windows attaches the correct date and time to the files you create and edit, and to e-mails you send.

You can place a *password* on your computer to prevent others from reading, changing or deleting your files.

Before you can copy files to a floppy disk, you must *format* the disk. If you format a previously used disk, any files that may have been on the disk are no longer accessible.

Windows offers a feature called *Backup and Restore* that simplifies the process of making backup copies of your important folders and files, and, when necessary, copying the backups in place of damaged or missing originals.

Anything you print goes first to a file called a *print queue* that can hold multiple print jobs. It is then taken from the print queue by the selected printer. You can view your print queue to see what jobs are waiting in it, delete jobs from the queue, and reorder the sequence in which jobs are listed.

A *device driver* is a small program that controls a hardware device such as a printer. You cannot use the device without first installing the appropriate driver.

Word Processing

3

Back in the days when people thought they could predict the future, someone came up with the phrase 'paperless office'.

As computers found their way into more and more workplaces, the theory was that paper-based communication would disappear. Forever.

But alongside affordable computers came affordable printers. Result: computerisation has led to more rather than less paper usage. The office supplies people have never been busier.

In this Word Processing Module you will learn how to add further to the world's output of computer-generated paperwork.

You will discover how to create formal business letters and reports, and produce stylish posters and restaurant menus. We will even share with you the secrets of generating personalised form letters, (un)popularly known as junk mail.

Good luck with it.

Section 3.1: Your First Letter in Word

In This Section

There is a lot more to word processing than just typing and editing words. But these are the two basics. Read the material and follow the examples in this Section and you will have the foundation skills to move on to more advanced tasks.

You will also learn how to access and search through Word's online help, which is a great place to find answers and advice on using any of the program's features.

New Activities

At the end of this Section you should be able to:

- Start and quit Word
- Enter and edit text
- Recognise Word's non-printing characters
- Use the SHIFT, BACKSPACE, DEL, ARROW and TAB keys
- Type and print a standard letter
- Save, name, open, create and close Word documents
- Use online help to learn more about Word

New Words

At the end of this Section you should be able to explain the following terms:

- Document
- Paragraph Mark
- Wrap around
- Non-printing characters

Starting Word

Microsoft
Word

Double click on the Microsoft Word icon or choose **Start | Programs | Microsoft Word**. Word starts and displays a new window containing a new, blank document ready for you to type into.

Above: **A blank Word document ready to accept your text**

Word Document
A Microsoft Word file. For example, a letter or a report.

What? No New, Blank Document?

If starting Word did not automatically open a new, blank document, click on the New button at the top left of your screen

New

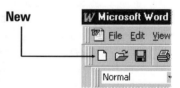

Text Cursor and Paragraph Mark

Text cursor

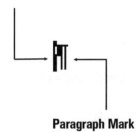

Paragraph Mark

Near the top-left corner of your document you can see two items:

- **Text cursor:** A blinking vertical line. Whenever you type text, Word places the text at the text cursor's location. Think of the cursor as a 'you are here' indicator, telling you where you are in a document.

- **Paragraph mark:** Every Word document contains one of these (it looks like a backwards letter P). Whenever you press the ENTER key to begin a new paragraph, Word inserts another one at that point. The paragraph mark appears on the screen only and not on printouts.

Paragraph Mark
Every document has at least one paragraph mark. Word displays another one each time you press ENTER.

What? No Paragraph Mark?	If Word does not display the paragraph mark in your document, click on the Show/Hide Paragraph Mark button at the top of the screen, near the top-right corner.

Actions You Need to Know

Here are the four basic operations in Word that you need to know: typing text, editing (changing) text you previously typed, using the SHIFT key to type upper-case (capital) letters, and using the ENTER key to type new paragraph marks.

You will practise each one in the following four Exercises.

Exercise 3.1: Typing Text to Word

1) Type the following number: 7

2) Press the SPACEBAR. Word displays a dot on the screen. This is Word's way of telling that you have typed a space. Word will not print the dot.

3) Type the following six letters: dwarfs

That's it. Congratulations! You have typed your first text to Word.

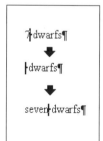

Exercise 3.2: Editing Previously Typed Text

Often you will want to change – or, perhaps, remove completely – text that you have typed. This is called editing.

1) Using the mouse, click to the right of the 7.

2) Press the BACKSPACE key. (You will find it directly above the ENTER key.)

3) Type the following word: seven

You have completed the editing Exercise.

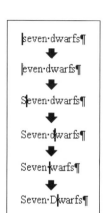

Exercise 3.3: Using the SHIFT Key

1) Click to the left of the letter s in seven.

2) Press the DEL key to delete the letter s.

3) Hold down the SHIFT key and type the letter s. Word displays an upper-case S.

4) Move the cursor to the right of the letter d in dwarfs.

5) Press the BACKSPACE key to delete the d.

6) Hold down the SHIFT key and type the letter d. Word displays an upper-case D.

Well done! Another Exercise completed.

John¶
Paul¶
George¶
Ringo¶

Exercise 3.4: Using ENTER to Type New Paragraphs Marks

Now you will use the ENTER key to end one paragraph and begin another.

1) Click to the right of the word Dwarfs, and press ENTER. This creates a new paragraph. Word places the cursor at the start of a new line.

2) Type John	6) Type George
3) Press ENTER.	7) Press ENTER.
4) Type Paul	8) Type Ringo
5) Press ENTER.	

You will not need the above text for future Exercises. So delete it as follows:

• Click to the right of the word Ringo.

• Press and hold down the BACKSPACE key until Word has removed all the text from the document.

Keys You Need to Know

Now is a good time to summarise the role of these important keys:

SHIFT: Pressed in combination with a letter, number or symbol key, this creates an upper-case character or symbol. You will find a SHIFT key at both sides of the keyboard.

BACKSPACE: Deletes the character to the *left* of the cursor. You will find the BACKSPACE key at the top-right of the keyboard, just above the ENTER key.

DEL: Deletes the character to the *right* of the cursor. You will find the DEL key in a group of six keys to the right of the ENTER key.

ARROW: Rather than use the mouse to move the cursor around your document, you can press any of the four ARROW keys, located to the right of the ENTER key. You may find this method faster than moving and clicking the mouse, as you need not take either hand away from the keyboard.

Typing a Letter

Now you are ready to type a longer piece of text, a letter.

Exercise: 3.5: Typing a Paragraph of a Letter

1) Type the following text:

I am writing to you in relation to our annual Sale of Work which will take place in our local Scout Den on 17 October next.

Your screen should look as follows.

I·am·writing·to·you·in·relation·to·our·annual·Sale·of·Work·which·will·take·place·in·our·local·
Scout·Den·on·17·October·next.¶

Notice how Word moved the cursor to the beginning of the next line when the text you were typing reached the right hand edge of the page.

On an old-style typewriter, you would have needed to press the ENTER (also called RETURN) key to move down to the next line. Word does this for you automatically. This feature is called wrap around, and Word is said 'wrap' the text to a new line once the previous line is full.

Wrap around

Word's ability to move the cursor to the beginning of a new line when the text reaches the end of the previous one.

Exercise: 3.6: Typing the Full Letter

In this Exercise, you will type the remainder of the letter.

1) Move the cursor to the beginning of the first line, just to the left of the I.

2) Press ENTER.

3) Type the following and press ENTER:
    24 Main Street,

4) Type the following and press ENTER:
    Anytown.

5) Type the following and press ENTER three times:
    333444

6) Type the following and press ENTER three times:
    1 October 1999

7) Type the following and press ENTER twice:
    Dear Ms Smith,

8) Move the cursor down to the last paragraph mark on the page, just after the full stop, and press ENTER twice.

9) Type the following and press ENTER twice:
    In previous years your company was kind enough to donate a prize for our wheel of fortune.

10) Type the following and press ENTER twice:
    Could we ask you to be as generous again this year?

11) Hold down the SHIFT key and press the hyphen key about twenty times. The hyphen key is the second key to the left of the BACKSPACE key.

   Then release the SHIFT key. When you print the letter, you will use the line created with the hyphen key to write your signature.

12) Press ENTER and type the following:
   Ken Bloggs

That's it. You have typed your first letter in Word. It should look as shown.

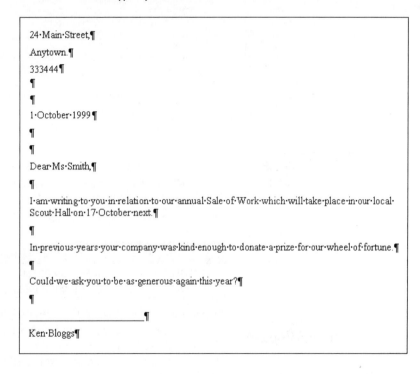

Moving Text with the Tab Key

There is a problem with your letter. The address, phone number and date at the top are in the wrong position. You need to move them to the right.

In Exercise 3.7 you learn how to use the TAB key to change the position of text on the page.

Above:
The TAB key

Exercise: 3.7: Using the Tab Key

1) Position the cursor at the top left of the page, just to the left of the 2.

2) Press the TAB key eight times. Word moves all text between the cursor and the paragraph mark to the right.

3) Repeat step 2) for the second address line, the phone number line, and the date line. Your screen should look as below.

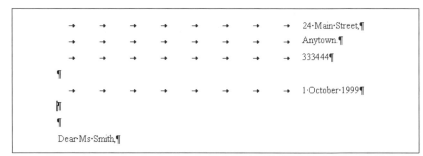

Non-printing Characters and Wavy Underlines

Each time you press the TAB key, Word inserts an arrow symbol on the screen. Like the paragraph mark that indicates a paragraph ending, and the dot between words that represents a blank space, the tab symbol is a non-printing character.

Non-printing characters
Symbols that Word displays on the screen to help you type and edit your document, but that are not printed out.

Ken·Bloggs¶

Depending on how Word is set up on your computer, you may see green and/or red wavy underlines beneath certain words or phrases. These have to do with Word's spell- and grammar-checking features, which are explained in Section 4.4. Until then, ignore them.

Printing Your Letter

Your letter is ready to be printed out. Choose **File | Print**. If your printer is set up correctly all you need do is click **OK** on the Print dialog box. You will learn more about printing in Section 3.3.

Word's Toolbars

Above the document window you can see Word's two main toolbars: the Standard Toolbar and the Formatting Toolbar.

The Standard Toolbar includes buttons for managing files – that is, Word documents – and for working with tables.

Word's Standard Toolbar

Word's Formatting Toolbar

| Normal | Times New Roman | 11 | **B** *I* <u>U</u> | ≡ ≡ ≡ ≡ | ≣ ≢ ≣ ≢ | □ ▾ ✎ ▾ A ▾ |

The Formatting Toolbar includes buttons for changing the appearance of text, and for inserting bullets.

Rather than introduce all these buttons at once, we will explain each one as it becomes relevant through the Wordprocessing Module.

Word's Undo Feature

Enter the wrong text? Press the wrong key? Word allows you undo your most recent text entry or document action if it has produced unwanted results:

- Choose **Edit | Undo** or click the Undo ↶ button on the Standard Toolbar.

Working With Word Documents

A Word document is a file containing text (and sometimes graphics too). The file names of Word documents end in .doc. This helps you to distinguish Word files from other file types.

Saving Your Document

In Word, as in other applications, always save your work as you go along. Don't wait until you are finished! To save a document:

- Choose **File | Save** or Click the Save 💾 button on the Standard Toolbar.

The first time you save a document file, Word asks you to give the file a name. The following Exercise shows you how.

Exercise 3.8: Saving and Naming a New Document

1) Choose **File | Save**. Word displays a dialog box similar to the one shown.

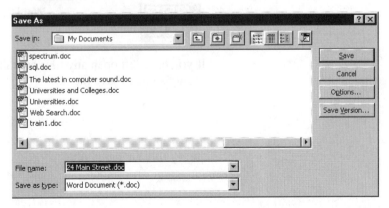

2) By default, Word suggests the first words of your document as the file name. Replace this file name with something that you will find easier to remember and recognise – such as your own name – and click the **Save** button.

Creating a New Document

To create a new Word file:

- Choose **File | New** or click the New  button on the Standard Toolbar.

Opening an Existing Document

To open an existing Word file:

- Choose **File | Open** or click the Open button on the Standard Toolbar. Select the file you want from the dialog box.

Closing a Document

To close a Word document:

- Choose **File | Close** or click the Close button on the document window.

 **———— Document Close button**

If you have made changes to your document since you last saved it, Word prompts you to save the changes before it closes the file.

Quitting Word

To leave Word:

- Choose **File | Exit** or click the Close button on the Word window.

———————— Word Close button

If you have left open any files containing unsaved work, Word prompts you to save them.

Online Help

Like Excel, Access, PowerPoint and other Microsoft applications, Word offers a searchable online help system.

- The 'help' in online help means that the information is there to assist you understand and use the program.

- The 'online' means that the material is presented on the computer screen rather than as a traditional printed manual.

You can search through and read online help in two ways: from the Help menu, or from dialog boxes.

Using Help Menu Options

Choose **Help | Contents and Index** to display the three tabs of the Help Topics dialog box. These are explained below.

Contents Tab

This offers short descriptions of Word's main features.

◆ Where you see a heading with a book symbol, double- click to view the related sub- headings.

? Double-click on a question mark symbol to read the help text.

Click a Show me arrow for Word to demonstrate how to perform a particular action.

Click a double-arrow to view step-by-step instructions.

Index Tab

Reading the material displayed on this tab is like looking through the index of a printed book.

Just type the first letters of the word or phrase you are interested in.

Word responds by displaying all matches from the online help in the lower half of the dialog box.

When you find the index entry that you are looking for, click the **Display** button.

Find Tab

Can't find what you are looking for in the Contents or Index tabs? Try this tab.

When you type a word or phrase, Word performs a deeper search of the online help.

Word also displays some related words to help you narrow your search.

When you find the item you are looking for, double-click on it to display it.

As you search through and read online help topics, you will see the following buttons at the top of the online help window:

- **Help Topics:** Click this to return to the Contents tab.

- **Back**: Click this to return to the previous help topic.

- **Options:** Click this to perform such actions as copying the online help text to a document, or printing it on your printer.

Using Help from Dialog Boxes

You can also access online help directly from a dialog box, as Exercise 3.9 demonstrates.

Exercise 3.9: Using Online Help in a Dialog Box

1) Choose **Edit | Find** to display the Find and Replace dialog box.

2) Click on the question mark symbol near the top-right of the dialog box. Word displays a question mark to the right of the cursor.

3) Move the mouse down and right, and click anywhere in the Find what: box.

4) Word displays online help text telling you about the purpose of the Find what: box.

Practise this Exercise with other dialog boxes in Word.

Section Summary: So Now You Know

A Word document is a file containing text (and sometimes graphics too). Word file names end in *.doc*.

Every new Word document contains a *text cursor*. Whenever you type text, Word places the text at the text cursor's location. You can move the text cursor with the mouse or with the ARROW keys.

Every new document also contains a *paragraph mark*. Whenever you press the ENTER key to begin a new paragraph, Word inserts another paragraph mark at that point.

You can edit text with the BACKSPACE key (removes text to the left of the text cursor) or the DEL key (removes text to the right of the text cursor). Press the SHIFT key in combination with a letter, number or symbol key to type an upper-case character or symbol.

Press the TAB key repeatedly to move text to the right. When typing a letter, for example, press TAB to position the address and related details at the top-right of the letter.

Word's *non-printing characters,* such as a single dot to represent a space, do not appear on printouts. They are displayed on the screen only.

Section 3.2: Formatting, Positioning and Copying Text

In This Section

Other than typing and editing text, there are two main types of action that you can perform with a word processor:

- You can change the *appearance* of the text.
- You can change the *position* of text on the page.

The first is called formatting. It includes such actions as making text bolder (heavier), placing a line under it, and putting it in italics. You can also change the text font and font size, format text as bullets, and apply coloured backgrounds and borders to text.

You have already learnt how to reposition text using the TAB key. Now you will discover two other methods: alignment and indenting.

New Activities

At the end of this Section you should be able to:

- Select text
- Format text (bold, italic and underline)
- Copy, cut and paste text
- Indent text from the left and right page margins
- Align text (left, right, centre and justified)
- Create text bullets
- Explain fonts and fonts sizes, and super- and subscripts
- Add borders and shading to text

New Words

At the end of this Section you should be able to explain the following terms:

- Select
- Clipboard
- Indent
- Alignment
- Bulleted text
- Font
- Superscript
- Subscript

Selecting Text

Typically, when you want to format or position some text, it is only a particular character, word, group of words or paragraph that you want to change.

You tell Word which part of the document you want to change by first *selecting* that text. Selecting a piece of text is sometimes called highlighting that text.

When you select text, Word displays that text in reverse (white text on black background), rather like the negative of a photograph.

Selected text ────────────────┐
                                   ↓

In ▐previous·years▌ your·company·was·kind·enough·to·donate·a·prize·for·our·wheel·of·fortune. ¶

Selecting Text
Highlighting a piece of text in order to perform an action on it, such as formatting or alignment.

Formatting and alignment are just two of the actions that you will learn how to perform on selected text. In later Sections, you will learn how to find and replace, and spell-check, selected text.

To select text within a Word document, first position the mouse at the beginning of the text that you want to select:

- To select text on a single line, drag the mouse to the right until you have selected the character(s) or word.

- To select text that is on more than a single line, drag the mouse to the right and down the page.

- To select your whole document, hold down the CTRL key and click in the left margin.

CTRL (Control) key

Exercise 3.10: Selecting Text

In this Exercise you will learn how to select characters, words and paragraphs.

1) Open the letter you saved in Section 3.1.

2) Position the cursor to the left of the letter D in Dear Ms Smith.

3) Drag the mouse to the right until you have selected the letter D. Release the mouse button.

You have learned how to select a single character. Now click anywhere on the page to deselect the letter D. Deselecting a piece of text does not remove the text; it just means that it is no longer selected.

4) Again, position the mouse to the left of the letter D, but this time keep dragging with the mouse until you have selected the entire word Dear.

   Release the mouse button.

5) Finally, position the mouse to the left of the letter D. Now drag the mouse down and right until you have selected the first paragraph of the letter.

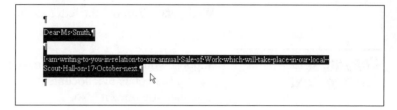

You have learned how to select several lines of text. Click anywhere outside the selected area to deselect it.

That completes the Exercise. But practice your text selection skills by clicking at any point in your document, and dragging the mouse in various directions.

Formatting Text

B *I* <u>U</u>

Format Buttons

Word's most commonly used formatting features are:

- **Bold**: Heavy black text, often used for headings

- *Italic*: Slanted text, often used for emphasis or foreign words

- <u>Underline</u>: A single line under the text, often used in legal documents and beneath signatures on letters.

You will find the relevant buttons on the Formatting Toolbar. In the next Exercises you will learn to apply the bold and italic formats.

Exercise 3.11: Applying the Bold Format

1) Place the cursor at the start of the first line of the address.

2) Drag right and down with the mouse until you have selected the two address lines and the phone number.

3) Click the Bold button or press CTRL+b (Hold down CTRL and type b).

4) Deselect the lines by clicking on any other area of the document.

Right:
Applying
the bold
format

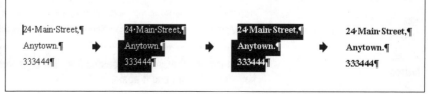

Exercise 3.12: Applying the Italic Format

1) Place the cursor at the start of the name, Ken Bloggs.

2) Drag right until you have selected the name.

3) Click the Italic button or press CTRL+i.

4) Deselect the name by clicking on any other area of the document.

Well done. Print out the letter again to inspect your work.

Copying and Pasting Text

Suppose you want to use the same text – word(s) or paragraph(s) – more than once in a document. Do you need the retype it each time that you need it? No.

With Word, you can type the text just once, and then insert it as many times as you need. This is a two step process:

- **Copy**: You select and then *copy* the text to the Clipboard, a temporary holding area.

- **Paste**: You insert or *paste* the text from the Clipboard into a different part of the same document, or even a different document.

> **Clipboard**
>
> *A temporary storage area to which you can copy text. You can paste that text to any location within the same or different documents.*

Exercise 3:13: Copying and Pasting Text Within a Document

1) Select the second paragraph of your letter.

> In·previous·years·your·company·was·kind·enough·to·donate·a·prize·for·our·wheel·of·fortune.¶

Copy button

2) Click the Copy button on the Standard Toolbar, or choose **Edit | Copy**.

3) Position the cursor at the left of the paragraph mark on the next line.

> In·previous·years·your·company·was·kind·enough·to·donate·a·prize·for·our·wheel·of·fortune.¶
> ¶

4) Click the Paste button on the Standard Toolbar, or choose **Edit | Paste**.

> In·previous·years·your·company·was·kind·enough·to·donate·a·prize·for·our·wheel·of·fortune.¶
> In·previous·years·your·company·was·kind·enough·to·donate·a·prize·for·our·wheel·of·fortune.¶

Paste button

Select the line that you have pasted from the Clipboard, and press the DEL key. You will not need it again.

About the Clipboard

Four points you should remember about the Clipboard:

- The Clipboard is temporary. Turn off your computer and the Clipboard contents are deleted.

- The same Clipboard is available to all Windows applications. For example, you can copy from Excel and paste into Word.

- The Clipboard can hold only a single, copied item at a time. If you copy a second piece of text, the second overwrites the first.

- Text stays in the Clipboard after you paste from it, so you can paste the same piece of text into as many locations as you need.

Exercise 3.14 Copying and Pasting Text between Documents

The line you copied in Exercise 3.13 is still in the Clipboard. In this Exercise you will copy it to a different document.

1) Click on the New File ▢ button to create a new, blank Word document.

   Word places the cursor at the beginning of the document.

3) Click the Paste button on the Standard Toolbar, or choose **Edit | Paste**.

4) Choose **File | Close** to close the new document. When Word asks you whether you want to save the new file, click **No**.

When you have more than one Word document open at a time, you can switch between them by choosing **Window |** (*document name)* command.

Cutting and Pasting Text

Sometimes, you may want to remove text from one part of a document and place it in a different part.

Rather than deleting the text and then retyping it elsewhere, Word allows you to move the text by cutting it from its current location and pasting it to the new location.

Cut button

Cut-and-paste differs from copy-and-paste in that Word removes the cut text, whereas copied text remains in its original location. You can cut selected text using the Cut button on the Standard Toolbar by choosing the **Edit | Cut** command.

Keyboard Shortcuts

You may find it quicker to use Word's keyboard shortcuts for copy, cut and paste operations as you need not take either hand away from the keyboard.

- To copy, press CTRL+c.
- To cut, press CTRL+x.

- To paste, press CTRL+v.

You can also right-click on your document to get a pop-up menu displaying the available commands for copying, cutting or pasting.

Formatted Documents

All Word documents are formatted, but some are more formatted than others. In the remainder of this Section you will discover the Word tools that enable you to design a highly-formatted poster: indents, alignment, bullets, fonts, borders and shading.

Left and Right Indents

The term indent means 'in from the margin'. Word's indenting feature lets you push a paragraph of text a specified distance in from the left margin, right margin, or both.

To indent a selected paragraph, choose **Format | Paragraph**, and enter the required left and/or right distances on the Indents and Spacing tab of the paragraph dialog box.

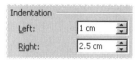

In long documents, you may sometimes see indenting used as a way of attracting attention to a particular part of the text. Here is an example that combines a left and right indent with italics:

> *Another successful year has seen revenues rise by 35% and profits by 47.5%. Our company is well placed to face the challenges of the future.*

> **Indent**
>
> *The positioning of a paragraph of text a specified distance in from the left and/or right margin.*

Aligning Text

Alignment Buttons

To align text means to 'line up' the text in a particular horizontal (left-right) way. Word gives you four choices:

- **Left**: The default, used for letters and business documents. Left-aligned text is generally the easiest to read.

- **Centre:** Places the text between the left and right margins. Used for headings.

- **Right**: Aligns the text against the right hand margin of the page. Used by graphic designers for decorative purposes.

- **Justify:** Both left and right aligned at the same time! It is used for narrow columns of text in newspapers and magazines.

Do not use justification when your text is in a single column across the width of the page (such as in letters), as it makes the text more difficult to read.

You can only align paragraphs. You cannot align selected characters or words within a paragraph.

To align a single paragraph, you don't need to select the text. You need only to position the cursor any place within the paragraph. You will find the four alignment buttons on the Formatting Toolbar.

Alignment
The horizontal positioning of lines in a paragraph in relation to one another. They can share a common centre-point, begin at the same point on the left, end at the same point on the right, or begin and end at the same points.

Bullets and Numbered Lists

Lists are good ways to communicate a series of short statements or instructions. Lists are of two types:

- *Bulleted:* Used when the reading order is not critical. The bullet character is typically a dot, square, diamond, line or arrow.

  To make a bulleted list, select the paragraph(s) and click the Bullets button on the Formatting Toolbar.

- *Numbered:* Used when the order of reading is important. For example, in directions and instructions. Each item is assigned a sequentially increased number.

  To make a numbered list, select the paragraph(s) and click the Numbering button on the Formatting Toolbar.

You can also make lists by choosing the **Format | Bullets and Numbering** command. Word offers you a wide range of options, such as the style of bullet character, and the distance between the bullet character and the bulleted text.

Bulleted and Numbered Lists
A list of short statements. The statements can be bulleted (preceded by a dot or other symbol) or numbered (preceded by a sequentially increasing number).

Fonts

Above:
Viewing the fonts on your computer

A font or typeface is a particular style of text. What fonts are installed on your computer? Click the arrow on the drop-down Font box on the Formatting Toolbar to see.

Do you need to remember the names and characteristics of all these fonts? No. You need remember only two points about fonts:

- There are really just two kinds (families) of fonts: *serif* and *sans serif*. Sans serif just means without serifs.

- Serif fonts are good for long paragraphs of text (what is called body text). Sans serif fonts are good for short pieces of text, such as headlines, headers, captions and maybe bulleted text.

You can tell which family a font belongs to by looking at it. Do its characters have serifs (tails or squiggles) at their edges?

Above:
A serif font

Above:
A sans serif font

Serif Fonts

Word's default font is a serif font called Times New Roman. It takes its name from *The Times* newspaper of London, where it was developed in the 1930s.

Other popular serif fonts include Garamond and Century Schoolbook.

- This text is written in a font called Garamond.

- This text is written in Century Schoolbook.

Sans Serif Fonts

Word's default sans serif font is Arial. It is based on another font, Helvetica, which was the world's most popular font in the 1970s.

Other common sans serif fonts include Futura and Avant Garde.

- This text is written in a font called Futura.

- This text is written in a font called Avant Garde.

Font
A typeface: a particular style of text. The two main font families are serif and sans serif.

Font Sizes

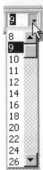

Font size is measured in a non-metric unit called the point, with approximately 72 points equal to one inch.

- For the body text of letters or longer business documents such as reports, 10, 11 or 12 points is a good choice. For headings, use larger font sizes in the range 14 to 28 points.

- Headers, footers, endnotes, footnotes and captions are often in 8 or 9 point font size.

To change the font size of selected text, click the required font size from the Font Size drop down list box on the Formatting Toolbar.

Font Properties

Word's **Format | Font** dialog box enables you apply a number of properties to fonts: style, effects, colour and spacing.

Font Style

You have already applied these options using Bold and Italic buttons on the Formatting Toolbar.

Underline

A lot of choices here. Single is the both the simplest and most commonly used. It is also the type of underline applied with the Underline button on the Formatting Toolbar.

Font Colour

Have you a colour printer? Then you may want to select a text colour other than Auto. Even without a colour printer, you may want to print your headings in grey.

What colour is Auto? Auto is black, unless the background is black or a dark grey, in which case Auto switches to white.

Font Effects

You can experiment with the various font effects by selecting any of the Effects checkboxes and viewing the result in the Preview area at the bottom of the dialog box.

One important effect you need to know about is superscript.

Effects		
☐ Strikethrough	☐ Shadow	☐ Small caps
☐ Double strikethrough	☐ Outline	☐ All caps
☐ Superscript	☐ Emboss	☐ Hidden
☐ Subscript	☐ Engrave	

This raises the selected text above the other text on the same line, and reduces its font size. It is used most commonly for mathematical symbols. For example:

$2^2, x^8, 10^{-3}$

> **Superscript**
>
> *Text that is raised above other text on the same line and is reduced in font size. Commonly used in maths for indices.*

The opposite of superscript is subscript. You will find subscripts used in typing chemical formulas, for example:

H_2O and H_2SO_4

> **Subscript**
>
> *Text that is lowered beneath other text on the same line and is reduced in font size. Commonly used in chemistry for formulas.*

Font Spacing

You can expand or condense the space between characters by using the options on the Character Spacing tab of the Font dialog box.

Here is a line of text that is expanded by 1 point.

You may want to use this spacing effect for document headings.

Font Borders and Shading

You brighten up your document with borders (decorative boxes) and shading (coloured backgrounds), using the options available with the **Format | Borders and Shading** command.

Word offers a range of border settings, with Box and Shadow the most common choices. Use the Preview section on the right of the dialog box to select the edges that you want bordered. The default is all four edges.

Pay attention to the Apply to: drop-down box at the bottom right. Your choice affects how Word draws the border. See the example below.

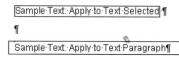

Setting:

None

Box

Shadow

3-D

Custom

Above: **Border setting options**

To apply shading, select the text, choose **Formats | Borders and Shading**, and then select your required Fill, Style and Colour options from the Shading Tab of the dialog box.

- *Fill:* This is the colour. If placing a grey shade behind black text, use 25% or less of grey. Otherwise, the text is difficult to read.

- *Style:* This allows you apply tints (percentages) or patterns of the selected fill colour.

- *Colour:* If you have selected a pattern in the Style box, select the colour of the lines and dots in the pattern here.

You can apply a border and shading to one or more characters, words or paragraphs. You need not apply both, but generally the border and shading features tend to be used together.

Example 3.15: Designing Your Poster

Practice makes perfect. In this Exercise you will apply the formatting (fonts, bullets, borders and shading) and text positioning (alignment and indenting) skills that you have learned in this Section. Your aim is to write and design a poster.

1)   Open a new document and type the following text.

¶
Annual·Sale·of·Work¶
¶
In·aid·of·Local·Scout·Troop¶
¶
¶
Wheel·of·Fortune¶
Raffle¶
Cakes¶
Books¶
Children's·Play·Area¶
¶
¶
¶
Where:¶
Local·Scout·Hall,·Main·Street¶
¶
When:¶
2pm¶
Sunday,·17·October¶
¶
Admission·Free¶
¶
All·Welcome¶

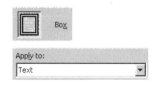

Above:
Diamond style
bullet character

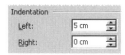

2) Select the text: Annual Sale of Work.

Using **Format | Font**, make it Times New Roman, 28 point. Using **Format | Borders and Shading**, select a Setting: of Box and select Text as the Apply to: option. On the Shading tab, select a shading of 15% Grey. Also, centre-align the text using the centre-align button on the Formatting Toolbar.

3) Select the text: In aid of Local Scout Troop Centre align it, and make it Arial Black, 14 point.

4) Select the five attractions: Wheel of Fortune, Raffle, Cakes, Books and Children's Play Area. Make them Arial, 20 point.

Choose **Format | Bullets and Numbering**. On the Bulleted tab, select the diamond bullet character style.

5) You want to place the bullets where they will get attention: in the centre of the page between the left and right page margins.

But *do not* apply centre alignment, as shown on the right, as the bullets are easier to read if they are left aligned.

```
◆→Wheel·of·Fortune¶
    ◆→Raffle¶
    ◆→Cakes¶
    ◆→Books¶
◆→Children's·Play·Area¶
```

6) With the five attractions still selected, select the **Format | Paragraph** command and apply a left indent of 5 cm. Your bulleted text remains left-aligned, but is now in the centre of the page.

7) Select the text: Where: Local Scout Hall, Main Street.

Make it centre aligned, Arial, 20 point. Make the 'Where' bold.

8) Repeat step 6) for the text: When: 2pm, Sunday, 17 October

9) Select the text: Admission Free.

Make it Arial, Bold, 20 point.

10) Select the text: All Welcome.

Make it Arial, italic, 20 point.

11) Finally, select any paragraph, choose **Format | Borders and Shading**, and select the Page Border tab.

Select a Setting: of Box and, in the Apply to: field, select Whole Document.

Your poster is now complete and should look like the sample shown.

Annual Sales of Work

In aid of Local Scout Troop

- ◆ Wheel of Fortune
- ◆ Cakes
- ◆ Books
- ◆ Children's Play Area

Where:

Local Scout Hall, Main Street

When:

2pm,
Sunday, 17 October

Admission Free

All Welcome

Section Summary: So Now You Know

Before you format or align text, you must first *select* that text. You do so by clicking and then dragging with the mouse. Word displays selected text in reverse (white text on black background).

Bold, italic and underline are Word's most commonly used *formatting* features. Buttons for these options are provided on the Formatting Toolbar.

You can *copy* text from one part of a document and then *paste* it to another part (or even to a different document) using the *Clipboard*, a temporary storage area. You can also *cut* and paste text, in which case Word deletes the text from its original location.

Indenting is a way of moving text in a specified distance from the left or right margin of the page – or from both. *Alignment* is a way of positioning text in a paragraph so it lines up beside the left margin, beside the right margin, beside both left and right margins (justification) or away from both left and right margins (centering). Buttons for the alignment options are provided on the Formatting Toolbar.

Use lists to communicate short statements or instructions. *Bulleted lists*, in which each item is preceded by a symbol such as a square or diamond, are suitable when the reading order is not critical. *Numbered lists*, in which each item is preceded by a sequentially increasing number, are used for instructions and directions, where the order of reading is important.

Fonts (typefaces) are styles of text. Serif fonts are better for long paragraphs. Use sans serif fonts for shorter text items, such as headlines or captions. Two important font effects are *superscript* (used for writing mathematical indices) and *subscript* (used for chemical formulas).

You can brighten up your documents by adding decorative *borders* and background *shading*.

Section 3.3: Long Documents, Little Details

Both for the writer and reader, long documents present problems that shorter ones do not. Word offers features to make life easier for both.

To help you edit long documents, Word includes a spell-checker, grammar-checker, and a find and replace feature.

You can help readers navigate their way through long documents by using Word's header, footer and page numbering options.

Also in this Section, you will discover how to control vertical spacing between lines and paragraphs, how to create new types of indents to highlight breaks between paragraphs, and how to insert line and page breaks.

New Activities

At the end of this Section you should be able to:

- Change the spacing between lines and between paragraphs
- Apply a first line indent to a paragraph
- Apply a hanging indent to a paragraph
- Find and replace text, text with formatting, and special characters
- Adjust page margins and page orientation
- Create headers and footers, and apply page numbering
- Insert manual line breaks and page breaks
- Use Word's spell- and grammar-checkers

New Words

At the end of this Section you should be able to explain the following terms:

- Inter-line spacing
- Inter-paragraph spacing
- First line indent
- Hanging Indent
- Margin
- A4
- Header and footer

Creating Your
Long Document

To learn how to work with long documents in Word, you need a sample long document to practise on. You begin this Section by copying some text from Word's online help.

Exercise 3.16: Copying Text from Word Online Help

1) Choose **Help | Contents and Index**. On the Contents tab of the Help Topics dialog box, double-click the topic: Working with Longer Documents.

2) Word displays a list of sub-topics. Double-click on: Automatically Summarising Your Document. You are shown a further sub-listing. Double-click on: Automatically summarise a document.

3) On the help screen displayed, select the two paragraphs of text shown below by dragging the mouse over them.

4) Choose **Options | Copy**. Close the online help window by clicking on the close box in its top-right corner.

5) Click the New File button on the Standard Toolbar to create a new Word document. The cursor is positioned at the start of the first line.

6) Choose **Edit | Paste** to paste the online help text into the new document.

7) Move the cursor to the start of the first line of the first paragraph. Press ENTER to create a new line, and move the cursor up to the start of that line.

How·does·AutoSummarize·determine·what·the·key·points·are?·AutoSummarize·analyzes·the·document·and·assigns·a·score·to·each·sentence.·(For·example,·it·gives·a·higher·score·to·sentences·

8) Type the following: Heading One

Heading·One¶
How·does·AutoSummarize·determine·what·the·key·points·are?·AutoSummarize·analyzes·the·document·and·assigns·a·score·to·each·sentence.·(For·example,·it·gives·a·higher·score·to·sentences·

9) Move the cursor to the left margin of the page where there is no text. Hold down the CTRL key and click. This selects all the text in the document.

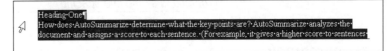

10) Choose **Edit | Copy** to copy the text to the Clipboard. Deselect the text by clicking anywhere on the page outside the selected text.

11) Move the cursor down to the end of the second paragraph, and press ENTER twice to move down the cursor a further two lines.

reports,·articles,·and·scientific·papers.¶
¶

12) The text you copied from Word's online help is still in the Clipboard. Choose **Edit | Paste** to paste it again.

13) Repeat steps 11) and 12) fifteen times to create three pages of sample text.

14) Choose **File | Save** to save the document with a name that you will find easy to remember. If your initials are KB, for example, call it KBlong.doc.

Inter-line Spacing

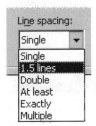

Inter-line spacing is the vertical space between lines within a paragraph of text. By default, Word applies single inter-line spacing. You can increase the inter-line spacing of a selected paragraph by choosing **Format | Paragraph**, and, in the Line Spacing: box, selecting 1.5 or Double.

Alternatively, enter a font size in the At: box, and select At Least: in the Line Spacing box. A good rule is to make inter-line spacing one point size larger than the font size. If your text is 10 point, for example, make inter-line spacing 11 point.

Right:
Examples of single, 1.5 and double inter-line spacing

How·does·AutoS document·and·as that·contain·word scoring·sentence ¶ Keep·in·mind·tha reports,·articles,·: ¶ How·does·AutoS document·and·as that·contain·word scoring·sentence that·contain·word scoring·sentence	How·does·AutoSu document·and·assi that·contain·words scoring·sentences· ¶ Keep·in·mind·that· reports,·articles,·an ¶ How·does·AutoSu	How·does·AutoS document·and·as that·contain·word scoring·sentence: ¶ Keep·in·mind·tha reports,·articles,·:

Inter-line Spacing

The vertical space between lines within a paragraph of text. Word's default is single line spacing

Inter-paragraph Spacing

Pressing the ENTER key to add a blank line between paragraphs of text is a crude – if effective – way of controlling the inter-paragraph spacing (spacing between paragraphs) in your documents.

For longer documents, you may instead wish to use the **Format | Paragraph** command, and enter an inter-paragraph space value in the Space Before: and/or Space After: boxes.

- For body text, enter a Space After: (slightly larger than the text font size) to separate the next paragraph from the current one.

- For headings, enter a value in the Space Before: box to place an extra area of blank space above the headings. This helps your headings to stand out from the rest of the text.

Right:
Inter-paragraph spacing, created with and without extra paragraph marks

How·does·AutoSi document·and·ass that·contain·word scoring·sentences ¶ Keep·in·mind·thai reports,·articles,·a ¶ How·does·AutoSi document·and·ass that·contain·word scoring·sentences	How·does·AutoSi document·and·ass that·contain·word scoring·sentences Keep·in·mind·that reports,·articles,·a How·does·AutoSi document·and·ass that·contain·word scoring·sentences

Inter-paragraph Spacing

The spacing between successive paragraphs of text.

Another option for long documents is to set inter-paragraph spacing for body text to zero, and to use instead first line indenting as a way of indicating where each new paragraph begins. See the next topic.

First Line Indents

In Section 3.2 you learned how to indent a selected paragraph from the left and/or right margins of the page. Word also lets you indent the first line of a paragraph only, so that it is in a greater distance from the left margin than the other lines of the same paragraph.

Exercise 3.17: Creating a First Line Indent

Here you will use a first line indent to separate two paragraphs of body text.

1) Select the second paragraph of your sample text.

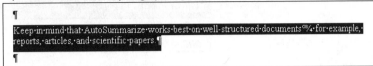

2) Choose **Format | Paragraph**.

3) On the Indents and Spacing tab, in the Special: box, select First Line. In the By: box, enter a value of 1 cm. Click **OK**.

4) Delete the extra paragraph mark above the indented paragraph. Your text should now look as below.

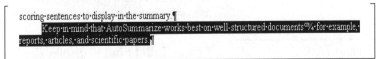

5) Undo the first line indent change by choosing **Edit | Undo**. Word's Undo reverses formatting and text positioning operations as well as typing and editing. Also, replace the extra paragraph mark to separate the two paragraphs.

Your sample text should look as it was before this Exercise.

First Line Indent

The positioning of the first line of a paragraph a greater distance in from the left margin than the remaining lines of the same paragraph.

If using first line indents to separate paragraphs, set inter-paragraph spacing to zero or to just 1 or 2 points. Do not use first line indents for the first paragraph after a heading.

Hanging Indents

A hanging indent is where all the lines of a paragraph are indented – except the first one. Hanging indents are sometimes used for lists such as bibliographies. Below is an example.

> *The·Memoirs·of·James·II* ·Translated·by·A.·Lytton·Sells·from·the·Bouillon·
> Manuscript.·Edited·and·collated·with·the·Clarke·Edition.·With·an·
> introduction·by·Sir·Arthur·Bryant.¶
>
> *The·History·of·England·from·the·Accession·of·James·II.* ·Lord·Macauley,·edited·
> by·Lady·Tevelyan.¶

Practise creating a hanging indent with the sample text by selecting a paragraph, choosing **Format | Paragraph**, selecting Hanging Indent from the Special: box, and  entering a value in the By: box. Undo any changes that you make.

Hanging Indent
Where all the lines of a paragraph are indented – except the first one. Sometimes used for lists.

Finding and Replacing Text

Need to locate quickly a particular word or phrase in a long document? Word's Find feature can take you straight to the text that you are looking for.

By default, Word searches the whole document. To limit the text that Word searches through, first select only that part of the document. When Word has finished searching the selected text, it asks whether you want to search the remainder or not.

Finding Text: The Basics

Choose **Edit | Find** to display the Find and Replace dialog box.

In the Find what: box, type or paste in the text you want to find, and choose **Find Next**.

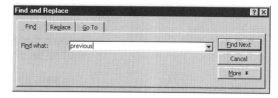

Word takes you to the first occurrence of the search text in your document. The dialog box stays open on your screen. Click **Find Next** to continue searching for further occurrences, or click **Cancel** to close the dialog box and end your search. Practise by searching for the word 'the' in your sample document.

Finding Text: Special Options

By default, Word finds parts of words as well as whole words. When you search for 'the', Word also finds 'then'. You can tell Word to find whole words only by clicking the **More** button, and then selecting the Find whole words only checkbox.

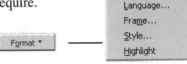

Another option is to select the Match case checkbox. So, for example, a search for 'The' does not find 'the' or 'THE'.

To find paragraph marks, tabs or other special or non-printing characters, choose the **Special** button and click on the relevant character.

Finding Text: Formats

You can tell Word to find only occurrences of text that is in a certain format. Click the **More** button, then the **Format** button, and select the formatting option that you require.

Finding and Replacing Text: The Basics

Sometimes you will want to find and replace all occurrences of a word or phrase in a document with a different word or phrase. You might have misspelled a word consistently throughout a document, for example, or maybe you want to substitute 'person' for 'man' or 'woman'.

To replace text, choose **Edit | Replace**. On the Replace tab, enter the text you want to replace in the Find what: box, and the new text you want to substitute for the replaced text in the Replace with box:

Finding and Replacing Text: The Two Methods

You are offered two options by the Replace tab of the Find and Replace dialog box.

- Word replaces your text one occurrence at a time. At each occurrence, you are asked whether you want to make the replacement or not. This is the 'safe' option.

- Word replaces all occurrences in a single operation. Use this option only if you are certain that you want to replace every instance of the text you are searching for!

Anything that you can locate with the Find command, you can replace with **Edit | Find and Replace** – including formatting, tabs and other special and non-printing characters.

Exercise 3.18: Finding and Replacing Text

In this Exercise you will practise finding and replacing text in your sample long document.

1) Look at the second of the two paragraphs that you pasted in from the online help text. Word incorrectly pasted the dash (–) after the word 'documents'.

2) Copy the following to the Clipboard: documents $^{o}3/_4$

3) Move the cursor to the start of the first line of the document. Choose **Edit | Find and Replace**.

4) On the Replace tab, paste the copied text in the Find what: box.

5) Type this in the Replace with: box: documents -

6) Choose the **Replace All** button.

Word performs the find-and-replace operation through the entire document. So much easier than correcting each occurrence of the error!

Exercise 3.19: Finding and Replacing Formatting

In this Exercise you will use Word's find and replace feature to reformat all occurrences of a heading in your sample long document.

1) Move the cursor to the start of the first line of the document. Choose **Edit | Find and Replace**.

2) On the Replace tab, type the following to the Find What box: Heading One.

3) Type this in the Replace with: box: Heading One.

4) Choose the **More** button and then the **Format** buttons.

5) Select the Font option, and specify a Font of Arial, a Font Style of Bold, and a Font Size of 14. Then click **OK**.

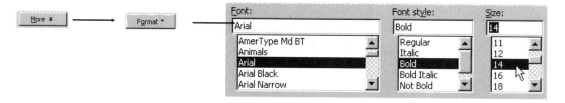

6) Choose the **Replace All** button.

Word reformats every occurrence of the heading.

Exercise 3.19: Finding and Replacing Special Characters

In this Exercise you will remove the extra paragraph that separates the paragraphs of the sample text.

1) Move the cursor to the start of the first line of the document. Choose **Edit | Find and Replace**.

2) On the Replace tab, click the **Special** button and select Paragraph Mark. Choose Special again and click Paragraph Mark. The Find what: box should contain Word's paragraph mark symbol twice (^ p ^ p).

3) Move the cursor to the Replace with: box, click the **Special** button and select Paragraph Mark.

4) Click **Replace All**.

Word replaces all occurrences of two consecutive paragraph marks with a single paragraph mark.

Exercise 3.20: Finding and Replacing Text Positioning

In this Exercise you will apply a first line indent to all occurrences of the second paragraph of sample text.

1) Move the cursor to the start of the first line of the document. Choose **Edit | Find and Replace**.

2) On the Replace tab, type the first word of the second paragraph of the sample text into the Find what: box: Keep

3) Type the same word into the Replace with: box.

4) With the cursor in the Replace with: box, click the **Format** button, then the **Paragraph** button, and specify a first line indent of 1 cm. Click **OK**.

14) Click **Replace All**.

Word indents the first line of every occurrence of the second paragraph.

Heading·One¶
How·does·AutoSummarize·determine·what·the·key·points·are?·AutoSummarize·analyzes·the·
document·and·assigns·a·score·to·each·sentence.·(For·example,·it·gives·a·higher·score·to·sentences·
that·contain·words·used·frequently·in·the·document.)·You·then·choose·a·percentage·of·the·highest-
scoring·sentences·to·display·in·the·summary.¶
    Keep·in·mind·that·AutoSummarize·works·best·on·well-structured·documents·-·for·example,·
reports,·articles,·and·scientific·papers.¶

Page Setup

You have learnt how to control where text appears on the printed page, using text alignment, indenting, inter-line spacing and inter-paragraph spacing.

But what about the page on which the text appears? What options does Word offer you?

Choose **File | Page Setup** to view the four tabs of page setup options. Only two of these tabs are relevant at this stage: Margins and Paper Size.

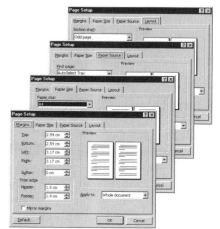

Above:
The four Page Setup tabs

The Margins Tab

A margin is the distance that the text and graphics are positioned in from the edge of the printed page.

Word's default margin values – top and bottom, 1 inch (2.54 cm), left and right, 1.25 inches (3.17 cm) – are acceptable for most letters and business documents.

You can change the margins at any stage, and make your new values the new defaults by choosing the **Defaults** button.

Above:
Margins indicated by dashed lines

> **Margin**
>
> *The distance of the text and graphics from the edge of the printed page. Word lets you specify separate top, bottom, left and right margins.*

Paper Size

For the Page size: box, accept the default of A4. This is the European standard paper size (21 cm wide and 29.7 cm high). A4 is used for almost all letters and other business documents.

> **A4**
>
> *The standard page size for letters and most other business documents throughout Europe.*

Orientation is the direction in which the page is printed. Your options are Portrait ('standing up') and Landscape ('on its side'). Letters and most other business documents are printed in portrait.

Headers and Footers

Above:
Word places headers and footers in the top and bottom page margins set with the File | Page Setup command

These are pieces of text that appear on the top and bottom of every page of a document (except the title and contents pages).

Looking at examples of published documents, you will see that headers and footers typically contain such details as document title, organisation name, author name, and perhaps a version or draft number.

Usually, headers and footers also contain page numbers. You will learn about page numbering in the next topic.

With Word, you need only type in header and/or footer text once, and the program repeats the text on every page. Any formatting that you can apply to text in your document – such as bold, italics, alignment, borders and shading – you can also apply to text in the headers and footers. You can also insert graphics, such as a company logo, in a header and footer.

Headers and Footers
Standard text and graphics that are printed in the top and bottom margins of every page of a document.

Here are a few facts about headers and footers and Word:

- You insert them with the **View | Headers and Footers** command.

- This command displays the header area (surrounded by a dashed border), the document text (which you cannot edit when working with headers and footers), and a Header and Footer Toolbar (giving you quick access to the commonly used commands).

Right:
Word's header area with Toolbar

- Word positions the paragraph mark at the left of the header area, ready for you to type text.

- Word inserts two preset tab stops to make it easy for you to centre-align or right-align headers. Press TAB once to centre a header, press TAB twice to line it up against the right margin.

Above:
The Switch
Between
Header and Footer
button

• Click the Switch between Header and Footer button to view the footer area when in the header area, and vice versa. The two areas are similar in appearance and operation.

• Place page numbers (discussed in the next topic) at the outside margin (left for left-hand side pages, right for right-hand pages) or at the centre of the header or footer area.

• Place text at the centre or at inside margin of the header or footer area.

Exercise 3.21: Creating a Header

In this Exercise you will insert header text in your sample document.

1) Choose **File | Page Setup**, select the Layout tab, ensure that the Header and Footer checkboxes are as shown on the right, and click **OK**.

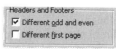

2) Choose **View | Header and Footer**. Word positions the paragraph mark at the left of the header area, ready for you to type text.

3) Type the following text: Annual Report

4) Click on the Next button on the Header and Footer Toolbar. Word takes you to the next page, the first even (left-hand) page of the document.

5) Press the TAB key twice to move the paragraph mark against the right-hand margin. Type the following text: ABC Limited

6) Click the **Close** button on the Header and Footer Toolbar.

Because you began this Exercise by selecting the Different odd and even: checkbox on **File | Setup**, Word allowed you to type separate headers for odd (right-hand) and even (left-hand) pages.

Exercise 3.22: Formatting a Header

In this Exercise you will place a border under the header text to help separate it from the main body of the document. You will also change the font and font size. Typically, the header font is 2 or 3 point sizes smaller than the body text. At that size, sans serif fonts such as Arial are easier to read than serif ones.

1) Choose **View | Header and Footer**.

2) Select the header text on the first page of your document.

3) Chose **Format | Font**, and select Arial, Regular, 8 point.

4) With the text still selected, choose **Format | Borders and Shading**.

5) On the Borders tab, select Box for Setting:, 1 pt for Width:, Paragraph for Apply to:, and choose a bottom border. Click **OK**.

6) Click on the Next page button on the Header and Footer Toolbar. Repeat steps 4) and 5) for the left-hand page.

7) Click the Close button on the Header and Footer Toolbar.

The top of your first page should now look as below.

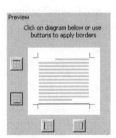

Above:
Apply a bottom border to the header text

Annual Report¶
_____

Heading·One¶
How··does·AutoSummarize·determine·what·the·key·points·are?·AutoSummarize·analyzes·the·

The top of your second page should now look as below.

→   →   ABC·Limited¶

Heading·One¶
How··does·AutoSummarize·determine·what·the·key·points·are?·AutoSummarize·analyzes·the·

Notice that the header text is 'greyed out', indicating that you cannot edit it when working with the main body of the document.

Page Numbering

You can insert a page number in the header or footer of a document. Word updates the page numbers as you add or remove document pages. The same formatting options are available for the page number as for header and footer text. You can align a page number at the left or right margin, or in the centre of the header or footer area.

Exercise 3.23: Inserting a Page Number

In this Exercise you will insert a centre-aligned page number in the footer of the document.

1) Choose **View | Headers and Footers**.

2) Display the footer area of the first page. Press TAB to move the cursor to the centre-aligned position.

Above:
**The Insert Page
Number button**

3) Click the Insert Page Number Button on the Header and Footer Toolbar. Word inserts the page number and displays it against a grey background.

4) Click the Next button on the Header and Footer Toolbar to move to the second page, the first even (left-hand) page of your document.

5) Repeat steps 2) and 3) to insert the page number in the centre-aligned position.

6) Click the Close button on the Header and Footer Toolbar. Save the document.

Page Numbering Options

Above:
**The Format
Page Number
button**

Click on the Format Page Number button on the Header and Footer Toolbar to display the page numbering options.

You can number the pages using numbers, letters, or Roman numerals. And you can start at a number other than one.

Manual Line and Page Breaks

Pressing ENTER at any stage inserts a new paragraph mark, and causes Word to begin a new paragraph. To insert a line break within a paragraph, press SHIFT+ENTER.

When text fills a page, Word automatically creates another page to hold the further text.

You can insert a page break manually at any point in a document by pressing CTRL+ENTER. Alternatively, choose the **Insert | Breaks** command, select the Page break option, and click **OK**.

Checking Your Spelling

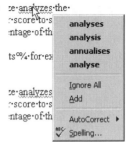

☑ Check spelling as you type

How's your spelling? Word can check your spelling and suggest corrections to errors in two ways:

- As you type and edit your document (the automatic option).

- Whenever you choose the **Tools | Spelling and Grammar** command (the on-request option).

To turn automatic spell-checking on or off, select or deselect the Check spelling as you type checkbox on the Spelling & Grammar tab of the Options dialog box. You display this dialog box with the **Tools | Options** command.

Spell Checking: The Automatic Option

As you type and edit, a wavy red line under words indicates possible spelling errors.

To correct an error, right-click the word with a wavy underline, and then select the correction you want on the pop-up menu.

Selecting the last menu option, Spelling, displays Word's Spelling dialog box.

The Spell Check Dialog Box

Whether automatic spell-checking is selected or not, you can spell check your document at any stage by choosing the **Tools | Spelling and Grammar** command.

If Word's spell-checker finds no errors, it displays a box telling you that the spell-check is complete.

If Word finds something it does not recognise, it displays the Spelling dialog box, and shows the relevant word in red.

Right:
The spell-check dialog box includes a Suggestions area that offers likely alternatives to queried words. Click on any suggested word to substitute it for the incorrect one.

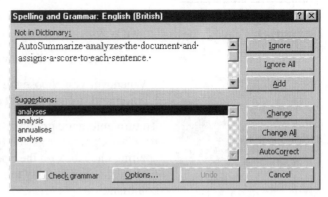

Whenever the spell-checker queries a word, your options include:

- **Ignore:** Leave this occurrence of the word unchanged.

- **Ignore All:** Leave this and all other occurrences of the word in the document unchanged.

- **Add:** Add the word to the spelling dictionary, so that Word will recognise it during future spell-checks of any document. Use this option for the names of people or places, or abbreviations or acronyms that you type regularly.

- **Change:** Correct this occurrence of the word, but prompt again on further occurrences.

- **Change All:** Correct this occurrence of the word – and all other occurrences without further prompting.

A word of caution: if the word that you have typed is correctly spelt but inappropriate – for example, 'their' instead of 'there'– your spell-checker will not detect it as an error. Therefore, you should always read over the final version of the document to ensure that it doesn't contain errors.

Watch Your Language

Before spell-checking your documents, choose **Tools | Language | Set Language** to display the current dictionary language. If it is incorrect (perhaps US English instead of British), select your required language and choose **Default**.

Checking Your Grammar

Word can check your grammar and suggest corrections to errors in two ways:

- As you type and edit your document (the automatic option).

- Whenever you choose the **Tools | Spelling and Grammar** command (the on-request option).

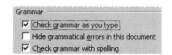

To turn automatic grammar-checking on or off, select or deselect the Check grammar as you type or the Check grammar with spelling checkbox on the Spelling & Grammar tab of the Options dialog box. You display this dialog box with **Tools | Options** command.

If automatic grammar-checking is turned on, a wavy green line under words indicates possible errors. You use Word's grammar checking features in the same way as its spell-checker.

Printing Options

Word offers a wide range of printing options. These include the ability to preview a document on your screen before you print it, and the choice of printing all your document, the current page, selected continuous or non-continuous pages, or the currently selected text.

Print Preview

This displays each page as it will appear when it is printed out on paper. To preview your document:

- Choose **File | Print Preview** or click the Print Preview 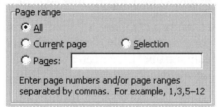 button on the Standard Toolbar. Click **Close** to return to your document.

Print Range Options

When you choose **File | Print**, you have the following options regarding which pages of your document you may print:

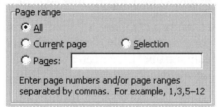

- **All:** Prints every page of your document.

- **Current Page**: Prints only the currently displayed page.

- **Selection:** Prints only the currently selected text.

- **Pages:** To print any one page of your document, enter its page number here.

  To print a group of continuous pages, enter the first and last page number of the group, separated by a dash. For example, 2-6 or 12-13.

  To print a non-continuous group of pages, enter their individual page numbers, separated by commas. For example, 3,5,9 or 12,17,34. You can combine continuous with non-continuous page selections.

Other options on the Print dialog box allow you specify how many copies you wish to print of your selected page(s), and indicate whether you want to print left or right pages only.

Section Summary:
So Now You Know

My Spell Checker

I have a spell checker
It came with my PC
It plane lee marks four my revue
Miss steaks aye can knot see

Eye ran this poem threw it
Your sure real glad two no
Its very polished in its own weigh
My chequer tolled me sew.

Cited in *Language and Technology:
From the Tower of Babel to the
Global Village*.
European Commission. 1996.
www.redact.ie/reports/langtech.htm

Above:
**This poem should warn you
against relying too heavily on
spell- and grammar-checkers.**

**Always check your document
for errors yourself, or ask
another person to check it for
you.**

You can increase or decrease Word's default *inter-line spacing* and *inter-paragraph spacing*.

You can highlight the start of each new paragraph by typing an extra paragraph mark (crude, but effective), by increasing inter-paragraph spacing, or by applying a *first line indent*. The opposite of a first line indent is a *hanging indent*, which is sometimes used for lists.

Word's *find and replace* feature enables you quickly to locate a particular piece of text, and replace it with an alternative piece of text. You can also find and replace text with specific formatting, and special characters such as paragraph marks and tabs.

The standard page size is *A4*, and pages can be oriented in *portrait* or *landscape*. A *margin* is the distance of the text (and graphics) from a particular edge of the page.

Headers and footers are small text items that reoccur on every page, and typically contain such details as the document title and author name. Either can also contain the automatically generated *page number*.

Word contains a *spell-checker* and a *grammar-checker*. You can set up these checkers so that they are permanently switched on, or you can run them only as you require.

Word's *print options* include a print preview feature and the ability to print one or a range of pages.

Section 3.4: Tables, Tabs and Graphics

In This Section

On most Word documents, text flows left to right across the width of the page. Sometimes, however, you may want to create narrow, side-by-side columns of text, numbers and graphics.

In this Section you will learn about Word's two options for creating such side-by-side columns: tables and tabs.

You will also discover how to insert and position graphics and images in Word, and how to insert one Word document inside another.

Finally, you are introduced to hyphenation – a way of splitting long words across lines to improve the appearance of justified text.

New Activities

At the end of this Section you should be able to:

- Create and format tables
- Insert and apply tabs and tab leaders
- Use Word's ruler to insert and change tabs
- Paste and insert graphics
- Move, reshape and resize graphics
- Apply automatic and manual hyphenation to justified text

New Words

At the end of this Section you should be able to explain the following terms:

- Table
- Tab
- Tab Leader
- Hyphenation

Using Tables in Word

A table consists of rectangular cells, arranged in rows and columns. Inside cells, text wraps just as it does on a page. As you type text into a cell, the cell expands vertically to hold each new line.

You can create a new, blank table, and enter text and graphics to its empty cells. Or you can convert existing paragraphs of text to a table.

> **Table**
>
> *An array of cells arranged in rows and columns that can hold text and graphics.*

Exercise 3.24: Creating a New Table

In this Exercise you create a table, and enter text to it.

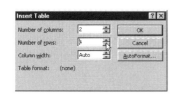

1) Click on the New button on the Standard Toolbar to create a new document. Click on the Save button to save it. Give your new document a name you will find easy to remember. If you initials are KB, for example, name it KBtable.doc.

2) Choose **Table | Insert Table**. In the Insert Table dialog box, select 2 columns and 4 rows. You can add or remove columns and rows later, as required.

    Accept the Column width default of Auto. This creates columns of equal size across the width of your page. Word displays a blank table as shown below.

¤	¤	¤
¤	¤	¤
¤	¤	¤
¤	¤	¤

3) Using the mouse, place the cursor in the top-left cell, and type: Sales Region

4) Press the TAB key. In a table, pressing TAB does not insert a tab stop. Instead, it moves the cursor to the next cell. SHIFT+TAB moves the cursor back to the previous cell. You can also use the ARROW keys or the mouse to move the cursor between different cells. (You cannot insert tabs in a Word table.)

    With the cursor in the top-right cell, enter the text: Number of Units Sold

5) Continue moving the cursor and typing text until your table looks like the one below.

    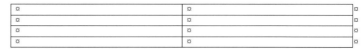

Sales·Region¤	Number·of·Units·Sold¤	¤
Europe¤	1234¤	¤
Latin·America¤	5678¤	¤
China¤	4321¤	¤

Selecting Table Cells

Congratulations. You have created your first table in Word.

You can format and align table text in the same way as text outside a table. Here are the rules on selecting table text:

- To select text in a cell, drag the mouse across the text.

- To select a single cell, click at the left edge of the cell.

- To select a row, double-click at the left edge of the left-most cell.

- To select a column, use the mouse to move the cursor to the top edge of the column, wait for the cursor to change to a thick, downward arrow, and then click to select the column.

- To select the entire table, click on any cell and choose **Table | Select Table**.

Table Operations

- To add a new row, select the row *beneath* the position where you want to insert the new row, and choose **Table | Insert Rows**.

- To add a new row at the end of a table, select the last end-of-row mark, and press ENTER.

- To add a new column, select the column to the *right* of where you want to insert the new column, and choose **Table | Insert Columns**.

- To add a new column at the right of a table, select the end-of-row marks and choose **Table | Insert Column**.

- To delete a row or column, select it, and choose **Table | Delete Rows** or **Table | Delete Columns**.

- To merge two or more selected cells from the same row into a single cell, choose **Table | Merge Cells**.

- To split a single, selected cell into two cells on the same row, choose **Table | Split Cells**.

- To apply borders and shading, select the cell(s), row(s), column(s) or entire table, and apply the **Format | Borders and Shading** command.

- To turn off a table's default borders (called *gridlines*) so that they appear only on the screen and not on the printout, select the table and choose **Table | Hide Gridlines**.

Example 3.25: Formatting and Changing Your Table

1) Select the top row of the table, choose **Format | Font**, select Arial, 12 pt, Bold, and click **OK**.

2) With the top row still selected, click on the Centre Align button on the Formatting Toolbar.

Sales·Region¤	Number·of·Units·Sold¤	¤
Europe¤	1234¤	¤

3) Place the cursor in the cell that contains Latin America. Choose **Table | Insert Row**. Type the following text into the new row.

South·Africa¤	581¤

4) Select the top row of the table, and choose **Table | Insert Row**.

5) With the new, inserted top row still selected, choose **Table | Merge Cells**.

6) Type the following text in the merged row: Sales Figures. Centre it.

7) Select the top, merged row, choose **Format | Font**, select Arial, 14 pt, Bold and Italic, and click **OK**.

8) By default, Word places a 1/2 pt black, single solid-line border around each cell. Select the top row, choose **Format | Borders and Shading** and place a double-line border under the first row.

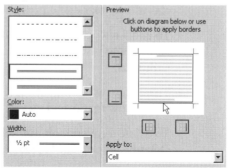

9) Select all rows except the top one, choose **Format | Borders and Shading**, click on the Shading tab, and select a 15% grey background. Your table should look as below.

Sales·Figures¤		
Sales·Region¤	Number·of·Units·Sold¤	¤
Europe¤	1234¤	¤
South·Africa¤	581¤	¤
Latin·America¤	5678¤	¤
China¤	4321¤	¤

Column Width, Spacing and Row Height

To change the width of a column, use the mouse to position the cursor over a vertical edge of the column. Then drag with the mouse until the column is the width that you require.

As you make a column wider or narrower, Word adjusts the width of the other columns so that the table width stays the same. If you hold down SHIFT while you drag a column edge, Word changes the width of the whole table accordingly.

You can change the height of cells in the same way.

Converting Text to a Table

If you have already typed into a Word document the text that you want placed in a table, select the text and choose **Table | Convert Text to Table**.

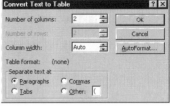

Select the number of columns and rows, and specify how Word is to recognise how the text for one cell is separated from text for the next cell. The most common separator is the paragraph mark.

The Table AutoFormat Option

Word's AutoFormat option offers a range of predefined formats for your table, including borders and shading. To apply AutoFormat, select your table and choose **Table | Table AutoFormat**. The Table AutoFormat dialog box offers a preview area where you can view the formatting effects on your table.

Right: Some examples of Word's AutoFormat options

Introduction to Tabs

Old-style typewriters had a key called TAB that, when pressed, changed the position at which the letter keys struck the page and printed text. Typically, there were about ten tab positions – called tab stops – usually about half-an-inch apart.

Pressing the TAB key once advanced the text position to the first tab stop, pressing TAB again moved it the second tab stop, and so on.

By typing text at the same tab position on successive lines, the typist could create vertical columns of text.

Right: **Tab stops used to position text in columns**

1	2	3	4	5	6	7	8	9	10
	Cajun·Heat·Fries				£1.45				
	Onion·Rings				£1.65				
	Bread·Sticks				£1.25				
	Fried·Cheese·Ravioli				£2.75				
	Primo·Mozzarella·Poppers				£3.25				
	Cream·Cheese·Poppers				£3.95				
	Breaded·Mushrooms				£2.95				
	Breaded·Zucchini·Sticks				£2.75				

The example above shows the second tab stop used to position menu items, and the sixth tab stop used to position menu prices.

As computers and wordprocessing software replaced the typewriter, the idea of tabs continued: computer keyboards include a TAB key, and Word, like other word-processing applications, offers a tab feature.

The effect of using tabs is similar to using tables: text appears in side-by-side columns rather than running continuously from the left to the right margin on the page.

Tabs
Predefined horizontal locations between the left and right page margins that determine where typed text is positioned. Using tabs on successive lines gives the effect of side-by-side columns of text.

If you want to position small amounts of text, such as the address lines at the top of a letter, tabs are quicker to use than tables. Also, tabs have a feature called leaders that tables do not have, which can make it easier to read text that is separated into different columns.

Using Tabs in Word

To view the tab stops set up on your copy of Word, choose **Format | Tabs** to display the Tabs dialog box. By default, Word has 10 preset tab stops, each a half-inch apart.

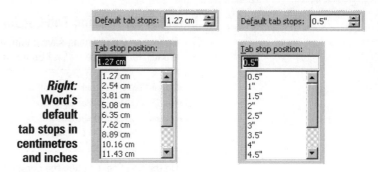

Right:
Word's default tab stops in centimetres and inches

Exercise 3.26: Using Tab Stops

1) Open the letter that you created and saved in Section 3.1.

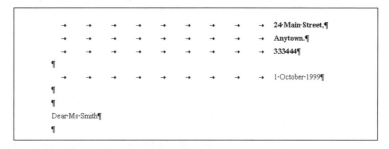

2) Move the cursor to the start of the first line and type: ABC Limited,

3) Move the cursor to the start of the second line and type: Unit 32A,

4) Move the cursor to the start of the third line and type: Smithstown Business Park.

   If your new text pushes any of the sender's address lines to the right or on to the next line, use the DEL key to remove tab stop(s) from the line until that address line returns to its original position.

5) Your new text picks up the bold formatting of the sender's address. Change its formatting back to normal. Your letter should now look as below.

Tab Leaders

Leader
- ⊙ 1 None
- ○ 2 ....
- ○ 3 -------
- ○ 4 ___

You can insert a line, called a tab leader, between text items that are positioned at adjoining tab stops. The Tabs dialog box offers a variety of leader formats.

Exercise 3.27: Using Tab Leaders

1) Open a new document, save it with a memorable name. If your initials are KB, for example, call it KBtabs.doc. Enter the following text:

> Cajun·Heat·Fries·£1.45·Primo·Mozzarella·Poppers·£3.25¶
> Onion·Rings·£1.65·Breaded·Zucchini·Sticks·£2.75¶
> Bread·Sticks·£1.25·Fried·Cheese·Ravioli·£2.75¶
> Cream·Cheese·Poppers·£3.95·Breaded·Mushrooms·£2.95¶

2) On the first line, position the cursor at the end of the word Fries, and press DEL to remove the space between Fries and £1.45. Press TAB repeatedly to move the £1.45 rightwards to the 5.08 cm default tab stop.

3) Repeat step 2) for the remaining three lines. Your text should look as below.

> Cajun·Heat·Fries → → £1.45·Primo·Mozzarella·Poppers·£3.25¶
> Onion·Rings → → → £1.65·Breaded·Zucchini·Sticks·£2.75¶
> Bread·Sticks → → → £1.25·Fried·Cheese·Ravioli·£2.75¶
> Cream·Cheese·Poppers→ → £3.95·Breaded·Mushrooms·£2.95¶

4) On the first line, position the cursor after £1.45, and press DEL to remove the space before Primo. Press TAB twice to move the Primo Mozzarella Poppers rightwards to the 7.62 cm default tab stop.

5) Repeat step 4) for the remaining three lines.

6) On the first line, position the cursor after Poppers, and press DEL to remove the space between Poppers and £3.25. Press TAB repeatedly to move the £3.25 rightwards to the 13.65 cm default tab stop.

7) Repeat step 6) for the remaining three lines. Your text should look as below.

> Cajun·Heat·Fries· → → £1.45→ → Primo·Mozzarella·Poppers → → £3.25¶
> Onion·Rings → → → £1.65→ → Breaded·Zucchini·Sticks → → £2.75¶
> Bread·Sticks → → → £1.25→ → Fried·Cheese·Ravioli → → → £2.75¶
> Cream·Cheese·Poppers→ → £3.95→ → Breaded·Mushrooms → → → £2.95¶

8) Select all the text and choose the **Format | Tabs** command.

9) Select the 2.54 cm tab stop, then select the Leader 2 option, and click the **Set** button.

10) Repeat step 9) for the following, other tabs stops: 3.81, 5.08, 11.43, 12.7, 13.65 and 13.97 cms.

Be sure to click **Set** every time you apply the Leader 2 option to a tab stop.

When finished, click **OK**.

Deselect the text. Your screen should now look as below.

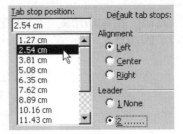

Cajun·Heat·Fries· ... → ... ... → .... £1.45→|	→	Primo·Mozzarella·Poppers...→... →. £3.25¶
Onion·Rings. →. ...→.... ...→.... £1.65→	→	Breaded·Zucchini·Sticks ....→... →.... £2.75¶
Bread·Sticks →. ...→.... ...→.... £1.25→	→	Fried·Cheese·Ravioli →. ...→.... →. £2.75¶
Cream·Cheese·Poppers→....→.... £3.95→	→	Breaded·Mushrooms →. ...→.... →. £2.95¶

Word displays small, white spaces at the tab stop positions. These appear on the screen only, and not on the printed copy.

Tab Leader

A solid, dotted or dashed line used to draw the reader's eye across the space between columns of text that are positioned using tab stops.

Using Tabs With the Ruler

You can display and amend Word's default tab stops by choosing **View | Ruler**. The ruler appears along the top of the document window. You can see the default tab stops at evenly- spaced positions along the base of the ruler.

You can change the position of a tab stop by dragging it left or rightwards to a new location on the ruler. The space between all default tab stop changes proportionately. As you drag a tab stop, Word displays a vertical, dashed line stretching down from the tab ruler to the document itself.

L   **Left**

⊥   **Centre**

⅃   **Right**

⅃·   **Decimal point**

At the top left of the slide window you can see the tab button. As you click on this, it cycles through four values: left-aligned (default), centre-aligned, right-aligned, and decimal point-aligned.

To add a new tab stop, click the tab button to display the type of tab you want, and then click the ruler where you want to place the tab.

Using Graphics in Word

You can illustrate your Word documents with graphics, such as drawings created in other computer applications or even scanned photographs.

Also, Word contains sixteen categories of standard or so-called clip art images that you can use and reuse in a wide range of documents. Examples of clip art would be Man Answering Phone, Woman Sitting at Desk, Handshake, Sunset and so on . Clip art is available on CD-ROMs and on the Internet.

Clip Art
Standard or stock images that can be used and reused in a wide range of documents.

Importing Graphics: Two Options

You have two options for inserting graphics: copy-and-paste, and file insert. Let's look at these two in detail.

Graphics: Copy and Paste

This option is possible only if you can open the file containing the relevant graphic. To do so, you need to have installed on your computer a software application that can read that graphic format.

For example, to copy into Word a graphic created in Adobe Photoshop, you would need Adobe Photoshop running on your computer. Or, failing that, another graphics program capable of opening Adobe Photoshop (.PSD) files.

When you have the graphic open in your graphics program, select it (or part of it, as you require), and choose **Edit | Copy** to copy it to the Clipboard. Then, switch to Word, position the cursor where you want the graphic to appear in your document, and choose **Edit | Paste**.

Graphics: File Insert

This option enables you to include a graphic in a Word document – even if you do not have installed the software package in which the graphic was created.

Position the cursor where you want the graphic to appear in your document, and choose **Insert | Picture | From File**. Locate the relevant graphic – it may be on your hard disk, on a floppy or on a CD-ROM – and click **OK** to insert the image.

To include any of Word's own set of clip art images, choose the **Insert | File | Clip Art** command, select the clip art category, then the individual image, and click **Insert**.

Working With Graphics

There are a number of common operations that you can perform on imported graphics, regardless of their type.

Moving a Graphic

To move a graphic, first select it by clicking anywhere inside it. Next, hold down the mouse button. Word changes the cursor to a cross. Then drag the graphic to its new location.

To move a graphic between documents, use the **Cut** and **Paste** commands on the **Edit** menu.

Changing the Shape and Size of a Graphic

You can change the shape and size of a graphic by selecting it and clicking on any of its six handles.

Hold down the mouse button and drag the edge of the graphic to change its shape. As you drag the object, Word changes its border to a dashed line.

To change the graphics' size but not its shape, hold down the SHIFT key as you drag with the mouse.

Exercise 3.28: Inserting a Word Clip Art Image

1) Open the poster document that you created in Section 3.2.

2) Position the cursor at the end of the last line, All Welcome. Press ENTER to insert a new paragraph mark.

3) Choose **Insert | Picture | Clip Art**, select the Category of Signs, click on the No Smoking symbol, and click **Insert**. Word creates a new, second page, and inserts the clip art image on it.

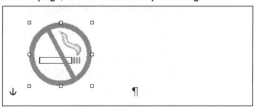

4) Select the graphic, reduce its size by a half, and drag it until it is under the All Welcome line. Delete the paragraph mark that you typed in step 2). The bottom of your poster should now look like that shown below.

Inserting One Document in Another

In addition to inserting graphic files into a Word document, you can also insert another, different Word document. To do so, place the cursor in the first document at the point where you want to insert the second document, chose **Insert | File**, select the second document, and click **OK**.

If you insert a second document at the end of the current document, this called *appending* the second document to the first one.

Hyphenating Justified Text

In Section 3.2 you learned about an alignment option called justification, whereby text is aligned against both the left and right margins. Justification is typically used for the narrow columns of text found in newspapers and magazines.

Justified columns can contain a lot of white (that is, blank) space, as Word spreads out the text in order to align it with both margins simultaneously. This is particularly true when the text contains a lot of long words.

Hyphenation – the process of breaking up long words and splitting them across two lines – gives justified text a more professional appearance. Consider the two examples below.

Hyphenation Off

Word spreads out the text in order to align it with both margins simultaneously. This is particularly true when the text contains a lot of long words.

Hyphenation On

Word spreads out the text in order to align it with both margins simultaneously. This is particularly true when the text contains a lot of long words.

Word applies two rules when hyphenating text: certain words are never hyphenated, and words that are hyphenated are split only in certain places.

Word allows you to hyphenate both justified and unjustified text.

> **Hyphenation**
> *The process of splitting a long word across two successive lines to avoid unsightly amounts of white space. Used mostly in narrow, justified columns of text.*

You can hyphenate text in two ways: automatically or manually.

Automatic Hyphenation

Word can hyphenate your document automatically as you type. To use this option, choose **Tools | Language | Hyphenation**, select the Automatically hyphenate document checkbox, and click **OK**.

☑ Automatically hyphenate document

Automatic Hyphenation Options

If you select automatic hyphenation, Word offers you a number of options that let you control how it applies hyphenation to your document.

- **Text in Capitals:** Typically, only headings are in capitals, so you can decide to turn automatic hyphenation off for capitalised text.

- **Hyphenation Zone:** The amount of space that Word leaves between the end of the last word in a line and the right margin. It applies only to unjustified text. Make the zone wider to reduce the number of hyphens, or narrower to reduce the raggedness of the right margin.

- **Consecutive Hyphens**: The number of consecutive lines that Word hyphenates.

Manual Hyphenation

If you don't want Word to insert hyphens in your text automatically, ensure that the Automatically hyphenate document checkbox is deselected.

The better option is to turn automatic hyphenation off, and run manual hyphenation after you have finished writing and editing, and adding and removing text.

Running Manual Hyphenation

To hyphenate your document (or a selected part of it) manually, choose **Tools | Language | Hyphenation** and click **Manual**.

Word scans through your text, and when it finds a word it thinks it should hyphenate, it displays a dialog box similar to the one below.

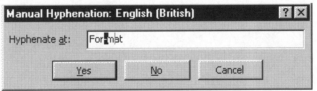

Click **Yes** if you want Word to insert a hyphen in the suggested location. If you prefer Word to insert the hyphen at a different location, move the cursor to that location, and then click **Yes**. Alternatively, click **No** to leave the word unbroken.

Section Summary: So Now You Know

A Word *table* consists of rectangular cells arranged in rows and columns. You can create a new table and enter text to it, or you can convert text in non-table form to table text.

As required, you can insert and delete rows and columns in a table, split a single cell into two cells, or merge multiple cells into a single cell. You can also change row and column height and width, apply formatting, and add borders and shading. Word's *AutoFormat* option provides quick way to improve the appearance of any table.

Tabs are prefined horizontal locations that, when used on successive lines, give the appearance of columns. *Tab leaders* are dashed, dotted or continuous lines that draw the reader's eye from one tabbed column to the next.

You can add *graphics* to a Word document in two ways: by copy and paste, or by inserting the graphic as a file. You can move, reposition, resize or change the shape of any graphic.

You can use Word's *hyphenation* feature to remove unsightly amounts of white space by splitting long words across successive lines. Hyphenation is applied mostly to narrow columns of justified text.

Section 3.5: Mail Merge and Templates

Bulk mail is the name given to mass-produced letters that contain individual names and addresses (as in 'Dear Ms Murray') but have the same basic text (as in 'Allow us to introduce our Spring Promotion...'). A more commonly used term might be junk mail.

How is it done? Each letter is basically the same, but clearly no one letter is just a copy of another, as each is slightly different. Read this Section to find out.

Hint: Each letter is the result of combining or *merging* two separate documents: one – the form letter – contains the basic text; the other – the data source – holds a list of names, addresses and other details.

Also in this Section you will learn about templates. These are quick, convenient ways to create documents that can contain ready-made text, images, formatting and page settings.

New Activities

At the end of this Section you should be able to:

- Create the two components of a merged letter: the form letter and the data source
- Select the appropriate merge fields and insert them in a form letter
- Merge a form letter with a data source to produce a mail merge
- Explain the two possible roles of a Word template: document model, and interface controller
- Choose an appropriate Word template for a document type
- Explain the relationship between styles and templates, and apply styles to selected text
- Attach a different template to a document, and create a new template

New Words

At the end of this section you should be able to explain the following terms:

- Form Letter
- Template
- Data Source
- Style
- Merge Field

Mail Merge:
The Components

Think of a mail merge as composed of two components: a *form letter* and a *data source*. And think of *merge fields* as the glue that binds the two together. Read on to discover what these three terms mean.

Form Letter

This holds the text that *remains the same* in every letter – plus punctuation, spaces and perhaps graphics.

You never type names or addresses in the form letter as these will be different on each copy of the final, merged letter.

Form Letter
A Word document containing information (text, spaces, punctuation and graphics) that remains the same in each copy of the merged letter.

Data Source

This holds the information that *changes* for each copy of the final, merged letter – the names and addresses of the people that you want to send the merged letters to.

You can create a data source in Word, or in a spreadsheet (such as Excel) or database (such as Access). Whichever file type you use, its contents must be arranged in a table. Along the top row must be the titles identifying the information categories in the columns underneath, such as Title or Last Name.

Data Source
A file containing information (such as names and addresses) that will be different in each merged copy of the final letter.

Merge Fields

«FirstName»¶

«Title»·«LastName»,¶

«Company».¶

Above:
Merge fields are enclosed within double angle brackets

In the merged letter, Word replaces the merge fields with the associated details from the data source.

These are special instructions that you insert in your form letter. They tell Word which details you want to merge from your data source, and where Word is to position them in your merged letter.

Merge fields have names such as Job Title, First Name and Town. When you merge the form letter and the data source, Word replaces the merge fields in the form letter with the associated details from the data source. For example, Word might replace the merge field called Town with Carrick-on-Suir, Castlebar or Clonmel on different copies of the merged letter.

Merge Field
An instruction to Word to insert a particular type of information, such as job title or a line of an address, in a specified location on the form letter.

Mail Merge: The Procedure

You can think of a mail merge as a five-step process. Steps one and two are about preparing the ingredients: the form letter and the data source.

In step three, you make the connection between the two by inserting the merge fields in your form letter – one merge field for every item of information that you wish to merge to the form letter from the data source.

Step four is optional, but recommended. Before you produce your merged letters, take a preview at the first one or two to check that the merge was worked successfully.

Finally in step five, print off your merged letters.

One: Prepare Your Form Letter

This is simply a Word document. Using the **Tools | Merge** command, you can:

- Create a new letter especially for the merge operation, or

- Select a letter you have already typed as the form letter.

Exercises 3.28 and 3.29 show you how to perform these steps.

Two: Prepare Your Data Source

Again, using the **Tools | Merge** command, you can:

- Create a new Word file and enter to it the names, addresses and other details of the people you plan to send the merged letter to, or

- Select a file created in another software program.

You will learn how to create a Word data source in Exercise 3.30.

Three: Insert Merge Fields in Your Form Letter

Whenever you open your form letter on screen, Word displays a special Mail Merge Toolbar. One of its buttons is called Insert Merge Field. This is one you use to select and then position the merge fields in your form letter. Exercise 3.31 shows you how to insert the merge field codes.

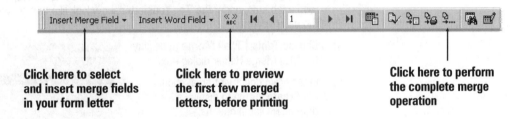

Click here to select and insert merge fields in your form letter

Click here to preview the first few merged letters, before printing

Click here to perform the complete merge operation

Four: Preview Your Merged Letters

Before you produce your (perhaps hundreds or thousands!) of merged letters, click on the Toolbar's View Merged Data button to preview the first one or two merged letters.

You will learn how to preview your merged letters in Exercise 3.32.

Five: Print Your Merged Letters

If you are happy with the preview, click on the Mail Merge button to perform the complete merge operation. Select the **Merge to Printer** option to output copies of your merged letters.

You will learn how to print your merged letters in Exercise 3.33.

Word gives you the option of saving all the merged letters in a single file. But you don't need to do this, as you can quickly recreate them at any stage by rerunning the merge operation.

Your Mail Merge Exercises

Exercises 3.29 to 3.33 take you, step-by-step, through a complete, worked example of a mail merge operation.

For these Exercises, we will assume that the merged letters are produced on pre-printed paper that already contains the sender's name and address. Only the recipients' names and addresses need therefore be inserted.

Exercise 3.28: Using an Existing a Document as a Form Letter

Do you still have on your computer the letter you saved from Exercise 3.26? If so, this Exercise shows you how to use that text as a basis for your form letter.

If not, proceed to Exercise 3.29 to create a new form letter from scratch.

1) Open the file that you saved in Exercise 3.26.

2) Remove the recipient's name and address from the top left of the letter, and remove the sender's address from the top right. Also delete the 'Ms Smith' after the word 'Dear'.

3) At the top right, type 'To': and press TAB. Insert three new lines, each with a tab stop, under the 'To': Your letter show look like that shown on the page opposite.

4) Choose **Tools | Mail Merge** to display the Mail Merge Helper dialog box.

5) In the Main document area, choose the **Create** button to display a drop-down list of options.

From this list, select the option called **Form Letters**.

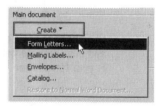

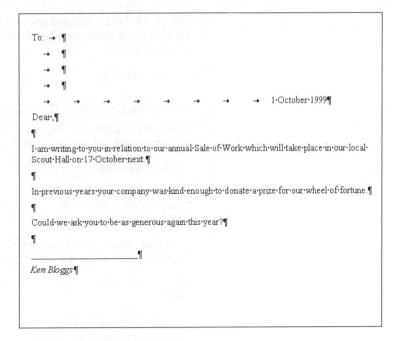

```
To:  →  ¶
     →   ¶
     →   ¶
     →   ¶
     →    →    →    →    →    →    →    →    1·October·1999¶
Dear·,¶
¶
I·am·writing·to·you·in·relation·to·our·annual·Sale·of·Work·which·will·take·place·in·our·local·
Scout·Hall·on·17·October·next.¶
¶
In·previous·years·your·company·was·kind·enough·to·donate·a·prize·for·our·wheel·of·fortune.¶
¶
Could·we·ask·you·to·be·as·generous·again·this·year?¶
¶
_____¶
Ken·Bloggs¶
```

6) On the next dialog box displayed, click the **Active Window** button.

7) Word next displays a dialog box that asks you to select or create a data source. Proceed to Exercise 3.30.

Exercise 3.29: Creating a New Form Letter

Follow this Exercise to create a new form letter for a mail merge operation.

1) Choose **Tools | Mail Merge** to display the Mail Merge Helper dialog box.

2) In the Main Document area, choose the **Create** button to display a drop-down list of options.

   From this list, select the option called **Form Letters**.

3) On the next dialog box displayed, click the **New Main Document** button, and click **Cancel**.

4) Word leaves a new document open on your screen for you to enter the text of your form letter. Type the text as shown in Exercise 3.28.

5) Click the File Save button and give your new document a name that you will find easy to remember. If you initials are KB, for example, name it KBformlet.doc.

Proceed to Exercise 3.30.

Exercise 3.30: Creating a Data Source

In this Exercise you create your data source to contain the names, addresses and other information that will vary on each copy of the final, merged letter.

Do not begin this Exercise until you have completed either Exercise 3.28 or 3.29.

1) If the Mail Merge Helper dialog box is not already open, choose **Tools | Mail Merge** to display it.

2) In the Data source area, choose the **Get Data** button to display a drop-down list of options.

From this list, select the option called **Create Data Source**.

3) Word now displays the Create Data Source dialog box. See below.

4) In the case of each of the following merge fields, click on the Field Name list and then click the **Remove Field Name** button to delete them: JobTitle, City, State, PostalCode, Country, HomePhone and WorkPhone.

5) You now have all the merge fields that you need. Click **OK**.

6) Word next asks you to name and save your Data Source file. If your initials are KB, for example, name it KBDataSource and click **Save**.

7) You are now shown the dialog box below. Click **Edit Data Source**.

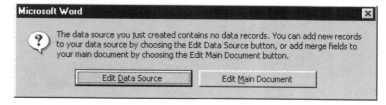

8) Word displays a Data Form dialog box. Enter the information as shown and click **Add New**.

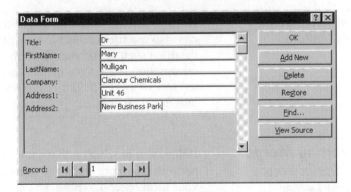

9) Enter a second set of details to the Data Form dialog box as shown below. Click **Add New** and then click **OK**.

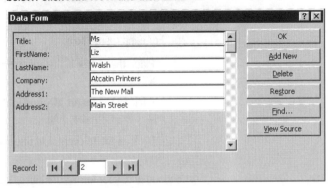

You have now created a Data Source with two records – enough for this Exercise. But you can easily imagine a Data Source with hundreds or thousands of records, each record holding the name, address and other information regarding a particular person or organisation.

Viewing Your Word Data Source

You can open, view and edit your data source file just as you can any other Word document. Open the data source you created in Exercise 3.30. It should look like that below.

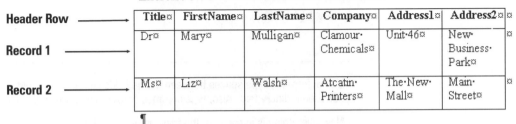

	Title¤	FirstName¤	LastName¤	Company¤	Address1¤	Address2¤	¤
Header Row →							
Record 1 →	Dr¤	Mary¤	Mulligan¤	Clamour· Chemicals¤	Unit·46¤	New· Business· Park¤	¤
Record 2 →	Ms¤	Liz¤	Walsh¤	Atcatin· Printers¤	The·New· Mall¤	Main· Street¤	¤

¶

You can see a header row containing the merge field names, such as FirstName and LastName. And under the header row are the records themselves, each in a row of its own.

*Using Non-Word
Data Sources*

Does your data source have to be a Word document? No. You can also use files created in a spreadsheet such as Excel or a database such as Access. The only requirement is that the information is arranged in the same type of table format: a single, top row of merge field titles, followed by other rows holding individual records.

Inserting Merge Codes in Your Form Letter

Before you moving on to the mail merge operation, you need to perform one more step. You must insert the merge field codes in your form letter. Exercise 3.31 shows you how.

Exercise 3.31: Inserting the Merge Field Codes

1) Open your form letter document.

2) For each merge field:

– Place the cursor in the appropriate position in your form letter

– Click on the **Insert Merge Field** button on the Mail Merge Toolbar, and

– Click on the relevant field title from the drop-down list.

Continue until your form letter looks like the sample shown.

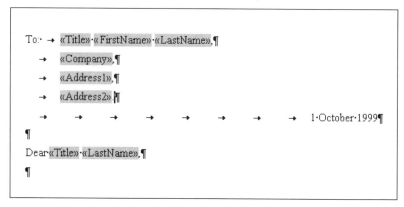

Do not forget to type spaces between merge fields just as you would between ordinary text. Also, type commas or full stops at the end of lines.

Now everything is in place for the mail merge operation.

Exercise 3.32: Previewing the Mail Merge

1) If your form letter is not already open, open it now and make it the active window.

View Merged Data button

2) Click the View Merged Data button on the Mail Merge Toolbar. Word displays the first merged letter. It should look as shown below.

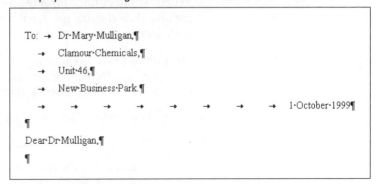

```
To:  →  Dr·Mary·Mulligan,¶
     →    Clamour·Chemicals,¶
     →    Unit·46,¶
     →    New·Business·Park.¶
     →    →    →    →    →    →    →    →    1·October·1999¶
¶
Dear·Dr·Mulligan,¶
¶
```

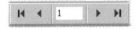

Arrow buttons

3) You can view the second merged letter by clicking the Forward Arrow button on the Mail Merge Toolbar.

You are now ready to perform the mail merge.

Exercise 3.33: Performing the Mail Merge

1) If your form letter is not already open, open it now and make it the active window.

Mail Merge button

2) Click on the Mail Merge button on the Mail Merge Toolbar to display the Merge dialog box. Select the options as shown below and click **Merge**.

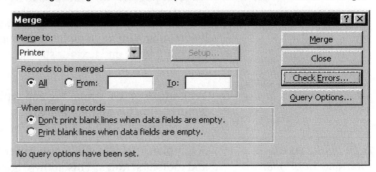

Your form letter and the two records from the data source are now merged to the printer.

Congratulations! You have performed your first mail merge in Word.

Word Templates

Microsoft Word is made up of three components: the Word software application itself, the document files that Word produces, and a third component you now meet for the first time: templates.

- **Word Application:** This provides the standard Word menus, commands and toolbars – the things you use to create and work with documents.

- **Document Files:** Look in any of these and you will find the text, graphics, formatting, and settings such as margins and page layout for that particular document.

- **Word Templates:** These have two main purposes. They can:

    - Provide a model for creating documents

    - Control Word's interface: the menus, commands and toolbars available to the user.

A Template as a Document Model

A template can act as a document model by storing:

- Built-in text and graphics, such as your company's name and logo. These are sometimes called 'boilerplate' text and graphics.

- Preset formatting (such as font settings) and text positioning (such as alignment, indents, tab stops, and inter-line and inter-paragraph spacing settings).

- Preset page settings (such as margins and page orientation).

For example, you could save everyone in your organisation time by creating a memo template that contained preset margins, the company logo, and text for standard headings such as 'Memo', 'To:' and 'From:'.

With much of the formatting and typing already done, users simply fill in the additional text.

A Template as an Interface Controller

A template can also store customised Word commands, menus and toolbar settings. This allows managers to remove unused and unnecessary features, and adapt Word to meet the needs of different levels of users.

For example, you could create a template that helped new Word users by displaying a customised toolbar with buttons and menus to lead them through everyday tasks.

Templates and Documents

Whether you realised it or not, every new Word document that you have created has been based on a template.

A single template can provide the basis for lots of documents. But each document can be based on only a single template at a time.

A template, like a document, is a Word file. Whereas document file names end in .doc, template file names end in .dot.

The Normal.dot Template

Unless you choose otherwise, every new Word document you create is based on a template called Normal.dot.

In addition to this standard, all-purpose template, Word provides templates for specific document types such as letters, memos and reports.

> **Word Template**
>
> *A file that can contain ready-made text, formatting and page settings, and interface controls. Every Word document is based on, and takes its characteristics from, a template of one kind or another.*

Templates and New Documents

In Section 3.1, you learned two ways to create a new document:

- Clicking on the New ▯ button on the Standard Toolbar

-or-

- Choosing the **File | New** command.

If you click the New button, Word automatically bases your new document on the Normal.dot template.

Choose **File | New**, however, and Word presents you with a wide range of templates to choose from. You will find the various templates on different tabs of the New dialog box.

Exercise 3.34: Previewing Word's Templates

1) Choose **File | New** to display the New dialog box.

2) Click on the various tabs to view the available templates.

3) Click on the various templates to view a miniature of them in the Preview area on the right of the dialog box.

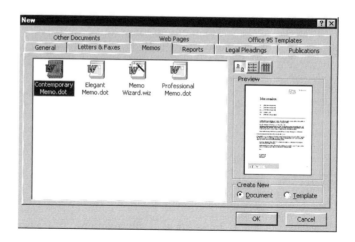

Templates and Styles

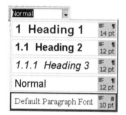

Above:
Style drop-down
list box

At the top-left of the Standard Toolbar is a drop-list list box containing items called Normal, Heading 1, Heading 2 and so on. These items are termed styles.

For ECDL, you need know only four things about *styles*:

- A style is a bundle of formatting and text positioning settings.

- You apply a style by first positioning the cursor in the text, and then clicking on that style from the drop-down list.

- Unless you choose otherwise, Word applies the style called Normal to all text you type in a document.

- Styles are linked to templates. For example, in one template the style called Heading 3 might be centre-aligned, Times, 10 point, italic. In another, Heading 3 might be left-aligned, Arial, 12 point, bold.

Exercise 3.35: Applying a Style to Text

In this Exercise you will open a document that you previously created and saved, and apply a style to its headings.

1) Open the document that you saved in Exercise 3.23.

2) Choose **Edit | Replace**, and on the Replace tab, type the text Heading One in both the Find what: and Replace with: boxes.

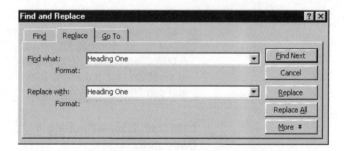

3) With the cursor in the Replace with: box, click the **More** button and then the **Format** button. Select the option **Style** from the pop-up menu, and then select the style Heading 1 from the list displayed. Click **OK**.

4) You are returned to the Find and Replace dialog box. Click **Replace All**.

Word now applies the style called Heading 1 to all the headings in your document. Unless you have at some stage changed the Heading 1 style that comes with Normal.dot, the Heading 1 font should be Arial 14 point, bold.

Why Use Styles?

Using styles to control the appearance of a document has three advantages:

- You can apply a bundle of formatting and text positioning settings to a piece of selected text in a single, quick operation.

- By changing the settings of a particular style, Word can automatically apply your new settings to all occurrences of text in that style throughout the entire document.

  For example, by changing the Heading 1 style from bold to italic, all text with the Heading 1 style changes from bold to italic. This is so much faster than individually selecting and then changing every heading.

- If you change the template on which a document is based, the document takes its style settings from the new template.

  You can therefore change the entire appearance of a document by linking it with a different template. Exercise 3.36 illustrates this point.

Style

A collection of formatting and positioning settings that you can apply to selected text in a single operation. Styles are linked to templates, and can have different settings in different templates.

Exercise 3.36: Attaching a Different Template to a Document

Professional
Report.dot

1) Select all the text in the document, and chose **Edit | Copy** (or CTRL+c).

2) Choose **File | New** to display the New dialog box. Click the Reports tab, and then click the template called Professional Report.dot. Finally, click **OK**.

3) Word opens a new document that is based on Professional Report.dot.

    This contains instructions which you can ignore. Hold down the CTRL key and click in the left margin to select everything in the new document, and then press DEL to delete the new document's contents.

4) Choose **Edit | Paste** (or press CTRL+v) to paste the text copied from your document into the new document.

Heading·One¶

How·does·AutoSummarize·determine·what·the·key·points·are?·AutoSummarize· analyzes·the·document·and·assigns·a·score·to·each·sentence.·(For·example,·it·gives· a·higher·score·to·sentences·that·contain·words·used·frequently·in·the·document.)·You· then·choose·a·percentage·of·the·highest-scoring·sentences·to·display·in·the·summary.¶
      Keep·in·mind·that·AutoSummarize·works·best·on·well-structured·documents·– for·example,·reports,·articles,·and·scientific·papers.¶

Notice how all text in your document with the Normal and Heading 1 styles changes in appearance. This is because such text is now taking its settings from the Professional Report.dot template – and not from the Normal.dot template on which the document was originally based.

Creating a New Template

Word offers a number of ways of creating a new template. Here is the easiest way:

- Create a document that has the features you want in your template – some boilerplate text, perhaps, or a particular margin setting.

- With the document open on your screen, save it not as a document but as a template.

In future, whenever you use the **File | New** command to create a document, your new template appears as an option on the General tab of the New dialog box.

Exercise 3.37 takes you through an example of this procedure.

Exercise 3.37: Creating a New Template

1) Create a new document and enter the following text in a table.

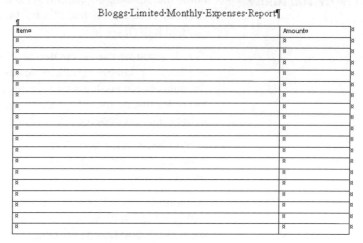

Apply the following settings:

– Page Orientation: Use the Paper Size tab displayed by the **File | Page Settings** command to change the page orientation to Landscape.

– Heading: Centre-align the heading, and make it Times New Roman, 20 point.

– Table: Create a two-column, 19-row table. Select the table and, using the Row tab displayed by the **Table | Cell Height and Width** command, set the row height to 20 point.

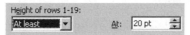

2) Choose **File | Save As**, and save the file as a template.

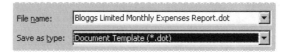

3) Choose **File | Close** to close your new template.

4) Choose **File | New** to display the General tab of the New dialog box, where you can see your new template as an option. Select your new template and then click **OK**.

Word creates a new document based on your template.

Section Summary: So Now You Know

Mail merge is the process of combining a *form letter* (which holds the unchanging letter text) and a *data source* (which holds the names, addresses and other details that are different in every merged letter).

The data source can be created in Word, or in a spreadsheet (such as Excel) or database (such as Access). Whichever the file type, the data source contents must be arranged in a table. Along the top row must be the titles identifying the information categories in the columns underneath, such as Title or Last Name.

Merge fields in the form letter indicate which details are taken from the data source, and where they are positioned on the final, merged letter.

A *template* can act as a *document model* by storing built-in text and graphics, such as your company's name and logo, preset formatting and text positioning, and, preset page settings. A template can also act as an *interface controller* by specifying which of Word's menus, commands and toolbars are available to the user.

A template, like a document, is a Word file. Whereas document file names end in .doc, template file names end in .dot.

Unless you choose otherwise, every new Word document you create is based on a template called Normal.dot. Word also provides templates for specific document types. You can create new templates, and change the template on which a document is based.

Styles, which are linked to templates, enable you to apply a bundle of formatting and text positioning settings to selected text in a single, quick operation.

4 Spreadsheets

Some things are easy to explain or describe – but difficult to use or operate. A spreadsheet is not one of those things. In fact, it's the very opposite.

At the end of this Module you will able able to build number-crunching, ECDL-exam passing spreadsheets for recording, analysing and graphing just about any kind of numbers you can think of.

Quarterly sales commission, annual rainfall or the monthly household budget: if you can count it now, you will be able to spreadsheet it later.

Along the way we will show the shortcuts that will help you get a lot of work done on long numbers, but with little typing and in a very short time.

But you will be no closer to being able to give a one-sentence definition of what exactly a spreadsheet is.

Perhaps it's because spreadsheets are about processing numbers rather than words that makes them so hard to define.

Think of this Module as your chance to count rather be counted. Good luck with it.

Section 4.1: Your First Steps in Excel

In This Section

'Why do I need to know all this ... What is the point ?' You may find yourself asking such questions when reading this Section.

But first lessons are like that – whether you are learning the guitar, karate or spreadsheets.

In your first hour you usually have the hard work of remembering new activities and words – but rarely the pleasure of putting your new knowledge into practice.

There is nothing in this Section that you will find difficult or complex. We have included only the material that you absolutely need to know, and we have introduced it as gently as possible.

Half-way through Section 4.2, when you discover the power and convenience of spreadsheets, you will be asking a very different question: 'How did I ever manage to organise my work or life without Microsoft Excel!'

New Activities

At the end of this Section you should be able to:

- Start and quit Excel

- Explain the difference between a worksheet and a workbook

- Enter numbers, text and cell references to a worksheet

- Edit and delete the contents of a cell

- Save, name, open, create and close Excel workbooks

New Words

At the end of this Section you should be able to explain the following terms:

- Worksheet
- Workbook
- Cell
- Active Cell
- Row

- Column
- Cell Reference
- Name Box
- Constant

Starting Excel

Double click on the Microsoft Excel icon.

-or-

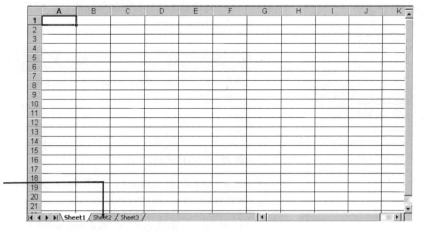

Microsoft
Excel

Choose **Start | Programs | Microsoft Excel**.

Excel starts and displays a new workbook with three worksheets ready for you to use.

Worksheets and Workbooks

This ECDL Module is about spreadsheets. But Excel does not use the word spreadsheet. Instead, it uses two other words – worksheet and workbook. Let's explain what these mean.

Worksheet
A page that is made up of little boxes arranged in rows and columns.

In Excel, a worksheet is a spreadsheet. A worksheet is much larger than your screen. You can see only a very small part of it at one time.

Workbook
A file containing worksheets.

When you create a new workbook, Excel creates three blank worksheets inside that workbook. Excel calls the worksheets Sheet1, Sheet2 and Sheet3.

To move from one worksheet to another, click on the tab displaying its name.

Above: **An Excel worksheet**

If three worksheets are not enough, you can add more to your workbook – up to a maximum of 256. Think of worksheets as pages in a book, and the workbook as the book containing those pages.

The Parts of a Worksheet

Now you will learn the names of the important parts of a worksheet.

Cells

The little boxes that make up a worksheet.

Cells are arranged in (horizontal) rows and (vertical) columns.

Active cell

The cell in which the cursor is currently located.

Only one cell on a worksheet can be the active cell at any one time. You will always know which cell is the active cell: Excel surrounds it with a thick border. You can make a cell active by clicking on it with the mouse.

The active cell  **A cell that is *not* the active cell**

When you open a new workbook, Excel makes the top-left cell of the first worksheet, Sheet1, the active cell.

Below:
A worksheet column

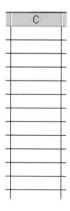

Column

A vertical line of cells from the top of the worksheet to the bottom.

Each worksheet contains 256 columns. Excel names each column with a letter or group of letters. The first 26 are named A to Z. The remainder are AA to AZ, BA to BZ, and continuing through to IA through to IZ.

Row

A horizontal line of cells that stretches left-to-right across a worksheet.

Above: **A worksheet row**

Each worksheet contains 16,384 rows. Excel gives each row a number, from 1 to 16,384.

The total number of cells in a worksheet is therefore 256 multiplied by 16,384 or 4,194,304!

Cell References and the Name Box

Each cell in a worksheet has a unique address or location known as its cell reference.

Cell Reference
The location or 'address' of a cell on a worksheet.

A cell reference is made up of two parts:

- The column letter (A, B, C, ...)   - The row number (1,2,3, ...)

When you open a new workbook in Excel, the active cell is the one on Sheet1 with the cell reference A1.

Remember: column letter first, row number second. For example, B6, C8 and J12.

Column Letters: Upper or Lower Case?

You will always see cell references written with the column letters in upper-case letters (for example, A1, B10 and W90) rather than in lower-case ones (for example, a1, b10 and w90). This is true for the Microsoft's Excel User Guide, Excel online help – and this book.

However, when you type a cell reference into Excel, as you will in Exercise 4.1, it does not matter whether you type the column letter in upper- or lower-case. Excel accepts either. You may find it easier to enter a column letter in lower-case, as you need type only the letter key, and not the letter key in combination with the SHIFT key.

Name Box
The rectangular area above the top-left corner of a worksheet in which Excel displays the cell reference of the active cell.

Name Box ⟶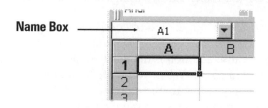

You can use the Name Box to move the cursor to any cell on the worksheet, making that cell the active cell.

To do so, type the cell reference in the Name Box and press ENTER.

Exercise 4.1: Name Box and Cell References

Perform this exercise to learn how to enter cell references to the Name Box.

1) Using the mouse, place the cursor in the Name Box and click once.

2) Type B2 and press ENTER.

Excel responds by making cell B2 the active cell.

As further practice, repeat these two steps for the following other cells: D8, A3, H5 and I19.

Entering Numbers to Cells

When you type something into a cell, Excel looks at your entry and asks:

- Is this a number?   • Is this text?

- Is this a cell reference?   • Is this a calculation?

Excel treats each type of entry in a different way. In this Section, we will deal with entering numbers, text and cell references. You will learn about entering calculations in Section 4.2.

Exercise 4.2: Entering a Number to a Cell

1) Using the Name Box or mouse, make B3 the active cell.

2) Type the number 2354.   3) Press ENTER.

	A	B
1		
2		
3		2354	
4		
5		

	A	B
1		
2		
3		2354
4		
5		

Why Does Excel Right-align Numbers?

In Exercise 4.2, Excel did two things after you pressed ENTER.

- It moved 2354 from the left of cell B3 to the right.

  This is because addition is the most common operation performed in Excel. When you write a list of numbers on paper to add them, you line up the numbers from the right. Excel right-aligns numbers for the same reason.

- It moved down the cursor to cell B4, the cell under B3.

  Again, this is because of addition. Excel assumes that you are creating a vertical list of numbers for adding together, and that you will want to enter another number directly under the previous one.

Entering Text to a Cell

You can enter text to a worksheet as well as numbers. By using text to identify the meaning or source of numbers, you make your worksheet easier to read and understand.

Exercise 4.3: Entering Text to a Cell

1) Move the cursor to cell A3, using the mouse or Name Box.

2) Type the word Conway.

3) Press ENTER.

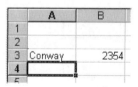

Notice how Excel responded after you pressed ENTER.

- Conway remained in the left of the cell A3.
  While Excel right-aligns numbers, it left-aligns text.

- It moved the cursor down to cell A4, the cell under A3.
  Excel assumes that this is the next cell that you will want to use.

Text used to describe a number on a worksheet is known as a label.

Label
A piece of text in a worksheet cell that provides information about the number in an accompanying cell, either below it or to its right.

Entering a Cell Reference to a Cell

Another type of entry you can make to a cell is a cell reference – that is, the address of another cell – preceded by an 'equal to' (=) sign . When you do so, Excel copies the content of that other cell to the active cell.

Exercise 4.4: Entering a Cell Reference to a Cell

1) If B3 does not contain the number 2354 from Exercise 4.2, enter it now.

2) Move the cursor to cell B10, type the following, and press ENTER:

   =B3

   That is, an 'equal to' sign (=) followed by cell reference B3.

Excel responds by displaying the current content of B3 (that is, number 2354) in B10.

Editing the Content of a Cell

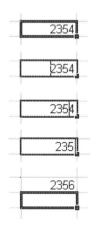

Sometimes, you will want to change the content of a cell. The following Exercise shows how you how.

Exercise 4.5: Editing the Content of a Cell

1) Move the cursor to cell B3, making it the active cell.

2) Double-click on B3.

   Excel makes the cell border cell thinner and displays a blinking cursor in the cell. (The location of the cursor within the cell depends on which part of the cell you double-clicked on.)

3) Using the ARROW keys, move the blinking cursor to the left of the 4.

4) Press DEL once, deleting the 4.

5) Type 6.

6) Press ENTER.

This moves the cursor out of B3 and down to B4. Excel has replaced 2354 with 2356. Notice that the number in B10 also changes.

The ARROW Keys

So far you have used the mouse and the Name Box to move the cursor around the worksheet. Another way of moving the cursor is by pressing the ARROW keys. You may find this method faster than moving and clicking the mouse, as you need not take either of your hands away from the keyboard.

F2: Excel's EDIT Key

In Step 2 of Exercise 4.5 above, you double-clicked on the active cell B3. This made the cell editable – that is, you were able to move the cursor within the cell and change the cell content.

Another way to make the active cell editable is to press F2. This is Excel's EDIT key. You may find this method faster than double-clicking with the mouse.

Deleting the Content of a Cell

Want to delete a number, text or cell reference from a cell? The following exercise shows you how.

Exercise 4.6: Deleting the Content of a Cell

1) Move the cursor to cell B10. From Exercise 4.4, this contains the cell reference =B3 and displays the number 2356.

2) Press BACKSPACE or DEL.

Excel removes the content of the cell. B10 is now empty.

Deleting and the ENTER Key	When you enter something to a cell, you must press ENTER to confirm the new content of the cell. Similarly, when you edit a cell, Excel makes the change only after you press ENTER.

When deleting a cell's content, however, you do not need to press ENTER to confirm the deletion. Just pressing BACKSPACE or DEL is enough. |

Deleting Cell Content – Not the Cell

Another way to delete the content of a cell is to right-click on the cell and choose **Clear Contents** from the pop-up menu.

Do not choose **Delete** from this pop-up menu. This command not only deletes the cell contents – it also removes the cell itself from the worksheet! As a result, other cells must change their position to fill the space left empty.

Standard and Formatting Toolbars

Only two of Excel's toolbars are relevant to this ECDL Module: The Standard Toolbar and the Formatting Toolbar.

The Standard Toolbar includes buttons for managing files and working with numbers in cells.

Excel's Standard Toolbar ———→

The Formatting Toolbar includes buttons for changing the appearance of text and numbers in cells.

Excel's Formatting Toolbar ———→

Rather than introduce all these buttons at once, we will explain each one as it becomes relevant through the remainder of the Module.

Excel's Undo

Enter the wrong data? Press the wrong key? Excel allows you to undo your most recent cell entry or worksheet action if it has produced unwanted results:

Choose **Edit | Undo**

-or-

Click the Undo ⟲ button on the Standard Toolbar.

Working With Excel Workbooks

An Excel workbook is a file containing a collection of worksheets. The file names of Excel workbooks end in .xls. This helps you to distinguish Excel files from other files types, such as Word files (ending in .doc).

Saving Your Workbook

In Excel, as in other applications, always save your work as you go along. Don't wait until you are finished! To save a workbook:

Choose **File | Save**

-or-

Click the Save 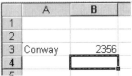 button on the Standard Toolbar.

The first time that you save a workbook file, Excel asks you to give the file a name. The following Exercise shows you how.

Exercise 4.7: Saving and Naming a New Workbook

1) Sheet 1 of your workbook should contain the text 'Conway' in cell A3 and the number 2356 in cell B3, as entered in this Section's Exercises.

	A	B
1		
2		
3	Conway	2356
4		

   If not, enter that data now. You will need it for the remaining Sections of this Module.

2) Choose **File | Save** or click the Save icon on the Standard Toolbar. Excel displays a dialog box similar to the one below.

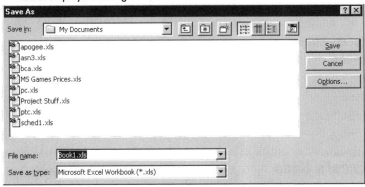

3) By default, Excel names the first workbook file you open and save as BOOK1.XLS. Replace this file name with something that you will find easier to remember and recognise – such as your own name – and click the **Save** button.

Creating a New Workbook	To create a new workbook file:
	Choose **File | New** or click the New 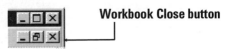 button on the Standard Toolbar.

Opening an Existing Workbook	To open an existing workbook file:
	Choose **File | Open** or click the Open  button on the Standard Toolbar. Select the file you want from the dialog box.

Closing a Workbook

Choose **File \| Close** or click the Close button on the workbook window.

Workbook Close button

If you have made changes to your workbook since you last saved it, Excel prompts you to save the changes before it closes the file.

Quitting Excel

To leave Excel:

Choose **File \| Exit** or click the Close button on the Excel window.

Excel Close button

If you have left open any files containing unsaved work, Excel prompts you to save them. You are then returned to the Windows desktop.

Section Summary: So Now You Know

An Excel *workbook* is a file containing spreadsheets, which Excel calls *worksheets*. Workbook files end in *.xls*.

A worksheet is made up of *cells*, arranged in *columns* and *rows*. Each cell has a unique *cell reference*, consisting of its column letter and row number. For example, B3 and G47.

Only one cell is the *active cell* at any one time. You make a cell active by moving the cursor to it, using the mouse, ARROW keys or *Name Box*.

You can enter a number, text (to *label* a number) or a cell reference to any cell. Press ENTER to confirm your entry. Excel *left-aligns text* but *right-aligns numbers*.

To *edit* the active cell, first make it editable. You do so by double-clicking it with the mouse or by pressing F2.

You can *delete* the content of the active cell (but not the cell itself) by pressing DEL.

Section 4.2: Arithmetic With Excel

Prepare to be impressed. In Section 4.1 you learnt the names for the important parts of an Excel worksheet, and practised the simple operations of entering numbers, text and cell references to cells.

Now you have the basics you need to discover the power of spreadsheets in this Section 4.2.

You will very quickly discover why people who work with numbers – such as accountants, statisticians, engineers and project managers – rely on spreadsheets to perform tedious calculations quickly and easily.

In the practical Exercises you will use fewer than a dozen numbers. These simple examples differ from the multi-page financial reports of a large corporation in size only. The principles are the same. Learn the principles here in Section 4.2 and you will never meet an amount of data too large or too complex for you to master with your spreadsheet skills.

New Activities

At the end of this Section you should be able to:

- Use Excel formulas to add, subtract, multiply and divide numbers
- Use Excel functions to find sums and averages
- Recognise error messages from formulas and functions
- Apply the rules of arithmetic to calculations in Excel
- Use the formula bar

New Words

At the end of this Section you should be able to explain the following terms:

- Calculated cell
- Operator
- Function
- Argument
- Formula
- Formula Bar

Formulas in Excel

In Section 4.1 you learnt how to enter numbers, text and cell references to worksheet cells. Now it's time to discover a fourth type of cell entry, called a calculation.

Calculations are the reason that you enter numbers to cells, because calculations enable you to perform arithmetic – addition, subtraction, multiplication and division – on your entered numbers.

Excel accepts two kinds of calculations: formulas and functions. Exercise 4.8 below shows you how to add three numbers using a formula. You will learn about functions later in this Section.

Exercise 4.8: Adding Three Numbers with an Excel Formula

1) Open the workbook that you saved in Exercise 4.7. If cells A3 and B3 do not contain Conway and 2356, enter that data now.

	A	B
1		
2		
3	Conway	2356
4		
5		

2) Enter the data below.

	A	B
1		
2		
3	Conway	2356
4	Murphy	4923
5	Sullivan	2903
6		
7		

3) Move the cursor to B6 and type:

=B3+B4+B5

	A	B
1		
2		
3	Conway	2356
4	Murphy	4923
5	Sullivan	2903
6		=b3+b4+b5
7		

4) Press ENTER when finished

	A	B
1		
2		
3	Conway	2356
4	Murphy	4921
5	Sullivan	2903
6		10182
7		
8		

Excel displays in B6 the sum of the contents of the three cells B3, B4 and B5.

Congratulations! You have performed your first calculation in Excel.

Calculations and Recalculations

In Exercise 4.8 you learnt how to use your £1,000 computer as a £10 pocket calculator! You have added just three numbers – but you can imagine how you could use the same method to record and add hundreds or even thousands of numbers on a worksheet.

The power of a spreadsheet is not so much the ability to calculate as the ability to *recalculate*. Excel will recalculate the result of an addition (or other type of operation) whenever any of the numbers that make up the operation are changed.

For example, if you change the content of B3, B4 or B5 from Exercise 4.8, Excel recalculates C6 and displays the new result. Let's try it and see.

Exercise 4.9: Recalculating with an Excel Formula

1) Double-click on cell B4.

2) Replace 4923 with 4921.

3) Press ENTER when finished.

	A	B
1		
2		
3	Conway	2356
4	Murphy	4921
5	Sullivan	2903
6		10180
7		

Excel recalculates the sum so that cell B6 now displays 10180 instead of 10182.

Calculated Cells and Arguments

Cell B6 in Exercises 4.8 and 4.9 is very different from cells B3, B4 and B5. These three cells each:

- Contain a number, and

- Display a number.

In other words, what they contain and what they display are the same.

B6, however, contains one thing (a formula) but displays another (a number). B6 is an example of what Excel calls a calculated cell.

Calculated Cell

A cell that contains a calculation but displays the result of that calculation.

You can think of a calculated cell as an 'answer cell'.

Formula

An equation that performs operations such as addition, subtraction, multiplication or division on data that is stored in a worksheet.

Note the following about formulas:

- Always begin formulas with the equal to (=) sign.

- Always press ENTER to confirm your formula.

The components of a formula are called arguments. Consider the following sample formula:

=C2+D4+E12

In this case, the arguments are C2, D4 and E12. Cell references are just one type of argument. As you will see, you can also use numbers as arguments.

Argument
The inputs to a calculation that generate the result in a calculated cell.

The Four Arithmetic Operations

The table below shows the four arithmetic operations that you can perform with Excel, and lists the keys you need to press for each type of operation.

Operation	Operator	Key(s) to Press	Example
Addition	+	⇧ ＋=	=C2+C3
Subtraction	-	-	=B4-B5
Multiplication	* (not x)	⇧ *8	=D5*F19
Division	/ (not ÷)	?/	=A4/F2

Operators
Symbols that specify the type of calculation you want to perform on the arguments of a formula. Excel's four main arithmetic operators are +,-, and /.*

Excel offers other, more complex, operators that are beyond the scope of this ECDL Module.

Formulas: Using Constants

Excel formulas can contain numbers as well as (or instead of) cell references. Excel calls these numbers 'constants'.

Constant
An argument in a formula that is a fixed number.

Here are some examples of formulas containing both cell references and constants:

=C26*109

=45*(A12+3)

=B2/100-B3/50

You can even enter formulas that contain only constants and no cell references, as shown in Exercise 4.10 below.

Excel 4.10: Entering Constant-Only Formulas

1) Enter the following to cell B8:   2) Press ENTER.

=32/4

Excel displays the result of the formula, 8, in cell B8. Delete the calculation from B8 when finished with Exercise 4.10. You will not need it again.

Exercise 4.11: Entering Complex Formulas

In this Exercise you will practice entering and working with formulas that contain the various types of arithmetic operators.

1) Enter the following formulas to cells A8, A9 and A10 respectively.

=B3-C3

=B5-B3/5

=B4*B5

Cells A8 to A10 should display the results shown on the right: 2356, 2431.8 and 14285663.

	A	B
1		
2		
3	Conway	2356
4	Murphy	4921
5	Sullivan	2903
6		10180
7		
8	2356	
9	2431.8	
10	14285663	
11		

Delete the calculations from A8, A9 and A10 when finished with Exercise 4.11. You will not need them again.

Formulas: The Rules of Arithmetic

Excel allows you to combine addition, subtraction, multiplication and division in a single formula. For example:

=C5*(A4+A7) -(C4/C7)

Excel follows the rules of arithmetic in calculating such formulas:

- Multiplication and division are done first, addition and subtraction second.

  For example, the following formula gives a result of 11 because Excel first multiplies 2 by 3 (resulting in 6) and then adds 5.

  =5+2*3

- You can use parentheses (brackets) to force Excel to calculate your formula in a particular order.

  For example, the following formula gives a result of 21 because Excel first adds 5 and 2 (because they are within parentheses) and then multiplies that result by 3 to give 21.

  =(5+2)*3

  Ensure that you follow every opening bracket you type with a matching closing bracket.

If you have difficulty remembering that:

= (A1+A2)*B1

gives a different result from:

= A1+(A2*B1)

Here's a way to help you remember the order of precedence among arithmetical operators:

My Dear Aunt Sally!
(Multiplication, division, addition, subtraction.)

Error Messages: When Bad Things Happen

If a formula cannot properly calculate a result, Excel displays an error message in the calculated cell indicating the type of error that has taken place.

Here are the main error messages that you are likely to meet in following this ECDL Module.

#####

Your cell contains a number or formula that gives a result which is too wide for the cell to display. This is not really an error: Excel has the correct information, it just can't display it. You will learn about adjusting column width in Section 4.3.

#VALUE!

Your formula contains text (or a cell reference that points to a cell containing text) instead of a number. Edit the formula or cell to fix the problem.

#DIV/0!

You have tried to divide a number by zero, or by a cell reference that points to a cell containing a zero.

You will see the same error message if you try to divide a number by a cell reference that points to an empty cell. Excel interprets a blank cell as containing a zero.

#REF!

Typically, your formula contains a cell reference that points to a cell which has been deleted.

Excel Functions

You have learned how Excel's formulas can add, subtract, multiply and divide numbers.

Excel offers a second way to work with numbers: functions.

Function
A predefined formula built-in to Excel and used for a specific purpose.

Most Excel functions are of interest only if you are using a spreadsheet for specialised purposes, such as statistical analysis. But two – SUM and AVERAGE – are useful to almost everyone.

The SUM
Function

In Exercise 4.8 you added three numbers by using the following addition formula:

=B3+B4+B5

You can imagine that the addition formula would become very awkward if there were a larger number of arguments. For example, if there were 100 cells to add rather than just three.

Excel's SUM function allows you to calculate the total of a row or column by entering just three items:

- The name of the function (in this case, SUM)

- The reference of the first cell

- A colon (:)

- The reference of the last cell.

The following Exercise shows the SUM function in action.

Exercise 4.12: Using the SUM Function

1) Make B6 the active cell and, using DEL or BACKSPACE, delete the formula from the cell.

2) Type the following function in B6:   3) Press ENTER.

=SUM(B3:B5)

	A	B
1		
2		
3	Conway	2356
4	Murphy	4921
5	Sullivan	2903
6		=sum(b3:b5)
7		

	A	B
1		
2		
3	Conway	2356
4	Murphy	4921
5	Sullivan	2903
6		10180
7		

Well done! You have used Excel's SUM function to add numbers. Keeps this data for Exercise 4.13.

The AutoSum
Button

Σ

As SUM is such a commonly used function, Microsoft put it on the Standard Toolbar.

Exercise 4.13: Using the AutoSum Button

1) Delete the SUM function from cell B6.

2) With B6 as the active cell, click on the AutoSum button on the Standard Toolbar.

3) Excel tries to 'guess' which cells you want to add together. In this example, it assumes that the cells to sum start at B3 and end at B5.

	A	B
1		
2		
3	Conway	2356
4	Murphy	4921
5	Sullivan	2903
6		=SUM(B3:B5)

4) Press ENTER to confirm that B3, B4 and B5 are the cells for adding.

	A	B
1		
2		
3	Conway	2356
4	Murphy	4921
5	Sullivan	2903
6		10180
7		
8		

SUM Tolerates Text and Spaces

Excel's SUM is a tolerant function. It ignores:

- Cells containing text
- Empty cells

For example, the function =SUM(W12:W16) adds whatever numbers it finds in the cells W12, W13, W14, W15 and W16.

If any of the cells contains text instead of a number, or is empty, the SUM function does not display an error message. It just ignores the non-number cells and carries on adding up the numeric ones.

The AVERAGE Function

This Excel function – you guessed it – finds the average of a group of numbers.

As with the SUM function, the AVERAGE function begins with the = sign. Then follows the function name, and finally the arguments within parentheses.

Exercise 4.14: Using the AVERAGE Function

1) Make B7 the active cell and type the following:

=AVERAGE(B3:B5)

	A	B	C
1			
2			
3	Conway	2356	
4	Murphy	4921	
5	Sullivan	2903	
6		10180	
7		=average(b3:b5)	
8			

3) Press ENTER.

	A	B
1		
2		
3	Conway	2356
4	Murphy	4921
5	Sullivan	2903
6		10180
7		3393.333
8		
9		

Excel displays the result of the average calculation in B7. Delete the AVERAGE function from B7 when finished Exercise 4.14.

Exercise 4.15: Adding More Numbers and Text

In this Exercise you will add more numbers and text to your worksheet.

1) Enter two further columns of numbers in columns C and D.

2) Enter a row of labels (text) across the top of the the columns, B, C, D and E.

3) Use the SUM function to total columns C, D and E, and rows 3, 4 and 5.

	A	B	C	D	E
1					
2		January	February	April	Totals
3	Conway	2356	3621	4560	10537
4	Murphy	4921	4055	3542	12518
5	Sullivan	2903	3308	3622	9833
6		10180	10984	11724	32888
7					

The Formula Bar

Located just above the column headings of the worksheet and below the Formatting Toolbar is part of the Excel screen known as the Formula Bar.

Formula Bar ─────────────────────┘

Formula Bar
Displays the contents of the active cell – whether a number, text, cell reference or calculation.

You do not need to use the Formula Bar to use Excel. But some users find it a convenient way of working.

Exercise 4.16: Using the Formula Bar

You can not only use the Formula Bar to view the contents of the active cell. You can also enter a number, text or a calculation directly into the formula bar, as follows:

1) Move the cursor to a cell, for example, cell D6, making it the active cell.

2) Move the cursor to the formula bar. Notice that D6 remains the active cell.

3) Enter a number, text or a calculation to the formula bar.

4) Click on the tick buttor ☑ or press ENTER.

Excel enters the number, text or calculation in the active cell.

Section Summary: So Now You Know

You can enter *calculations* to worksheet cells in two ways: using formulas and using functions. A *formula* begins with an 'equal to' symbol (=) and contains an *operator* – for example, addition (+), subtraction (-), multiplication (*) or division (/). The components or *arguments* of a formula can be cell references, numbers or both.

A sample formula would be:

=A12+B12+3

Excel follows the rules of arithmetic in calculating formulas: multiplication and division are done first, addition and subtraction second. You can use parentheses (brackets) to force Excel to calculate your formula in a particular order. The following two formulas, for example, gives different results:

=(A1+A2)*B1

=A1+(A2*B1)

A *function* is a predefined formula for specific purposes, such as addition (SUM) and averaging (AVERAGE). In each case, you need only enter the cell reference of the first and last cell in the calculation. Functions also begin with the 'equal to' symbol (=). For example.

=SUM(S2:S12) and =AVERAGE(C23:C27)

A fast way to apply the SUM function is to click on the AutoSum button on the Standard Toolbar.

$$\boxed{\Sigma}$$

Excel stores the result of a calculation in a *calculated cell*, which contains the formula or function but displays the calculation result.

Located just above the worksheet column headings, Excel's *Formula Bar* displays the contents of the active cell – whether a number, text, cell reference or calculation. You can also type cell entries to the Formula Bar rather than directly to the cells themselves.

Section 4.3: Formatting, Aligning and Moving Data

In This Section

When you work with numbers, it's important to get the right answers. But it's also important that your answers look good, and that they are in the correct locations on your worksheet.

Excel provides a wide range of formatting and alignment features to help you give your worksheets a professional appearance. Excel also allows you to cut, copy and paste cell contents, so that you can control which data appears where on your worksheet.

New Activities

At the end of this Section you should be able to:

- Format and align cells

- Select adjacent and non-adjacent cell ranges

- Insert and delete rows, columns and cells

- Adjust row height and column width.

- Copy, cut and paste the contents of cells

- Sort cells

New Words

At the end of this Section you should be able to explain the following terms:

- Selected cell

- Adjacent cell range

- Non-adjacent cell range

- Marquee

Formatting and Aligning Single Cells

Format Buttons

Alignment Buttons

You begin this Section 4.3 by learning how to format and align the cells on Sheet1 of the workbook that you saved in Section 4.2.

	A	B	C	D	E
1					
2		January	February	April	Totals
3	Conway	2356	3621	4560	10537
4	Murphy	4921	4055	3542	12518
5	Sullivan	2903	3308	3622	9833
6		10180	10984	11724	32888
7					

Above: Sheet1 from Exercise 4.15

Exercise 4.17 Formatting and Aligning Cells

1) Open your saved workbook and make B2 the active cell (using the mouse, ARROW keys or Name Box).

2) Click the Bold button on the Formatting Toolbar. Excel displays the word January in bold.

3) Click the Centre-Align button on the Formatting Toolbar. Excel centre-aligns the word January.

4) Make A3 the active cell, and then click the Italic button on the Formatting Toolbar. Excel displays the word Conway in italics.

Formatting and Aligning Cell Groups

You can save time and mouse-clicks by formatting or aligning a group of cells in one, single operation. Before you can do so, you must first select the group of cells.

You can select a group of cells by clicking on the top-left cell in the group, and then dragging the mouse across the other cells. Exercise 4.18 shows you how.

Exercise 4.18 Formatting and Aligning a Cell Range

1) Select cell C2. (That is, make C2 the active cell.)

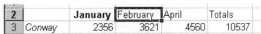

2) Drag the mouse across to cell E2.

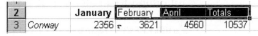

3) Click on the Bold button on the Formatting Toolbar.

	2		January	February	April		Totals	
	3	Conway	2356	3621	4560		10537	

4) Click on the Centre-Align button on the Formatting Toolbar.

	2		January	February		April	Totals	
	3	Conway	2356	3621		4560	10537	

5) Select cell A4.

6) Drag the mouse down to cell A5.

7) Click on the Italic button on the Formatting Toolbar.

Your worksheet should look as shown below.

	A	B	C	D	E
1					
2		January	February	April	Totals
3	Conway	2356	3621	4560	10537
4	Murphy	4921	4055	3542	12518
5	Sullivan	2903	3308	3622	9833
6		10180	10984	11724	32888

Cell Ranges

In Excel, a group of cells in a worksheet is known as a cell range.

Cell Range

A group of cells on a worksheet.

Cell ranges are of two kinds: adjacent and non-adjacent.

Adjacent Cell Range

Adjacent Cell Range

Group of cells that are directly beside or above or below one another. Adjacent cells are sometimes called contiguous cells.

You identify an adjacent cell range by:

- The cell reference of the top-left cell
- A colon (:)
- The cell reference of the bottom-right cell.

For example, the adjacent cell range A1:B2 includes the following four cells: A1, A2, B1 and B2.

Adjacent cell ranges may also include cells in one column only (for example, B2:B5) or in one row only (for example, D9:F9).

Can you select cells that are located on different parts of a worksheet as a single range? Yes. This is what Excel calls a non-adjacent cell range.

Non-adjacent Cell Range

Group of cells that are not directly beside, or above or below, one another. Also called non-contiguous cells.

A non-adjacent cell range can consist of individual cells dotted around the worksheet. Or, as in Exercise 4.19, it can contain a number of smaller, sub-groups of adjacent cells.

You select a non-adjacent cell range by selecting the first cell (or first sub-group of adjacent cells) and then holding down the CTRL key when selecting further cells (or adjacent ranges).

Exercise 4.19: Selecting a Non-Adjacent Cell Range

1) Select the first cell or sub-group of adjacent cells. For example, B2:B6 (that is, cells B2, B3, B4, B5 and B6).

	A	B	C	D	E
1					
2		January	February	April	Totals
3	Conway	2356	3621	4560	10537
4	Murphy	4921	4055	3542	12518
5	Sullivan	2903	3308	3622	9833
6		10180	10984	11724	32888
7					

2) Hold down the CTRL key.

3) Select the next cell or next sub-group of adjacent cells. For example, cell range E2:E6.

	A	B	C	D	E
1					
2		January	February	April	Totals
3	Conway	2356	3621	4560	10537
4	Murphy	4921	4055	3542	12518
5	Sullivan	2903	3308	3622	9833
6		10180	10984	11724	32888
7					

You can continue this process until you have selected all the cells in the non-adjacent range that you want to select.

Click anywhere outside the cell range to cancel the selection.

Selected Cells and the Active Cell

One active cell

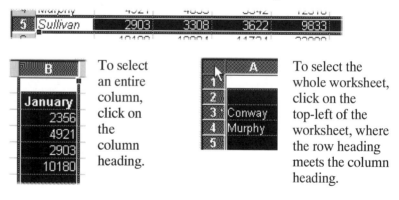

Four selected cells

In Section 4.1 you learnt how to select a single cell – by clicking on it with the mouse, moving the cursor to it with the ARROW keys, or entering its cell reference in the Name Box. That cell is then the active cell.

So, for a single cell, the terms 'active cell' and 'selected cell' mean the same thing. And 'Select a cell' is simply another way of saying 'Make a cell the active cell'.

While you can select any number of cells at one time, only one cell can be the active cell. Excel displays selected cells in reverse (white text on-black background). The active cell is shown as black text on a white background.

F8: Excel's SELECT Key

In Exercises 4.18 and 4.19, you selected cell ranges by selecting the first cell, and then dragging the mouse across the other cells in the range.

An alternative method is to select the first cell, press F8, and press the ARROW keys to extend the selected area over the other cells. F8 is Excel's SELECT key. You may find this method faster than using the mouse, but you can use it only for selecting adjacent cell ranges.

Selecting Columns, Rows or the Entire Worksheet

To select an entire row, click on the row heading.

To select an entire column, click on the column heading.

To select the whole worksheet, click on the top-left of the worksheet, where the row heading meets the column heading.

A fast way to delete the contents of all cells on a worksheet is to select the entire worksheet, and then press DEL.

Cancelling a Selection

Select the wrong cell or cell range? To cancel a selection, click anywhere outside the selected cell or range.

Cancelling a selection does not delete the cell or range from the worksheet. It just de-selects the selected cell(s).

Inserting and Deleting Rows

With over four million cells on a single worksheet, why would you want to add some more? Answer: Sometimes you need to insert a row or column to hold new data within a range of cells that already contain text and numbers.

Exercise 4.20: Inserting a New Row

1) Select the heading of the row immediately below where you want to insert the new row. For example, to insert a new row above row 5, click on the heading of row 5.

	A	B	C	D	E
1					
2		January	February	April	Totals
3	Conway	2356	3621	4560	10537
4	Murphy	4921	4055	3542	12518
5	Sullivan	2903	3308	3622	9833
6		10180	10984	11724	32888
7					

2) Choose **Insert | Rows**. Excel inserts a new row of blank cells.

	A	B	C	D	E
1					
2		January	February	April	Totals
3	Conway	2356	3621	4560	10537
4	Murphy	4921	4055	3542	12518
5					
6	Sullivan	2903	3308	3622	9833
7		10180	10984	11724	32888

3) Enter new text and numbers as shown below. Excel recalculates the column totals automatically as you add the new numbers in cells B5, C5 and D5.

4) In cell E5, enter the following SUM function to add the cells of row 5:

=SUM(B5:D5)

Excel recalculates E7, the total of the Totals column, to include E5, the sum of the numbers that you have entered in row 5.

	A	B	C	D	E
1					
2		January	February	April	Totals
3	Conway	2356	3621	4560	10537
4	Murphy	4921	4055	3542	12518
5	Smith	3872	2441	4949	11262
6	Sullivan	2903	3308	3622	9833
7		14052	13425	16673	44150
8					
9					

4) To make your worksheet more readable, insert a blank row above the column totals, as shown.

	A	B	C	D	E
1					
2		January	February	April	Totals
3	Conway	2356	3621	4560	10537
4	Murphy	4921	4055	3542	12518
5	Smith	3872	2441	4949	11262
6	Sullivan	2903	3308	3622	9833
7					
8		14052	13425	16673	44150

To delete a row, select the row heading and choose **Edit | Delete**.

Inserting and Deleting Columns

Inserting a new column in a worksheet is very similar to inserting a new row. Exercise 4.21 shows you how.

Exercise 4.21: Inserting a New Column

1) Select the heading of the column immediately to the right of where you want to insert the new column.

   For example, to insert a new column to the left of column D, click on the heading of column D.

2) Choose **Insert | Columns**. Excel inserts a new column of blank cells.

3) Enter new text and numbers as shown below.

   Excel recalculates the row totals automatically as you add the new numbers in column D. You need to enter the SUM function in cell D8 to calculate the March total.

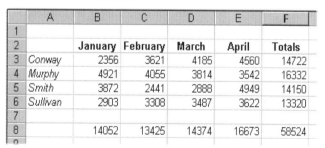

	A	B	C	D	E	F
1						
2		January	February	March	April	Totals
3	Conway	2356	3621	4185	4560	14722
4	Murphy	4921	4055	3814	3542	16332
5	Smith	3872	2441	2888	4949	14150
6	Sullivan	2903	3308	3487	3622	13320
7						
8		14052	13425	14374	16673	58524

4) To make your worksheet more readable, insert a column to the left of the Totals row, as shown.

	A	B	C	D	E	F	G
1							
2		January	February	March	April		Totals
3	Conway	2356	3621	4185	4560		14722
4	Murphy	4921	4055	3814	3542		16332
5	Smith	3872	2441	2888	4949		14150
6	Sullivan	2903	3308	3487	3622		13320
7							
8		14052	13425	14374	16673		58524

To delete a column, select its heading and choose **Edit | Delete**.

Inserting and Deleting Cells

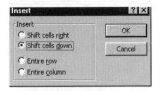

You can insert individual cells on a worksheet by first selecting a cell immediately below or to the right of where you want to insert the new cell, and then choosing **Insert | Cells**.

Be careful about inserting a new cell, as Excel adjusts the position of the surrounding cells to make room it. Excel prompts you to choose whether the surrounding cells should move right or down.

Adjusting Column Width and Row Height

You can change the appearance of your worksheet by adjusting the width of one or more columns, or the height of one or more rows.

To change the width of a column, use the mouse to position the cursor on the column address bar at the dividing line between the column and the one to the right. Next, drag the mouse sideways until the column is the width you want. See Exercise 4.22.

To change row height, position the cursor on the row address bar at the dividing line between the row and the one beneath it, and drag the mouse up or down until the row is the height you want.

Exercise 4.22 Adjusting Column Width

In Step 4 of Exercise 4.21, you inserted an extra, blank column to separate the April column from the Total column. This blank column is wider than it need be.

1) In the column heading, click on the dividing line between columns F and G.

2) Drag the dividing line to the left, making column F narrower.

	E	F	G
	April		Totals
	4560		14722

	E	F	G
	April		Totals
	4560		14722

Copying and Pasting Cell Contents

Suppose you have text or a number in one cell, and you want to copy it to another cell. How do you do it?

Excel offers two main ways to copy and paste within the same worksheet: drag-and-drop and right-clicking. You will learn about each method in the next two Exercises.

Exercise 4:23: Copy and Paste with Drag-and-Drop

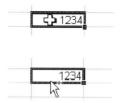

1) Select the cell you want to copy from. For example, enter 1234 in cell B9, and then select B9. See how the cursor is shaped like a plus sign (+).

2) Move the cursor to the bottom edge of the selected cell. Excel changes the cursor from a plus sign to an arrow with a smaller plus sign.

   (You can move the cursor to any edge of the selected cell – it doesn't matter which edge. The cursor still changes shape.)

3) Holding down the CTRL key, drag the cell to the destination cell that you want to paste to – for example, D9.

   If there is already something in D9, Excel asks if you want to replace it or not.

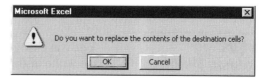

5) Choose **OK**.

6) You can now delete the contents of D9 in preparation for Exercise 4.24.

Exercise 4:24: Copy and Paste by Right-Clicking

1) Select the cell whose contents you want to copy, as in Exercise 4.23.

2) Right-click with the mouse.

3) Choose **Copy** from the pop-up menu. Excel places the contents of B9 in the clipboard.

4) Select the cell D9.

5) Right-click with the mouse.

6) Choose **Paste**.

If there is already an entry in cell D9, Excel over-writes it with the pasted data. Delete the contents of B9 and D9. You will not need them for future Exercises.

| The Flashing Marquee | When you select a cell and choose **Copy**, Excel surrounds the selected cell with a flashing rectangle called a marquee. |

> **Marquee**
>
> *A flashing rectangle that Excel uses to surround a cell, or cell range, that you have copied to the clipboard.*

You can remove a marquee at any stage by pressing ESC or clicking on another cell.

If you remove a marquee, Excel removes the contents of the selected cell or cell range from the clipboard.

| Copying and Pasting to Multiple Cells | You can use the pop-up menu to copy the contents of one cell to any number of other cells on a worksheet. |

Select the cell you want to copy from, right-click, choose **Copy** from the pop-up menu, select the cell range that you want to paste to, right-click on any cell in the selected cell range, and choose **Paste** from the pop-up menu. You can paste to an adjacent or non-adjacent cell range.

Cutting and Pasting Cell Contents

To cut and paste using the drag-and-drop method, do not hold down the CTRL key while dragging the cell contents to their new cell location. To cut and paste using the pop-up menu, choose **Cut** rather than **Copy**.

Sorting: Reordering Cells by Content

The order in which you typed entries to a worksheet may not be the order in which, later on, you would prefer to display or print that information. Suppose, for example, that you have entered ten numbers to a column of a worksheet.

By selecting the cell range and choosing the Sort Ascending (or Sort Descending) button, you can rearrange the cells so that Excel displays them in order of increasing (or decreasing) value. The reordered list may now be easier to read than the original, unsorted one.

> **Sorting**
>
> *Rearranging columns of cells based on the values in the cells. Sorting does not change the content of cells, only their location.*

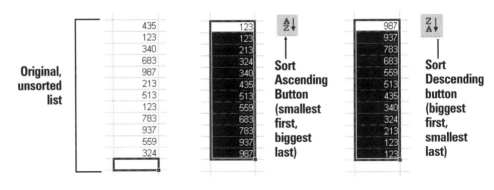

Original, unsorted list		Sort Ascending Button (smallest first, biggest last)		Sort Descending button (biggest first, smallest last)
435	123		987	
123	123		937	
340	213		783	
683	324		683	
987	340		559	
213	435		513	
513	513		435	
123	559		340	
783	683		324	
937	783		213	
559	937		123	
324	987		123	

Excel offers a number of sequencing options, called sort orders.

Sort Order

A particular way of ordering cells based on value. A sort order can be alphabetic or numeric, and can be in ascending (0 to 9, A to Z) or descending (9 to 0, Z to A) sequence.

The two Sort buttons give you a quick, one-click way of reordering a cell range. As you will discover in Exercise 4.25, Excel's **Data | Sort** menu command provides an additional option: you can sort a cell range based on the values in more than a single column. This is called a 'multiple sort'.

Exercise 4.25: Sorting Cells

The rows of your worksheet are currently arranged in alphabetic sort order according to surname: Conway first, then Murphy, Smith and, lastly, Sullivan.

	A	B	C	D	E	F	G
1							
2		January	February	March	April		Totals
3	Conway	2356	3621	4185	4560		14722
4	Murphy	4921	4055	3814	3542		16332
5	Smith	3872	2441	2888	4949		14150
6	Sullivan	2903	3308	3487	3622		13320
7							
8		14052	13425	14374	16673		58524

1) Select row 7 by clicking on its row heading, and choose **Insert | Rows**. Next, press CTRL+Y twice. This is the keyboard shortcut for Excel's REPEAT command. Excel inserts three new, blank rows under row 6.

6	Sullivan	2903	3308	3487	3622	13320
7						
8						
9						
10						
11		14052	13425	14374	16673	58524

2) Enter to rows 7, 8 and 9 the text and numbers as shown on the screen below.

	A	B	C	D	E	F	G
1							
2		January	February	March	April		Totals
3	Conway	2356	3621	4185	4560		14722
4	Murphy	4921	4055	3814	3542		16332
5	Smith	3872	2441	2888	4949		14150
6	Sullivan	2903	3308	3487	3622		13320
7	Rafferty	2512	2864	3290	3741		12407
8	Higgins	3463	3981	4210	4974		16628
9	Smith	5951	6226	6481	6852		25510
10							
11		25978	26496	28355	32240		113069

In row 11, edit the arguments of the SUM functions to include the three new rows. For example, to B11 enter the function =SUM(B3:B9).

Enter new SUM functions in G7, G8 and G9 to calculate the row totals. For example, to G8 enter =SUM(B8:E8).

2) Select column B by clicking on its column heading, and choose the **Insert | Columns** command.

In the new column, enter the first names as shown.

	A	B	C	D	E	F	G	H
1								
2			January	February	March	April		Totals
3	Conway	John	2356	3621	4185	4560		14722
4	Murphy	Robert	4921	4055	3814	3542		16332
5	Smith	Zowie	3872	2441	2888	4949		14150
6	Sullivan	Andrew	2903	3308	3487	3622		13320
7	Rafferty	Aidan	2512	2864	3290	3741		12407
8	Higgins	Tracey	3463	3981	4210	4974		16628
9	Smith	Catherine	5951	6226	6481	6852		25510
10								
11			25978	26496	28355	32240		113069

3) Select cell range A3:H9, and choose **Data | Sort**.

By default, Excel shows the first column in the selected range, column A, in the Sort by drop-down box.

In the Then by drop-down box. select Column B.

Next, select the sort order of Ascending for both columns A and B, and click OK.

Your worksheet should now resemble the following.

	A	B	C	D	E	F	G	H
1								
2			January	February	March	April		Totals
3	Conway	John	2356	3621	4185	4560		14722
4	Higgins	Tracey	3463	3981	4210	4974		16628
5	Murphy	Robert	4921	4055	3814	3542		16332
6	Rafferty	Aidan	2512	2864	3290	3741		12407
7	Smith	Catherine	5951	6226	6481	6852		25510
8	Smith	Zowie	3872	2441	2888	4949		14150
9	Sullivan	Andrew	2903	3308	3487	3622		13320
10								
11			25978	26496	28355	32240		113069

The multiple-column sort is useful where one column has duplicate entries. In this Exercise 4.25, cells A5 and A9 both initially contain the same text entry of 'Smith'.

Changing Fonts

Excel's Formatting Toolbar gives you access to the fonts installed on your computer. You can change the font of any cell or cell range on a worksheet by first selecting the cell(s) and the choosing a font from the drop-down list.

Our advice: don't. Excel's default font of Arial is an excellent choice for worksheets. Anything else is a disimprovement.

Changing Font Sizes

You can change the font size of any cell or cell range by first selecting the cell(s) and the choosing a font size from the drop-down list.

You will use the font size option in Exercise 4.30 of Section 4.4.

Adding Borders and Patterns

Excel provides a wide choice of borders and patterns that you can use to highlight particular cells – such as cells containing headings or totals – on a worksheet. You access these options with the **Format | Cells** command, as Exercise 4.26 demonstrates.

Exercise 4.26: Placing a Border Around a Cell Range

1) Select the cell range C11:H11.

| 25978 | 26496 | 28355 | 32240 | 113069 |

2) Choose **Format | Cells**, and on the dialog box, select the Border tab.

3) On the Border tab of the dialog box, select the Outline button. This places a continuous border around the C11:H11, as shown below.

| 25978 | 26496 | 28355 | 32240 | 113069 |

Navigating Your Worksheet

So far you have learnt how to move the cursor to a cell by using the:

- Name Box
- Mouse
- ARROW keys.

Read the table below to discover some other keys and key combinations that you can use to navigate (move around) your worksheet.

To...	Press
Move to the edge of a group of cells that contains data.	CTRL+ARROW
Move to the beginning of a row	HOME
Move to the top-left cell (A1) of a worksheet	CTRL+HOME
Move to the last cell that contains data in a worksheet	CTRL+END
Move down or up one screen	PAGE DOWN or PAGE UP

Section Summary: So Now You Know

A *cell range* is a group of cells on a worksheet. You can *select* an *adjacent* cell range by dragging the mouse across it. Select a *non-adjacent* cell range by selecting the first cell (or first sub-group of adjacent cells) and then holding down the CTRL key when selecting further cells (or adjacent ranges).

Selected cells can be *formatted* (bold or italic), *aligned* (left, right or centre) or *sorted* (in ascending or descending order). You can also add *borders* and *background* patterns, and change *font* and *sizes*.

Use the **Insert** menu commands to insert rows, columns or individual cells, and the **Edit** menu commands to delete them. You can adjust *column width* and *row height* by dragging the cell dividing lines in the row and column headings.

You can *copy and paste* cells by drag-and-drop with CTRL, or by choosing the commands from the pop-up menu. Similarly, without the CTRL key, you can *cut and paste* cells.

Section 4.4: More About Numbers, Text and Calculations

In This Section

In Sections 4.1 and 4.2 you learnt the basics of working with numbers, cell references and text. Now it's time to build on what you know.

Here you will discover that there are really four types of number and two types of cell reference, and that Excel treats the different types in different ways.

You will also learn more about entering text, and meet AutoFill, a convenient, time-saving feature for entering data in cells.

New Activities

At the end of this Section you should be able to:

- Choose the appropriate number format for the type of numbers that you want to enter and store in your worksheet

- Enter text across multiple columns

- Enter numbers as text

- Recognise the type of numbers that should be entered in calculations as absolute rather than relative cell references

- Use AutoFill to copy numbers and text, and to increment number series and special entries (dates, days, months and years)

- Use AutoFill feature to copy calculations that apply to multiple rows or columns

New Words

At the end of this Section you should be able to explain the following terms:

- Number format
- Relative cell reference
- General format
- Absolute cell reference
- Comma style
- Increment
- Currency style
- AutoFill
- Per cent style

Numbers: The Four Different Formats

In Section 4.1 you learnt that a number was one of the four kinds of entries you could type in a worksheet cell – the others were text, cell references, and calculations (formulas and functions).

In fact, Excel recognises many types of numbers, but four are all you need to know about for this ECDL Spreadsheet Module.

Excel calls each type a number format. Do not confuse this term with the use of the word format for bold and italics.

The number format affects only the appearance of a number – the way it appears on screen and on printouts – and not its content.

Number Format
The way in which Excel displays a number on screen and on printouts.

The General Format

123.4	**Left:**
345.75	**Example of**
9383.5	**General**
45	**Format**

Excel's default number format is called the General Format. Unless you change to a different number format, Excel applies this format to every number you enter.

The General Format has two disadvantages: it ignores zeros after the decimal point, and does not automatically insert commas to separate thousands. This makes it unsuitable for displaying amounts of money.

General Format and Trailing Zeros

A zero you enter as the last digit after a decimal point is called a trailing zero.

123.0	**Left:**
456.70	**Examples**
45.450	**of Trailing**
	Zeros

Enter 123.40, for example, and Excel's General Format displays 123.4.

General Format and Thousands Separators

The General Format does not automatically insert the comma symbol (,) to separate thousands. Enter 2500, for example, and Excel displays it as 2500, not 2,500.

General Format and Currency Symbols

If you type a currency symbol (such as IR£) before a number (such as 123), Excel treats the entry as text rather than a number. As a result, you cannot use your entry of IR£123 in a calculation – if you do, Excel displays the #VALUE! error message.

The Comma Style

Above:
**Comma style
button**

Change to this number format for Excel to insert a comma to separate thousands. Excel also displays all numbers to two places of decimals. Exercise 4.27 demonstrates the comma style.

Exercise 4.27: Changing Number Format to the Comma Style

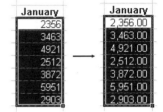

1) Open your worksheet and select cell range C3:C9.

2) Click on the Comma Style button on the Standard Toolbar.

Excel inserts commas and two places of decimals in the selected cell range.

Choose **Edit | Undo Style** (or press CTRL+z) to revert to General Format.

The Currency Style

Above:
**Currency
style button**

Change to this number format when your numbers represent amounts of money. Exercise 4.28 demonstrates the currency format.

Exercise 4.28: Changing Number Format to the Currency Style

1) On your worksheet select cell range C3:H11.

2) Click on the Currency Style button on the Standard Toolbar.

	A	B	C	D	E	F	G	H
1								
2			January	February	March	April		Totals
3	Conway	John	IR£ 2,356.00	IR£ 3,621.00	IR£ 4,185.00	IR£ 4,560.00		IR£ 14,722.00
4	Higgins	Robert	IR£ 3,463.00	IR£ 3,981.00	IR£ 4,210.00	IR£ 4,974.00		IR£ 16,628.00
5	Murphy	Tracey	IR£ 4,921.00	IR£ 4,055.00	IR£ 3,814.00	IR£ 3,542.00		IR£ 16,332.00
6	Rafferty	Andrew	IR£ 2,512.00	IR£ 2,864.00	IR£ 3,290.00	IR£ 3,741.00		IR£ 12,407.00
7	Smith	Aidan	IR£ 3,872.00	IR£ 2,441.00	IR£ 2,888.00	IR£ 4,949.00		IR£ 14,150.00
8	Smith	Zowie	IR£ 5,951.00	IR£ 6,226.00	IR£ 6,481.00	IR£ 6,852.00		IR£ 25,510.00
9	Sullivan	Catherine	IR£ 2,903.00	IR£ 3,308.00	IR£ 3,487.00	IR£ 3,622.00		IR£ 13,320.00
10								
11			IR£ 25,978.00	IR£ 26,496.00	IR£ 28,355.00	IR£ 32,240.00		IR£ 113,069.00
12								

Excel inserts the currency symbol (IR£), the thousands separator (,) and trailing zero(s).

The Percent Style

Above:
Percent style
button

This number format performs two actions. It:

- Multiplies the selected cell or cell range by 100

- Places the percent sign (%) after each selected number.

Use it to display decimal fractions (such as 0.0525) as more readable percentages (such as 5.25%). See Exercise 4.29.

Exercise 4.29: Changing Number Format to the Percent Style

In this Exercise you will add a new column to your worksheet. It will show each person's total as a proportion of the overall total. You will also add a new row to show each month's total as a proportion of the overall.

In each case, you will display the proportion as a percentage, using the percent style number format.

1) Enter the percent symbol (%) in cells I2 and B13, and make the symbols bold and centre-aligned.

2) In I3, enter the formula =H3/H11 to calculate the percentage of the total contributed by John Conway. Enter similar formulas for cells I4:I9. For example, to I5 enter = H5/H11 and to I7 enter =H7/H11.

3) Select the range I3:I9 and click the Percent Style button. Excel multiplies each cell by 100 and inserts the % symbol after it.

4) With range I3:I9 selected, click on the drop-down arrow to the right of the Fill Colour button on the Formatting Toolbar.

5) From the colour palette, choose Grey 25%.

6) In C13, enter the formula =C11/H11 to calculate the percentage of the total contributed in January.

   Enter similar formulas for cells D11:F11. For example, to D11 enter = D11/H11.

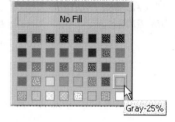

7) Select the range C11:F11 and click the Percent Style button.

8) Repeat steps 4) and 5) for C11:F11, filling the cells' background with 25% grey.

9) Select C15:F15 and centre-align the cells.

Your worksheet should now look as shown.

	A	B	C	D	E	F	G	H	I
1									
2			January	February	March	April		Totals	%
3	Conway	John	IR£ 2,356.00	IR£ 3,621.00	IR£ 4,185.00	IR£ 4,560.00		IR£ 14,722.00	13%
4	Higgins	Robert	IR£ 3,463.00	IR£ 3,981.00	IR£ 4,210.00	IR£ 4,974.00		IR£ 16,628.00	15%
5	Murphy	Tracey	IR£ 4,921.00	IR£ 4,055.00	IR£ 3,814.00	IR£ 3,542.00		IR£ 16,332.00	14%
6	Rafferty	Andrew	IR£ 2,512.00	IR£ 2,864.00	IR£ 3,290.00	IR£ 3,741.00		IR£ 12,407.00	11%
7	Smith	Aidan	IR£ 3,872.00	IR£ 2,441.00	IR£ 2,888.00	IR£ 4,949.00		IR£ 14,150.00	13%
8	Smith	Zowie	IR£ 5,951.00	IR£ 6,226.00	IR£ 6,481.00	IR£ 6,852.00		IR£ 25,510.00	23%
9	Sullivan	Catherine	IR£ 2,903.00	IR£ 3,308.00	IR£ 3,487.00	IR£ 3,622.00		IR£ 13,320.00	12%
10									
11			IR£ 25,978.00	IR£ 26,496.00	IR£ 28,355.00	IR£ 32,240.00		IR£ 113,069.00	
12									
13		%	23%	23%	25%	29%			

Changing from the General Format

There are two ways that you can change Excel's number format:

- First enter the numbers, and then change the number format.
- Change the number format of the blank cells first, and then enter the numbers.

The second method is better. If you are creating a new worksheet to enter financial amounts, select the whole worksheet and change the number format to currency style before entering any numbers. The currency style will affect only the entered numbers and not any text entries.

Excel and Text

Two further items you need to know about Excel and text: you can enter text that displays across several columns of a worksheet, and you can enter numbers as text.

Text Across Multiple Columns

Sometimes you may want to enter a line of text that is longer than the width of a single cell. Excel allows you do this – provided that the text does not run into any cell which has data in it.

Exercise 4.30 provides an example of entering and displaying text that stretches across several columns.

Exercise 4.30: Entering Text Across Multiple Columns

1) Select row 1 of your worksheet by clicking on the row heading.

2) Choose **Insert | Rows**.

3) Press CTRL+y to repeat the row insertion. You now have two new, blank rows at the top of the worksheet.

4) In C2, enter the following text:

    First Quarter Sales Figures for 1999

5) Select C2, click on Font Size drop-down box, and select 14 point.

6) With C2 still selected, click on the Bold and Italic buttons on the Formatting Toolbar.

The spreadsheet title should now look as shown.

	A	B	C	D	E	F
1						
2			*First Quarter Sales Figures for 1999*			
3						

Entering Numbers as Text

Why would you ever want Excel to treat a number as anything other than a number? The answer is when the number is not an amount but an identifier of some kind. Examples include part and model numbers (such as 010-34 or M5339), ID numbers (such as 99-10837), and telephone and fax numbers.

If you find it hard to think of a telephone number as anything other than a number, imagine how ridiculous it would be to add two telephone numbers together!

To enter a number as text, you must first apply the Text format to the empty cells, and then enter the numbers, as shown in Exercise 4.31. If you enter the numbers first, Excel will not apply the Text format to them – you will need to reenter all the numbers!

Below:
Selecting the Text Format

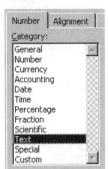

Exercise 4.31: Formatting Numbers as Text

1) Select cells B20:B23.

2) Choose **Format | Cells**.

3) On the Number tab, select Text from the Category list, and click **OK**.

4) Enter the numbers in cells B20:B23 as shown on the right.

010-56
M56-47N
091-10000
W1-S9

Excel treats the numbers as text. You can now delete the four entries from the worksheet.

Cell References: The Two Kinds

In Section 4.1, you learnt that each cell on a worksheet has a unique reference, written in the form A1 – column letter first, row number second.

In fact, Excel supports two kinds of cell references: relative (the A1 type you know already) and absolute (the $A$1 type you have not met yet).

Why is one type of cell reference not enough? The answer lies in the way that Excel copies and pastes calculations that contain cell references. The difference between the two is shown in Exercises 4.32 and 4.33.

Exercise 4.32: Copying a Relative Cell Reference

This Exercise demonstrates what happens when you copy a function that contains a relative cell reference.

1) Select cell H11 and press DEL.

IR£ 25,510.00	26%
	0%

2) Select H10. This calculated cell contains the following function:

   = SUM(C10:F10)

3) Copy H10 and paste it to I10.

IR£ 25,510.00	23%
IR£ 13,320.00	12%

   Notice that I10 now contains the following function:

   = SUM(C11:F11)

Excel changed the relative cell range from C10:F10 to C11:F11 when you pasted the SUM function to its new location.

> **Relative Cell Reference**
>
> *A reference to a cell or cell range in the format A1. Excel changes a relative cell reference when you copy a formula or function containing such a reference.*

Exercise 4.33: Copying an Absolute Cell Reference

This Exercise demonstrates what happens when you copy a function that contains an absolute cell reference.

1) Double-click in cell I10 and change the arguments of its SUM function to the following:

   =H10/$H$13

   You have now changed the relative cell reference of H13 to an absolute cell reference of $H$13.

2) Select cell I11 and press DEL to delete its contents.

3) Select I10 and copy it to I11. Cell I11 contains the following function:

=H11/$H$13

Excel changed the relative cell reference of H10 to H11 as you copied and pasted it from one cell to another. However, Excel did not change absolute cell reference $H$13.

Use absolute cell references in formulas and functions when giving the references of cells that contain fixed factors such as tax rates, sales commission percentages and so on. You can make part of a reference absolute and part relative. For example, G$13 or $D7.

Absolute Cell Reference
A reference to a cell or cell range in the format $A$1. Excel does not change an absolute cell reference when you copy a formula or function containing such a reference.

Excel's AutoFill Feature

Excel provides a very convenient feature called AutoFill for copying or incrementing (increasing in a defined sequence) the entries in a cell or range.

Exercise 4.34: Using AutoFill To Copy and Increment Numbers and Text

1) Enter the following to cell range B19:F19, C20.

19	12	12	Hello	Jan	Mon
20			13		

2) Click on cell B19 and position the cursor over the fill handle – the black square at the bottom-right of the selected cell.

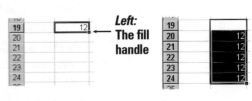

Left: The fill handle

3) Drag the fill handle down to cell B24. Excel copies the contents of cell B19 to the other selected cells.

4) Select cell range C19:C20 and drag the fill handle down to C24.

5) Select D19 and drag the fill handle down to D24.

6) Select E19 and drag the fill handle down to E24.

7) Select F19 and drag the fill handle down to F24.

Your worksheet should now look as shown.

19	12	12	Hello	Jan	Mon
20	12	13	Hello	Feb	Tue
21	12	14	Hello	Mar	Wed
22	12	15	Hello	Apr	Thu
23	12	16	Hello	May	Fri
24	12	17	Hello	Jun	Sat

AutoFill and Single Numbers, Text

For cell ranges B19:B24 and D19:D24, you began by selecting a single cell containing a number (12) and text item (Hello). As you dragged the fill handle, Excel copied the number and text into the cells that you dragged over.

AutoFill and Number Series

For cell range C19:C24, you began by selecting two cells. Excel recognised that they contained two numbers in an increasing series, (12 and 13). As you dragged the fill handle, Excel placed increments of the series (14, 15 and so on) into the cells that you dragged over.

AutoFill and Months, Days, Times and Years

For cell ranges E19:E24 and F19:F24, Excel recognised that the single cell you selected contained the name of a month and a day. As you dragged the fill handle, Excel placed increments of the series (Feb, Mar ... and Tue, Wed ...).

Excel also recognises times (such as 9:00 or 12:30), dates (such as 1-May or 10-April) and years (such as 1996 or 2001).

AutoFill and Calculations

Columns or rows of a worksheet often need the same action applied to them; for example, summing or averaging. Use AutoFill in a two-step process to avoid entering calculations (formulas and functions) individually to sum or average each row or column.

- Enter the calculation for one row or column, using relative cell references.
- Use AutoFill to copy the formula or function to the adjacent cells.

Excel adjusts the cell references as it copies the calculation.

Exercise 4.35: Using AutoFill To Copy Calculations

1) Select cell range H6:I11, and press DEL to delete their contents.

2) Drag the fill handle down to range H11:I11.

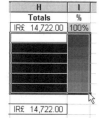

AutoFill works across rows as well as down columns, as you will learn in steps 3) and 4) of this Exercise.

3)   Select cell range D13:F13, and press DEL to delete their contents.

| IR£ 25,978.00 | | IR£ 113,069.0(|

4)   Select C13 and drag the fill handle to the right to cell F13.

| IR£ 25,978.00 | IR£ 26,496.00 | IR£ 28,355.00 | IR£ 32,240.00 | IR£ 113,069.00 |

Save your worksheet.

AutoFill Keyboard Shortcut

You may find it quicker to apply AutoFill using the keyboard short cuts rather than dragging the fill handle with the mouse. Follow these steps:

- Select the cell(s) you want to fill from.

- Drag the mouse down (or right) to select the cells(s) you want to fill.

- Press CTRL+d to fill down or CTRL+r to fill right.

AutoFill
An Excel tool for quickly copying or incrementing (increasing in a defined sequence) the entries in a cell or range.

Section Summary:
So Now You Know

Excel's default number format, the *general format*, does not display trailing zeros, does not automatically insert commas to separate thousands, and is unsuitable for entering financial amounts.

The *comma style* automatically inserts a comma to separate thousands, and displays all numbers to two places of decimals.

The *currency style* automatically inserts your national currency symbol, and follows your currency's convention for decimal places.

The *percent style* multiplies numbers by 100, and places the percent sign (%) after each one.

When changing to a non-default number format, it is better to do so *before* you enter your numbers. Only numbers and not text are affected by number formatting.

You can enter *multi-column text* (provided the other, over-typed cells are blank) and format *text as numbers*. This can be useful when the numbers are identifiers (part numbers, phone numbers and so on) rather than amounts.

In calculations, cells can have *relative references* or *absolute references*. Excel changes relative cell references when you copy the calculation to another cell; absolute references are unchanged by copying. Use absolute cell references for cells containing fixed factors such as tax rates.

AutoFill copies the contents of a cell to other, selected cells in the same row or column. AutoFill can also increment a series of numbers, times, dates, days, months, and years.

Section 4.5: Charting with Excel

In This Section

So far you have used Excel to enter, edit, calculate, format and re-position cells on your worksheets.

In this Section you will learn how to present the contents of your worksheet cells in what Excel – an American product – calls a chart. On this side of Atlantic, we would more commonly use the term 'graph' or 'diagram' rather than chart.

New Activities

At the end of this Section you should be able to:

- Use Excel's Chart Wizard to create charts that are based on the numbers, text and calculations in your worksheet

- Choose the appropriate options from the following four dialog boxes of Excel's Chart Wizard:

    - Chart type
    - Chart source data
    - Chart options
    - Chart location

New Words

At the end of this Section you should be able to explain the following terms:

- Chart
- Bar chart
- Data Point
- Column chart
- Data series
- Pie chart

Charting: The Two Steps

You follow two main steps to creating a chart in Excel:

- Select the cells whose contents you want to chart.
- Select and run Excel's Chart Wizard.

> ### Excel Chart
> *A graphic or diagram based on the numbers, text and calculations that are located in the rows and columns of an Excel worksheet.*

The Four Dialog Boxes to an Excel Chart

When you run the Chart Wizard, Excel presents you with a series of four dialog boxes. These are:

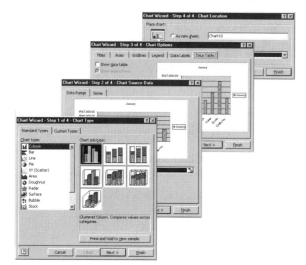

Chart Type: Excel offers lots of different chart types. You decide which is best for your data.

Chart Source: What data do you want to chart – all the cells on your worksheet, or just a selected cell range?

Chart Options: How do you want your chart to look? Excel offers a variety of choices.

Chart Location: Where you want the chart stored – on your current worksheet, on a different worksheet, or in a new workbook? You decide.

Above:
The four dialog boxes of Excel's Chart Wizard

Does this seem like a lot of dialog boxes to learn about? Don't worry. All four dialogs offer a default option that in most cases will create an impressive-looking, ECDL-exam-passing chart. So, when in doubt, just click the **Next** button on the first three dialog boxes, and the **Finish** button on the fourth.

Creating Your First Chart in Excel

Perform the following Exercise to make yourself familiar with charting in Excel.

Exercise 4.36: Creating a Simple Excel Chart

1) Open the worksheet that you saved in Exercise 4.35.

2) Select the non-adjacent cell range A4:A11, C4:C11. Do this by using the mouse to select A4:A11. Then hold down the CTRL key and select C4:C11.

Above:
Excel's Chart
Wizard button

	A	B	C	D	E	F	G	H	I
1									
2			First Quarter Sales Figures for 1999						
3									
4			January	February	March	April		Totals	%
5	Conway	John	IR£ 2,356.00	IR£ 3,621.00	IR£ 4,185.00	IR£ 4,560.00		IR£ 14,722.00	13%
6	Higgins	Robert	IR£ 3,463.00	IR£ 3,981.00	IR£ 4,210.00	IR£ 4,974.00		IR£ 16,628.00	15%
7	Murphy	Tracey	IR£ 4,921.00	IR£ 4,055.00	IR£ 3,814.00	IR£ 3,542.00		IR£ 16,332.00	14%
8	Rafferty	Andrew	IR£ 2,512.00	IR£ 2,864.00	IR£ 3,290.00	IR£ 3,741.00		IR£ 12,407.00	11%
9	Smith	Aidan	IR£ 3,872.00	IR£ 2,441.00	IR£ 2,888.00	IR£ 4,949.00		IR£ 14,150.00	13%
10	Smith	Zowie	IR£ 5,951.00	IR£ 6,226.00	IR£ 6,481.00	IR£ 6,852.00		IR£ 25,510.00	23%
11	Sullivan	Catherine	IR£ 2,903.00	IR£ 3,308.00	IR£ 3,487.00	IR£ 3,622.00		IR£ 13,320.00	12%
12									
13			IR£25,978.00	IR£26,496.00	IR£28,355.00	IR£32,240.00		IR£ 113,069.00	
14									
15		%	23%	23%	25%	29%			

3) See the button towards the right on the Standard Toolbar? That's Excel's Chart Wizard button. Click on it.

4) Excel displays a series of four dialog boxes. On the first three, click the **Next** button. On the fourth and last, click **Finish**.

Congratulations. You have drawn your first chart in Excel!

To move your chart to a different position on your worksheet, click on a blank area of the chart margin and drag with the mouse.

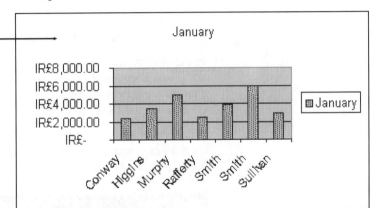

5) Unfortunately, Excel positions your chart on top of your data, so you cannot see both at the same time. Move the chart by clicking on any blank part of the chart margin – Excel calls this the Chart Area – and then dragging the chart to the right and down until you can see your data.

Finally, delete your chart by selecting it and pressing DEL.

Charts: Two Ideas You Need to Know

All charting – in Excel or with pen and paper – is based on two very basic ideas: the *data point* and the *data series*.

You will see these two terms a lot on Excel's charting dialog boxes and online help screens. Understand these two ideas and you will be able to exploit fully Excel's charting possibilities.

About Data Points

Data point: the idea is so simple you will wonder why anyone bothered even to give it a name. Consider the four examples below.

Item	Value
Apples	4
Pears	3
Bananas	6

Item	Value
January	IR£ 1,965.34
February	IR£ 2,451.50
March	IR£ 8,301.49

Item	Value
Mary	15.00%
Catherine	50.00%
Margaret	35.00%

Item	Value
Sales	IR£4,954,032.00
Costs	IR£394,823.00
Overheads	IR£25,068.00

Each example consist of individual items (or people) being measured. They are types of fruit, months of the year, people and amounts of money.

The items each have a number that is their measured value. A *data point* is a single item and its related value.

In the first example, the three data points are: Apples and 4, Pears and 3 and Bananas and 6. Other data points from the above examples are February and IR£2,451.50, Catherine and 50%, and Overheads and IR£25,068.00

A data point always has two parts: the item and the value. On its own, a number is not a data point, nor is it an item. You need both for a data point.

Data Point

An item being measured and its measured value.

About Data Series

A single data point does not tell us very much. A chart is useful only if there is more than one data point. A collection of data points is called a data series.

For instance, you may want to create a chart that shows the company's sales figures for different months. Or a chart that compares one month's sales figures for different departments.

Data Series

A group of related data points. For example, your data series may compare different items measured at the same time, or single items measured at different times.

Single Data Series Charts

We used the word 'simple' to describe the chart that you created in Exercise 4.36. More precisely, it is an example of a single data series chart.

Here are some other single data series charts from your worksheet. Practise your charting skills by creating these yourself.

Data Series: A4:A11, F4:F11   **Data Series: A4:A11, I4:I11**

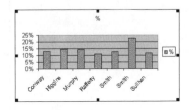

Data Series: C4:F4, C15:F15   **Data Series: B4:B11, H4:H1**

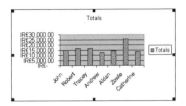

Creating a Multiple Data Series Chart

You can have more than one data series in a collection of related information.

Consider the part of your worksheet shown on the right. How many data series can you see? Answer: two.

There is one data series for January, and a second for February.

	January	February
Conway	IR£ 2,356.00	IR£ 3,621.00
Higgins	IR£ 3,463.00	IR£ 3,981.00
Murphy	IR£ 4,921.00	IR£ 4,055.00
Rafferty	IR£ 2,512.00	IR£ 2,864.00
Smith	IR£ 3,872.00	IR£ 2,441.00
Smith	IR£ 5,951.00	IR£ 6,226.00
Sullivan	IR£ 2,903.00	IR£ 3,308.00

***Right:*
Two data series, one for each of the two months**

	January
Conway	IR£ 2,356.00
Higgins	IR£ 3,463.00
Murphy	IR£ 4,921.00
Rafferty	IR£ 2,512.00
Smith	IR£ 3,872.00
Smith	IR£ 5,951.00
Sullivan	IR£ 2,903.00

	February
Conway	IR£ 3,621.00
Higgins	IR£ 3,981.00
Murphy	IR£ 4,055.00
Rafferty	IR£ 2,864.00
Smith	IR£ 2,441.00
Smith	IR£ 6,226.00
Sullivan	IR£ 3,308.00

Exercise 4.37: Creating a Two Data Series Chart in Excel

1) Select the cell range A2:A6, C2:D6.

2) Click on the Chart Wizard button and accept the default options in the sequence of four dialog boxes. Your chart should look as below.

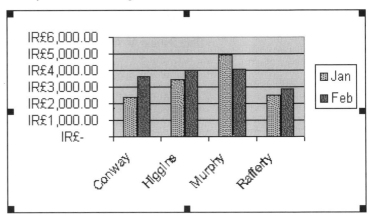

When Excel draws a chart with more than a single data series, it uses a different colour to represent different items.

Finally, delete your chart.

Exercise 4.38: Creating a Three Data Series Chart in Excel

1) Select the cell range A2:A6, C2:E6.

2) Click on the Chart Wizard button and accept the default options in the sequence of four dialog boxes. Your chart should look as below.

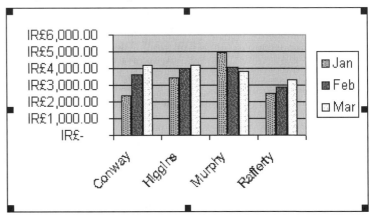

3) Drag the chart down the worksheet so that it does not block the view of your data.

More About Excel's Chart Wizard

In your charting Exercises you accepted the default options presented by Excel's Chart Wizard. Next, we will look closely at the other options available with the Chart Wizard.

Chart Type (Step 1)

Use this to decide which type of chart you want to illustrate your data. Excel offers 13 chart types, with several choices within each type. But only three are relevant here.

 Column Chart: Items are shown horizontally and values vertically.

 Bar Chart: A 'sideways column chart' that shows items horizontally and values vertically.

 Pie Chart: Shows the proportion of each item that makes up the total. For a single data series only.

Source Data (Step 2)

You can use this dialog to change the cell range on which your chart is based. You can also swap the rows with the columns.

Chart Options (Step 3)

Use this dialog to control the appearance of your chart. The relevant dialog box tabs are:

- **Titles:** Add titles to horizontal and/or vertical axes.
- **Gridlines:** Control whether and how Excel displays gridlines.

Chart Location (Step 4)

Where do you want Excel to put your chart? The default is the worksheet that contains the data on which the chart is based.

You can use this dialog box to place your chart within a different worksheet of the same workbook.

Or, in a new workbook.

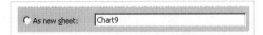

Editing Your Chart

When you create a chart, don't think of it as fixed forever. You can change just about every aspect of a chart.

Resizing a Chart

Changing your chart's size can affect its appearance dramatically. Click once on your chart to select it. Handles (small black squares) appear around its edges. Click on any of the handles and hold down the mouse button as you drag the chart to a different shape.

If you drag on a corner handle, the chart expands and contracts proportionally to its current size; if you drag on an edge handle, the chart expands or contracts in that direction.

Changing Chart Data

You can amend the worksheet data on which your chart is based; as soon as you change that data, Excel updates the chart to reflect your changes.

Changing Chart Format

Double-clicking on any part of a chart displays a pop-up menu that offers you a range of such formatting options as borders, patterns, fonts, colours and text positioning.

Exercise 4.39: Formatting a Pie Chart

1) Select the cell range A4:A11, C4:C11.

2) Click on the Chart Wizard button.

3) In the Chart Type dialog box, select Pie Chart and click **Finish**. Your chart should look as below.

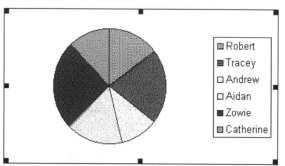

4) By default, Excel does not display percentages to show how much each 'slice' of the pie chart contributes to the total. You will insert these in the next step.

5) Double-click on the pie chart itself (not the surrounding area) to display the Format Data Series dialog box.

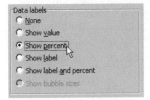

6) On the Data Labels tab, select the option Show percent, and click **OK**.

7) Your pie chart should now look as below.

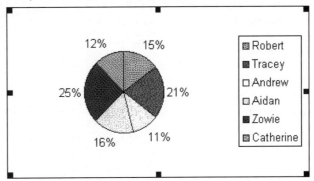

Section Summary: So Now You Know

To draw a chart in Excel, first select the cells with the numbers and text that you want to chart, and then run Excel's *Chart Wizard*. The Wizard's default options on its four dialog boxes are acceptable in most cases.

If you change any of the data on which a chart is based, Excel updates the chart to reflect the changes.

By default, Excel positions your chart on top of your worksheet data. You can move the chart by clicking on any blank part of the chart margin, and then dragging the chart to a new position.

Charting is based on the ideas of data points and data series. A *data point* is a single item and its related value (for example, the sales figure in January), while a *data series* is a group of related data points (for example, monthly sales figures over a year). You can chart more than one data series at one time.

Excel offers a wide range of *chart types*, with column, bar and pie charts being the most commonly used. You can *format* your chart in a variety of ways by adding gridlines, data labels, chart patterns, colours and borders.

Databases

You can never be too rich, too thin, or too informed.

And the best kind of information to have is that which is organised in such a way that you can find the facts you need quickly and easily. It's also important to be able to store away new items you come across.

Databases – structured collections of facts about a particular topic – existed long before computers. Address books, card indexes and telephone directories are all examples of databases.

But by storing your facts in a database file on a computer, you gain the power to manage and manipulate that information – even seriously large amounts of information – in a variety of ways.

You will discover how to view information in your database file from different perspectives, sort and select particular pieces you are interested in, and produce printed reports.

Think of this Module as your chance to file rather than be filed. Good luck with it.

Section 5.1: What Is a Database?

In This Section

This Section deals with the basic concepts of databases, and introduces the terminology you will need to make sense of the rest of the Module.

New Activities

At the end of this Section, you should be able to:

- Say what a database is, and what it is used for
- Use and understand the terminology associated with databases
- Understand that data in a database can be presented in a number of different forms

New Words

At the end of this Section, you should be able to explain the following terms:

- Database
- Table
- Record
- Field
- Datasheet
- Form

The word 'database' is really only a fancy word for a file. It is a collection of information relating to the same subject matter. It is usually organised in such a way you can easily find the bits you are interested in, and you can file away the new bits of information that you come across.

Database
A database is an organised collection of related information.

A database does not have to be kept on a computer: for example, address books, card indexes, and telephone directories are all databases (even though very few people would call them that!).

However, storing a database on a computer enables you to manipulate the information easily and quickly. For example, using a (paper-based) telephone directory, it is relatively easy to find a person's telephone number, but it is very difficult (but not impossible) to find the person's name if you only have their telephone number. A computer-based directory would enable you to find that information quickly and easily. And you could also find the names of everyone who lives on a particular road, or everyone whose first name was Paul. Or you could print a report showing the five most common surnames. The possibilities are endless.

Computer-based databases are flexible: they enable you to deal with information – even very large quantities of information – in a variety of ways.

Database Management System

A database management system enables you to collect information on a computer, organise it in different ways, sort and select pieces of information of interest to you, and produce reports.

In a database, individual pieces of information (such as a telephone number) are called *fields*; the set of information relating to one individual is called a *record*; and a collection of such records is called a *table*.

Field

A field is a single piece of information about a subject. More precisely, it is the space where that information is held.

Record

A record is one complete set of fields relating to the same subject.

Table

A table is a collection of records that contain the same fields.

In a simple database, the table *is* the database. More complex databases can contain several tables.

Note that the term *table* is used in Access, but not in every database program: some use the term *file*, and some just use the term *database*. The reason that Access makes a distinction between a database and a table is that Access is a *relational database* system.

In a relational database, you can maintain a number of separate tables containing related information. For example, you might maintain a table of suppliers (with their address and telephone number), and a table of purchase orders (with only the supplier name). This would enable you to store the supplier address and telephone number only once, but to print them out on every order confirmation. Using a separate table for each topic helps to eliminate duplicated data: the database requires less memory; when the information changes, it only has to be changed once;

and there is less likelihood that errors will be introduced when the information is being entered.

Different Ways of Looking at the Same Thing

With Access, and with most database systems, you can view and manipulate information in two ways: in a datasheet, or in forms.

A *datasheet* shows the information arranged in columns (one for each field) and rows (one for each record); it is similar in appearance to a spreadsheet. See below.

Order ID	Product	Unit Price	Quantity	Discount
10248	Queso Cabrales	£14.00	12	0%
10248	Singaporean Hokkien Fried Mee	£9.80	10	0%
10248	Mozzarella di Giovanni	£34.80	5	0%
10249	Tofu	£18.60	9	0%
10249	Manjimup Dried Apples	£42.40	40	0%
10250	Jack's New England Clam Chowder	£7.70	10	0%
10250	Manjimup Dried Apples	£42.40	35	15%
10250	Louisiana Fiery Hot Pepper Sauce	£16.80	15	15%
10251	Gustaf's Knäckebröd	£16.80	6	5%
10251	Ravioli Angelo	£15.60	15	5%
10251	Louisiana Fiery Hot Pepper Sauce	£16.80	20	0%
10252	Sir Rodney's Marmalade	£64.80	40	5%
10252	Geitost	£2.00	25	5%
10252	Camembert Pierrot	£27.20	40	0%
10253	Gorgonzola Telino	£10.00	20	0%
10253	Chartreuse verte	£14.40	42	0%
10253	Maxilaku	£16.00	40	0%
10254	Guaraná Fantástica	£3.60	15	15%
10254	Pâté chinois	£19.20	21	15%

Datasheet

A datasheet presents information from a database as rows and columns, so that you can see several records at the same time.

A *form* presents selected information for one record. The form can be laid out in a format that is easier to read, perhaps with explanatory text. You can structure the form in such a way that it looks like a paper form, with the fields in the corresponding place on the screen.

Bird Name	Gannet
Date Seen	12/06/98
Place Seen	Ireland's Eye

Form

A form shows the information relating to one database record.

Section Summary: So Now You Know

A *database* is a collection of information, typically held on a computer, and organised in such a way that you can find what you are looking for quickly and easily.

A database holds at least one *table* of information; each table has a number of *records*; and each record has a number of *fields*.

With a computer-based *database management system*, you can present your information in different ways: as a *datasheet* (which shows the information in tabular layout, with a row for each record, and a column for each field), or as a *form* (which presents the records one at a time).

Section 5.2: Your First Access Database

In This Section

In this section, you will use Microsoft Access to create a simple database.

New Activities

At the end of this Section, you should be able to:

- Start and quit Access
- Decide on a structure for a simple database
- Create a new database
- Use a table to add records to a database
- Save, name, open, and close Access databases
- Edit and delete database records

New Words

At the end of this Section, you should be able to explain the terms *key* and *data type*, and understand the difference between the following data types:

- Text
- Number
- Currency
- Yes/No
- Memo
- Date/Time
- AutoNumber

Starting Access

Double-click on the Microsoft Access icon.

-or-

Choose **Start | Programs | Microsoft Access**.

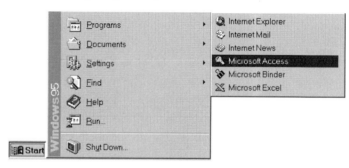

The dialog box gives you the choice of opening an existing database, or of creating a new database.

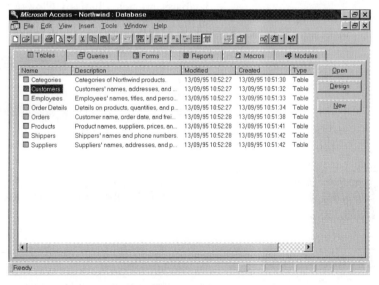

Opening an Existing Database

Access comes with three sample databases: Northwind, Orders, and Solutions. Select **Open an Existing Database**. The sample databases may be listed in the box below: if they are, select northwind.mdb and then click **OK**.

If the sample databases are not listed, select **More Files**. You can then navigate through the directories on your PC to find them: they are most likely in the Samples subdirectory of your Access directory (MSOffice\Access\Samples). Use Windows Explorer if necessary. When you find northwind.mdb, select it, and then click **OK**. (If you are presented with a welcome screen, click **OK** to close it.)

This is the Database screen: it shows six tabs: Tables, Queries, Forms, Reports, Macros, and Modules. These are all sets of files that are associated with the database in some way: Access calls them *objects*. In this Module, you will learn about the first four of them: you don't need to worry about Macros and Modules for the ECDL.

You will see this screen a lot when you are working with Access: from here, you can open any of the database objects – to work with them or to change them – and when you are finished with that object, Access returns you to this Database screen, from where you can access any of the other objects easily.

The exercises in this Module take you through many Access features, but as you follow the exercises, you should also try to familiarise yourself with other features, so that you see the possibilities that the program offers. Don't be afraid to experiment. If you get lost, simply close the object you are working on, don't save the changes you have made, and start again from there. You will quickly become comfortable with Access, and will be better equipped to work with it when you have finished this book.

When you first open a database, the Tables tab is normally on top. If it isn't, simply click the **Tables** tab, and it comes to the top.

Notice that the Northwind database has a number of tables listed. Open any one of these, either by selecting it and clicking **Open**, or by double-clicking on its name or icon. Have a look at the type of information it contains. This will give you a good idea of how databases are actually used. Close it by clicking the Close button on the top right of the Table window.

If you have made any changes to the table, Access prompts you to save the changes before it closes the file. For the moment, don't save any changes.

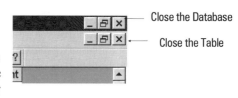

Close the Database

Close the Table

Closing a Database

Choose **File | Close**, or click the Close button on the database window.

Quitting Access

To leave Access:

Choose **File | Exit**, or click the Close button on the Access window.

If you have left open any files containing unsaved work, Access prompts you to save them. You are then returned to the Windows desktop.

Creating a New Database

Design Considerations

Before you even touch the computer, give some thought to the kind of information you want to put into your database, and how you want to use it. The boxed panels on the following pages give a number of examples of simple databases and how they can be used. The examples supplied with Access are more complex.

Example 1: The Wine Buff

Henry is interested in wine. He reads the wine column in the newspapers and notes the recommendations. When he goes to the supermarket, he brings a list with him, so that he can select wine based on the recommendations. When he buys wine, he might have it in the house for some time before he tastes it, and he likes to record his impressions and compare notes with the original review.

Henry might include the following *fields* in his database:

- Wine Style (Red, White, Rosé, Sparkling, Sweet)

- Name	- Country/Region
- Grower	- Grape Varieties
- Vintage	- Recommended by
- Review comments	- Available from (shop)
- Price	- Number bought
- Date bought	- Date tasted
- Tasting notes	- Buy again?

With such a database, Henry could print out a separate list for each shop, he could list all the red wines, he could list all the white wines that cost less than £10, he could find where the wines by a particular grower were available, he could view the comments on different vintages of the same wine, and so on.

Example 2: The CD Collector

Michelle plays the piano, and has a large collection of CDs. When she is learning a new piece, she likes to listen to other people playing it. She has built a database with the following fields:

- CD Title
- Artist
- Track Number
- Name of tune
- Composer
- Date recorded

By sorting the database on the Name of the Tune, she can quickly identify the particular CDs that include the tune she is working on.

Example 3: The Household Manager

Oscar started his database for insurance purposes: it enabled him to build up a detailed record of his house contents. It included the following fields:

- Room
- Item
- Category
- Date Purchased
- Price Paid

With this database, he was able to provide an accurate inventory to the insurance company to support a claim. He could provide the original cost, along with the depreciated value, and the replacement value, based on the original cost and the elapsed time since the purchase. He could also quickly give a value for all the paintings in the house, the value of all the clothes in the upstairs rooms, or all the contents of a particular room.

Example 4: The Bird Spotter

Every weekend, Clara goes out with her field glasses and notebook, and spends some time watching birds. When she comes home, she puts details of what she has seen into a database. The database has the following fields:

- Bird Name
- Size
- Migratory?
- Date Seen

- Predominant Colour (Male)
- Predominant Colour (Female)
- Where Seen

Clara has entered into her database the basic information for the first five fields, based on her reference books, and she records her sightings every week. If she sees a bird that she is unable to identify, she can look up all birds of a certain colour and size. (Obviously this is not enough for identification, but it helps her find the right bird in her reference books.) She can then record the date and place of the sighting. After a while, she will be able to identify the best places and times of the year to spot the different species.

When you are deciding on the fields in the database, think carefully about how they are to be used. If, for example, you want to sort or select wines by country of origin, you should have a column for country: while you might know that Bordeaux is in France, Access doesn't. If you want to find all the albums produced by Nick Lowe, you have to record that information, and preferably in a consistent way (for example, last name followed by first name).

All the fields in a record should relate specifically to that record. For example, the weather in Bordeaux in a given year is not a function of a particular wine, so it should not feature in the wine table: a separate table could be created, with details of the weather in different regions in different years, and this could then be linked to the wine table.

First Steps

In the rest of this Module, you will create a simple database, similar to the one that Clara uses to record her bird-watching activities.

Access includes a number of features to simplify the process of creating a database: we will use the Wizard and other automated features to do some of the work, and we will do some of it the 'hard way', so that you will learn more about how the software works.

Start Access, by double-clicking on the Microsoft Access icon, or by choosing **Start | Programs | Microsoft Access**.

This time ...

... select **Database Wizard** ...

... then click **OK**.

Select the Blank Database icon ...

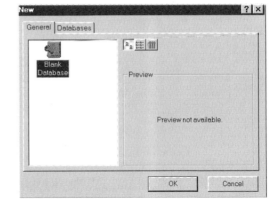

... and click **OK**.

Give your new database a name – birds.mdb – and indicate the directory in which you want to store it.

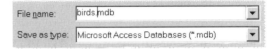

Click **Create**.

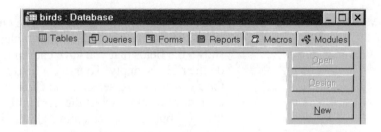

Normally, the Tables tab is on top at this point; if it isn't, click on the **Tables** tab to bring it to the top.

Click New.

There are five ways to create a new table. For this exercise, select **Table Wizard**.

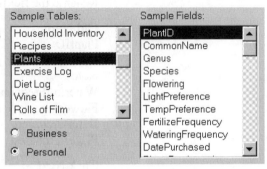

This will take you through the process step by step.

Click **OK**.

It would be impossible for anyone to anticipate precisely what you wanted to do with your database. So the Access Table Wizard offers you a wide range of choices at this point. The idea is that you pick the one that comes closest to matching your needs, and you modify it until it is exactly what you want.

Browse through the choices on offer. They are broadly categorized into Business and Personal. Click on **Business** and scroll through the list of fields that are suggested for the various business tables. None of these seem to be particularly appropriate for your needs.

Click on **Personal**. Again, there is nothing that relates to bird-watching, but one of the tables – Plants – could be relatively easily modified to suit the bird-watching application.

The screen shows two list boxes. The one on the left shows the fields that you can include in your table; the one on the right shows the fields that you have chosen to include. Initially, the one on the right is empty. To move a field from the left-hand box to the right-hand box, select it and click the `>` button. If you change your mind, select the field in the right-hand box and click the `<` button. You can move all the fields from one box to the other by clicking `>>` or `<<`.

Move the following fields from the left-hand box to the right-hand box:

PlantID
CommonName
Notes
WateringFrequency
Flowering
DatePurchased
PlacePurchased

To rename a field, select it in the right-hand box and click **Rename**. You can then type the new name for the field.

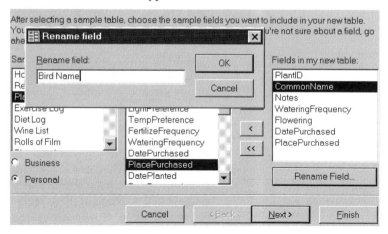

Rename the fields as follows:

Old Name	New Name
PlantID	Number
CommonName	Bird Name
Notes	Colour
WateringFrequency	Size
Flowering	Migratory?
DatePurchased	Date Seen
PlacePurchased	Place Seen

Click **Next >**.

Congratulations! You have just created your first Access table. Now you have to give it a name.

Apply all your imagination: call it Birds.

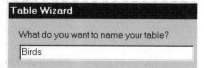

Table Wizard

What do you want to name your table?

Birds

You are then asked whether you want the Wizard to set a primary key, or whether you want to do it yourself. Okay, let's talk about keys.

Keys

In the telephone directory, there many people listed with the surname Murphy; a number of them share the same first name, John. To find the one you want, you need some more information: where do they live? Even that might not be enough – father and son might have the same name – and you might have to ask them some further question to confirm that you are talking to the right one. Well, in a computer system, that obviously is not satisfactory (you don't want to send a bill, or, worse still, a cheque to the wrong John Murphy), and so we give each record an identifier, called a *key*, which is unique to that record – it is not shared with any other.

> **Key**
>
> *A field (or combination of fields) in a database record that is used to uniquely identify that record.*

The question of specifying a key (called a *primary key* in Access) is particularly relevant in a database with a number of tables that have to be linked together: Access needs to know which John Murphy you mean.

However, our database is a simple one, and for the moment you can let the Wizard worry about setting the primary key.

Click **Next >**.

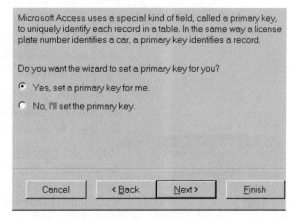

Microsoft Access uses a special kind of field, called a primary key, to uniquely identify each record in a table. In the same way a license plate number identifies a car, a primary key identifies a record.

Do you want the wizard to set a primary key for you?

○ Yes, set a primary key for me.

○ No, I'll set the primary key.

| Cancel | < Back | Next > | Finish |

You are then asked what you want to do next: do you want to modify the table design, enter data directly into the table, or enter data into a table using a form wizard. Well, a table with no data is pretty boring, so you probably want to enter data directly into the

table without further delay. Choose that option ...

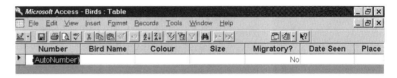

After the wizard creates the table, what do you want to do?

- ○ Modify the table design.
- ● Enter data directly into the table.
- ○ Enter data into the table using a form the wizard creates for me.

... and click **Finish**.

| Cancel | < Back | Next > | Finish |

Using a Datasheet to Enter Data into the Table

The table shows one row with a number of columns, one for each of the fields you defined. This is called the *Datasheet View* of the table.

Microsoft Access - Birds : Table

File   Edit   View   Insert   Format   Records   Tools   Window   Help

Number	Bird Name	Colour	Size	Migratory?	Date Seen	Place
(AutoNumber)				No		

Click in any field: you can then enter data in that field. You can move from field to field using the TAB key or the arrow keys. There is an exception: the Number field is automatically assigned by Access – you cannot enter a new number or change an existing one. You will learn more about this feature in the next section.

As soon as you start entering data for a record, a new line opens up underneath. So, no matter how many records you enter, there is always a blank record at the end where you can enter the next one.

Fill in the details of a number of birds, as on the next page. In the case of Migratory?, you indicate that a bird is migratory by clicking on the checkbox in the table. Leave the details of the sightings blank for the moment.

(If the entry under Migratory? in the blank line says 'No' instead of showing a checkbox, you change it by typing 'Yes' in place of the 'No'. We'll change it to a checkbox later.)

When you have entered the descriptive details of the birds into the datasheet, close it by clicking the Close button on the top right of the window. You are then returned to the Database screen, this time with one important difference: the table Birds is

Number	Bird Name	Colour	Size	Migratory?	Date Seen	Plac
1	Great Northern	Black/White	69	☑		
2	Great Crested (	Grey/White/Bro	46	☐		
3	Little Grebe	Black/Brown	24	☐		
4	Gannet	White/Black	85	☐		
5	Fulmar	White/Grey	45	☐		
6	Great Shearwat	White/Brown	42	☑		
7	Manx Shearwat	Black/White	30	☐		
8	Storm Petrel	Black/White	13	☐		
9	Cormorant	Black/White	83	☐		
10	Grey Heron	Grey/White	90	☐		
11	Mute Swan	White	144	☐		
12	Brent Goose	Black/White	56	☑		
13	Greylag Goose	Grey	76	☑		
14	Shelduck	White/Brown/Bl	57	☐		
15	Goldeneye	White/Black	41	☑		
16	Teal	Grey/Multicolou	34	☐		
17	Mallard	Green/White/Br	55	☐		
18	Sparrowhawk	Blue/White	28	☑		
19	Kestrel	Grey/brown	33	☐		
20	Pheasant	Red/Black	53	☐		
(AutoNumber)				☐		

Record: 18 of 20

Datasheet View

shown. That's it. You now know how to create a table and how to enter data into it using a datasheet.

Changing and Deleting Database Records

To change or delete a record in the Birds database, open Access, open the Birds database, then open the Birds table. It opens in Datasheet View, like the picture at the top of the page.

To change a field, click on that field and enter the new data. If you click on the leftmost position in the field, you immediately overwrite the whole field; if you click anywhere else in the field, you can use the BACKSPACE or DEL key to delete characters one by one, or you can insert new characters. Remember that you cannot change the Number field: that is assigned by Access. Change the Migratory? checkbox by clicking it: if it is already on, clicking it turns it off; if it is off, clicking it turns it on. (If the Migratory? field contains 'No', you can either leave it alone or change it to 'Yes'; no other input is accepted.)

To delete a record, select it by clicking on the little box to the extreme left: it shows a  beside the selected record, and the entire line changes colour. Choose **Edit | Delete**. You can then confirm that you want to delete the record, or change your mind and leave it alone.

Next, put in the details of some sightings. Notice that the Date Seen field only accepts valid dates, and forces you to input them in a standard way. Try putting in some invalid dates to see what happens: 44th October 1748, my birthday, Christmas day, 29th February 1999.

Bird Name	Colour	Size	Migratory?	Date Seen	Place Seen
Great Northern	Black/White	69	☑		
Great Crested (	Grey/White/Brc	46	☐	13/03/99	Dalkey
Little Grebe	Black/Brown	24	☐	04/09/98	Stephen's Gree
Gannet	White/Black	85	☐	12/06/98	Ireland's Eye
Fulmar	White/Grey	45	☐		
Great Shearwat	White/Brown	42	☑		
Manx Shearwat	Black/White	30	☐		
Storm Petrel	Black/White	13	☐		
Cormorant	Black/White	83	☐	12/06/98	Ireland's Eye
Grey Heron	Grey/White	90	☐		
Mute Swan	White	144	☐	14/06/99	Malahide
Brent Goose	Black/White	56	☑	12/12/98	Dollymount
Greylag Goose	Grey	76	☑		
Shelduck	White/Brown/Bl	57	☐		
Goldeneye	White/Black	41	☑		
Teal	Grey/Multicolou	34	☐		
Mallard	Green/White/Br	55	☐		
Sparrowhawk	Blue/White	28	☑	07/06/98	Enniskerry
Kestrel	Grey/brown	33	☐		

Then put in some valid dates, and note how you can enter them in a variety of formats, and Access converts them to a consistent format: 4 March 1999, 23/1/99, 29-2-00, 30 Jun 98.

When you are finished, close the table by clicking the Close button on the top right of the window. You are then returned to the Database screen.

One thing to note: if your database records contain an AutoNumber field, and you delete a record, the number assigned to the deleted record is *not* assigned to another record. Records keep the number initially assigned to them, and later additions are always assigned higher numbers than earlier ones.

The Different Data Types

At this stage, you're probably thinking that Access is reading your mind. How does it know that the Date Seen column should only contain dates? And how does it know that the Migratory? column is either ticked for Yes, or left blank for No? (Or that input in that field is limited to Yes and No.) Well the answer is in the table design, and, to be honest, we cheated a bit.

When you set up a table in Access, there are two things you have to do for each field: you have to give the field a *name*, and you have to give it a *data type*. In using the Wizard to set up the Birds table, you selected fields from the Plants table that had more or less the same characteristics as the fields in the Birds table. You changed the names of the fields to match the bird-watching application. However, because you chose fields carefully, you didn't have to change the data types.

The data type tells Access how to treat the field, how the data is to be stored, and what kind of data is allowed in it.

Data Type

The data type determines the kind of data that you can store in a field, and tells Access how to handle it.

Access recognises a number of different data types. For our purposes, the most important are:

Data Type	Used For	Examples
Text	Any sort of alphabetic or numeric data. Typically used where there is a limit on the amount of data. No more than 255 characters may be input. (If the data is numeric, it should not be intended for use in calculations.)	Surname, Colour, Zip Code, Telephone Number
Memo	Any sort of alphabetic or numeric data. Typically used for free-form input. Up to 64,000 characters may be input. (Again, if the data is numeric, it should not be intended for use in calculations.)	Description, Where Seen, Notes
Number	Numeric data that may be used in calculations.	Quantity in Stock, Number in Flock, Number Sold
Date/Time	Date or time data.	Date Bought, Arrival Time, Planting Date
Currency	Money values or other numeric data used in calculations where the number of decimal places does not exceed four.	Price, Current Value
AutoNumber	A number assigned to each new record automatically. Access assigns the numbers in sequence, starting with 1.	Sequence Number
Yes/No	Fields that can have simple yes/no, true/false, or on/off values only.	Migratory?, Buy Again?, Flowering?

Changing Data Types

It is easy to change the data type of a field, but ideally you should get it right at the design stage. If you try to change the data type after you have input a lot of data, you can confuse Access, and you may lose some of your data.

Try this:

1) Start up Access, and open the Birds database.

2) At the Database screen, select the Birds table, and click **Design**.

3) You then see the Design View of the table: this shows two main boxes. At the top is the list of field names with their data types.

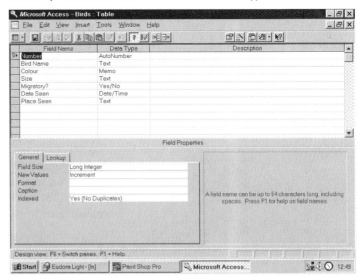

Click on any of the data type fields. Notice how a drop-down arrow appears beside the data type. Click on this arrow: you see the list of data types described above (along with a few others that we haven't discussed). To change a data type, you simply select the new one from that list.

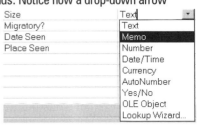

Try some experiments: change the data type of Migratory? from Yes/No to Number. Close the dialog box, and confirm that you want to save the changes. Then open the table. Notice how the data displayed under Migratory? has changed.

4) Go back into Design View. (To do this, close the table, and then click on **Design** again.) This time, change the Data Type of Migratory? to Date/Time. Then save the change and have a look at the effect of this change on the data displayed in the datasheet.

Notice how changing the data type after you have input data can yield surprising results.

Migratory?
☑
☐
☐

When you have finished experimenting, change the Data Type of Migratory? back to Yes/No.

Before you finish: remember how the Migratory? field contains *either* Yes or No *or* a checkbox? Well here's your chance to make it behave. Click again on the Migratory? field. Then, in the lower half of the Design View screen (Field Properties), choose the Lookup tab, and in Display Control, choose the option you want: either Check Box, or Text Box.

One other thing: later we will want to compare the sizes of different birds. To do this, the Size field must be numeric. Change its Data Type from Text to Number.

Finally, save your work.

Adding New Fields to a Table

You can add new fields to the database records at any time. But if you do, you may have to go back and edit all records you have already entered, particularly for numeric fields (where a blank field may be interpreted as 0), and Yes/No fields (where blank may be interpreted as No), but it is also important for any field that you will use for sorting or filtering. So it is better if you think about the fields you want when you are setting up the database, and modify the design as little as possible after that.

To add a field to the Birds table:

1) Open the table in Design View. If you already have the table open in Datasheet View, you can switch directly to Design View by clicking the Table View button ![icon] at the top left of the table. Alternatively, if you do not have the table open, select the table at the Database screen, and click **Design**. Note that when you are in Design View, you can go directly to Datasheet View by clicking the Table View button ![icon]. This enables you to switch quickly between the two views, so that you can see the effect of any design changes you make.

2) To add the new field at the end of the record, click on the next unused Field Name box.
   To add the new field between two existing fields, click on the title of the field that will end up on the right of the new field. For example, click on the Size field title. Then choose **Insert | Field**.

3) Enter the title of the new field: Colour F.
   (Change the title of the existing Colour field to read 'Colour M'.)

4) Specify the Data Type of the new field: Text.

Bird Name	Text
Colour M	Text
Colour F	Text
Size	Number
Migratory?	Yes/No
Date Seen	Date/Time

5) Click the Close button
-or-
Choose **File | Close**.
-or-
Hold down the CTRL key and type w.
-or-
Click the Table View button.

(Notice how Access – like most programs – offers you a number of ways of doing the same thing.)

Access asks you to confirm the change.

You can also insert a new field into a table while you are in Datasheet View: just click on the title of the field that will end up on the right of the new field and choose **Insert | Column**. This field will be assigned the Text Data Type. If that is what you want, fine. If it isn't, you will have to go into Design View to specify the Data Type you want.

Changing the Width of Columns in a Table

This is easy. By now you will have noticed that Access starts off by making all the columns the same width, which (a) doesn't always look very elegant, and (b) may push some of your data off the right of the screen, so that you have to use the left-right scroll bar to see it, and you can't see it all at the same time.

To change the width of a column, click on the dividing line between its title and the one to its right. Notice that the shape of the cursor changes. Drag the cursor left or right until the column is the right size.

Try this now with the Birds table to improve its overall appearance.

Before

Number	Bird Name	Colour	Size	Migratory?	Date Seen
1	Great Northern	Black/White	69	☑	
2	Great Crested (	Grey/White/Brc	46	☐	13/03/99
3	Little Grebe	Black/Brown	24	☐	04/09/98
4	Gannet	White/Black	85	☐	12/06/98

After

Num	Bird Name	Colour M	Colour F	Size	Migratory?	Date Seen
1	Great Northern Diver	Black/White		69	☑	12/12/98
2	Great Crested Grebe	Grey/White/Brown		46	☐	12/06/98
3	Little Grebe	Black/Brown		24	☐	
4	Gannet	White/Black		85	☐	12/06/98

You can make the column width adjust automatically to fit the longest entry in the field by double-clicking on the dividing line between its title and the one to its right.

Reordering the Fields in a Table

To change the order of fields in the Table, click on the title of the one you want to move. Then click on it *again* and drag it to the new location.

Click to select. ⌐ Click and drag to new location.

	Number	Bird Name	Colour M	Colour F	Size	Migratory?	Date Seen
▶	1	Great Northern Diver	Black/White		69	☑	
	2	Great Crested Grebe	Grey/White/Brown		46	☐	13/03/99 D:
	3	Little Grebe	Black/Brown		24	☐	04/09/98 St
	4	Gannet	White/Black		85	☐	12/06/98 Ir
	5	Fulmar	White/Grey		45	☐	
	6	Great Shearwater	White/Brown		42	☑	
	7	Manx Shearwater	Black/White		30	☐	

Section Summary: So Now You Know

Access offers a *Database Wizard* to simplify the process of creating a new database. A *Table Wizard* provides a number of sample tables. Choose one that resembles the table that you want to create. You can customise a particular sample table by selecting which of its fields you want to use, and then renaming the selected fields as required.

A *key* is a field (or combination of fields) in a database record that uniquely identifies that record. You can enter and change record data using Datasheet View. As soon as you enter a record, Access opens up a new line underneath, so that there is always a blank record at the end where you can enter the next one.

A field's *data type* tells Access how to treat the field, how the data is to be stored, and what kind of data is allowed in it. Commonly-used data types are: Text, Memo, Number, Data/Time, Currency, AutoNumber and Yes/No.

You can *change column* width manually at any stage, or make column width adjust automatically to the longest entry in the field. You can also change the *order* of fields in a table.

Before creating your database, consider the kind of information you want to put into your database, and how you want to use it.

Try to select the correct data type for each field before you enter data, as changing a field's data type at a later stage may result in data loss.

You can add new fields to the database at any time, but you may need to go back and edit all records that you have already entered, particularly for numeric fields (where a blank field may be interpreted as 0), and Yes/No fields (where a blank may be interpreted as No).

Section 5.3: Making the Database Work for You

In This Section

After the previous section, you might still be asking: Why bother? You can use a word processor to keep lists of things, and if you want to put them in neat columns, you can use a spreadsheet. Well this section should convince you that a database is a very useful tool for managing your information, and for quickly finding the particular pieces of interest.

New Activities

At the end of this Section, you should be able to:

- Reorder the database records

- Find a particular record or set of records

- Save and apply a query to a database

New Words

At the end of this Section, you should be able to explain the following terms:

- Sort
- Filter
- Query

Changing the Order of Records in the Table

Open the Birds table. Notice that the datasheet shows the records in the order you entered them: the Number field reflects that order – records you added later have higher numbers than ones you added earlier.

However, you can choose to display the records in a different order, by *sorting* them.

> **Sort**
>
> *The operation that you carry out on a file to change the order in which the records are displayed is called a sort.*

Suppose you want the records to be displayed alphabetically by bird name, or in order of size (biggest first, smallest last), how would you go about it? Easy. Click on any Bird Name. Then click the ⬇ button on the toolbar. Done! (This is called Sort Ascending.)

Click on any size field. Click the Z A↓ button. Again, done! (This is called Sort Descending.) What could be simpler?

Sorted by Name, Ascending   **Sorted by Size, Descending**

Number	Bird Name	C⟨	Colour M	Colour F	Size
12	Brent Goose	Black/V	Grey/White		90
9	Cormorant	Black/V	White/Black		85
5	Fulmar	White/(	Black/White		83
4	Gannet	White/E	Grey		76
15	Goldeneye	White/E	Black/White		69
2	Great Crested Grebe	Grey/W	White/Brown/Black		57
1	Great Northern Diver	Black/V	Black/White		56
6	Great Shearwater	White/E	Green/White/Brown		55
10	Grey Heron	Grey/W	Red/Black		53
13	Greylag Goose	Grey	Grey/White/Brown		46
19	Kestrel	Grey/br	White/Grey		45
3	Little Grebe	Black/E	White/Brown		42
17	Mallard	Green/\	White/Black		41
7	Manx Shearwater	Black/V	Grey/Multicoloured		34
11	Mute Swan	White	Grey/brown		33
20	Pheasant	Red/Bl⟨	Black/White		30
14	Shelduck	White/E	Blue/White		28
18	Sparrowhawk	Blue/W	Black/Brown		24

These kind of sorts are called simple, or *single criterion* sorts. Now imagine that you have more complex requirements: you want to sort all the birds by colour, and you want to show the biggest birds of any colour before the smaller ones. These are called *multiple criteria* sorts: you cannot use the sort buttons to perform them. Here's what to do:

1) Choose **Records | Filter | Advanced Filter/Sort**.

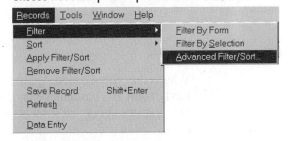

2) In the lower half of the screen, click on the list button in first column: a list of all the fields in your table is shown. Click on Colour M.

3) In the field below, the sort order is shown: use the list button and choose Ascending.

4) Click in the first field of the next column: a list button appears. Click on it, and choose Size from the list.

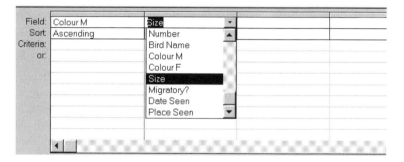

5) Click in the field below Size: a list button appears; click it and choose Descending.

6) Then click the Apply Filter button ▽, and the datasheet is shown, this time listing the birds in order of colour, and with the bigger birds of each colour shown before the smaller ones.

Number	Bird Name	Colour M	Colour F	Size	Migratory
3	Little Grebe	Black/Brown		24	☐
9	Cormorant	Black/White		83	☐
1	Great Northern Diver	Black/White		69	☑
12	Brent Goose	Black/White		56	☑
7	Manx Shearwater	Black/White		30	☐
8	Storm Petrel	Black/White		13	☐
18	Sparrowhawk	Blue/White		28	☑
17	Mallard	Green/White/Brown		55	☐
13	Greylag Goose	Grey		76	☑
19	Kestrel	Grey/brown		33	☐
16	Teal	Grey/Multicoloured		34	☐
10	Grey Heron	Grey/White		90	☐
2	Great Crested Grebe	Grey/White/Brown		46	☐
20	Pheasant	Red/Black		53	☐
11	Mute Swan	White		144	☐
4	Gannet	White/Black		85	☐
15	Goldeneye	White/Black		41	☑
6	Great Shearwater	White/Brown		42	☑
14	Shelduck	White/Brown/Black		57	☐

Why is the button called Apply Filter? Well, Access regards this kind of sort as a particular example of a filter. What's a filter? Don't worry about that for now: we'll be looking at filters in the next section.

Saving a Query

If you experiment with sorting, you'll see that you can view the information in your table in many different ways: you can separate the records into migratory and non-migratory birds; you can quickly identify the smallest bird you saw on a particular date; you can see what birds you have seen in Wexford – you get the idea.

It's quite likely that you will want to repeat some of these sorts regularly: for example, if you have several hundred birds in your database, sorting them by colour and size would help you identify unusual birds. You can enter the sort criteria each time you want to sort the table in this way, or you can make life easy for yourself, by saving the sort criteria as a *query*.

> **Query**
>
> *Queries are used to repeatedly view database records in a particular way defined by you.*

To save your sort criteria as a query, follow these steps:

1) Set up your sort criteria as in steps 1 to 5 of the previous exercise.

2) Then choose **File | Save as Query**

-or-

Click the Save button on the button bar.

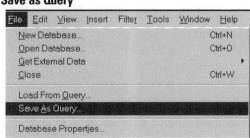

3) Give the query a name: say Colour/Size.

And that's it! Notice that the query shows up on the Query tab on the database screen. From now on, even after you have added more records to the database, or changed the ones that are already there, you simply open this query and the records in the table will be presented in the manner defined in the query.

Note that queries don't make any permanent change to the database; they simply extract information and present it in a certain way.

Restricting the Information Displayed

You can narrow down the amount of information displayed, either by showing fewer fields in each record, or by showing only those records that match certain criteria. This is called *filtering*.

Filter

A filter narrows down the display of your database information to records and fields that match criteria that you specify.

Suppose, for example, you want to concentrate on birds that you have seen in Wexford. Simply find any record that matches your criterion – in this case, one with Wexford in Where Seen? column. Click on the relevant field – Wexford – and then click on the Filter by Selection button in the button bar ![button] . The display is immediately restricted to records that match your selection – that is, ones that have Wexford in the Where Seen? column.

Number	Bird Name	Colour M	C	Size	Migratory?	Date Seen	Place See
16	Teal	Grey/Multicoloured		34	☐	28/09/98	Wexford
17	Mallard	Green/White/Browr		55	☐	28/09/98	Wexford
20	Pheasant	Red/Black		53	☐	27/09/98	Wexford
bNumber)					☐		

Don't panic: the rest of your records are still in the database. The filter just limits the amount of information in the display. To see all your records again, you remove the filter: click the Remove Filter button in the button bar ![button] .

A word of caution: Remember that you can change the information in the database at any time. And remember that you change a Yes/No field by clicking on it: a click turns it on if it was off, and off if it was on. If you are filtering based on a Yes/No field, you will change the information when you select it. So in the case of a Yes/No field, you will have to click on the field *twice* before you click on the Filter by Selection button. For example, suppose you want to study only migratory birds. As before, find one record of a migratory bird. Click on the Migratory? tick box: notice what happens – the box changes from ticked (Yes, migratory) to unticked (No, not migratory). Click it again, so that it shows the correct status, and then click the Apply Filter button. The display shows only migratory birds.

Bird Name	Colour M	C	Size	Migratory?	Date Seen	
Great Northern Diver	Black/White		69	☑		
Great Shearwater	White/Brown		42	☑		
Brent Goose	Black/White		56	☑	12/12/98	D(
Greylag Goose	Grey		76	☑		
Goldeneye	White/Black		41	☑		
Sparrowhawk	Blue/White		28	☑	07/06/98	Fr

When you select a field, and filter based on the contents of that field, the process is known as *Filtering by Selection*. Note that you don't have to select the whole field: you might be interested in all the Warblers, or all birds that have White somewhere in their colour. No problem. As before, find a record that has the characteristic you want – white in its colour. Drag the mouse over the part of the field that has the word (or part of word) that you want to match. Then click the Filter by Selection button. The display shows the White birds along with the Black/White and White/Grey ones (and so on).

Bird Name	Colour	Filter By Selection	Migratory?	Date Seen
Great Northern Diver	Black/White	69	☑	
Great Crested Grebe	Grey/White/Brown	46	☐	13/03/99 Dâ
Gannet	White/Black	85	☐	12/06/98 Irɛ
Fulmar	White/Grey	45	☐	
Great Shearwater	White/Brown	42	☑	
Manx Shearwater	Black/White	30	☐	
Storm Petrel	Black/White	13	☐	
Cormorant	Black/White	83	☐	12/06/98 Irɛ
Grey Heron	Grey/White	90	☐	
Mute Swan	White	144	☐	14/06/99 Mâ
Brent Goose	Black/White	56	☑	12/12/98 Dɾ
Shelduck	White/Brown/Black	57	☐	
Goldeneye	White/Black	41	☑	
Mallard	Green/White/Brown	55	☐	28/09/98 W
Sparrowhawk	Blue/White	28	☑	07/06/98 Er

Filtering by Selection includes the ideas 'Beginning with ...' and 'Ending with ...'. If you select the first letter in a field and Filter by Selection, Access displays all records in which the field *begins with* that letter. Similarly, if you select the last letter in the field, Access displays the records in which the field *ends with* that letter.

So if you want to filter based on the first word or the last word in a field, only include the first letter or the last letter if you want to restrict the display to records that begin with or end with the selection. If you want all records that include the word anywhere in the field, select only *part* of the word – a part in the middle of the word, such as 'hit' for White or 'lac' for Black.

Try Filtering by Selection yourself: remove the colour filter, and this time restrict the display to Grebes.

If you want to further restrict the records displayed – say to all green-coloured birds spotted in Wexford – you simply repeat the steps above. First, find all the birds spotted in Wexford, then *from that list* find all the green birds. Alternatively, start by finding all the green birds, then further restrict that list to ones spotted in Wexford.

Bird Name	Colour M	C	Size	Migratory?	Date Seen	Place Seen
Mallard	Green/White/Brown		55	☐	28/09/98	Wexford

Section Summary: So Now You Know

A *sort* is an operation that you carry out on a table to change the order in which the records are displayed. Access allows you to perform *single criterion* and *multiple criteria* sort operations.

If you perform a particular sort regularly, you can save the sort details as a *query*. You can use queries to repeatedly view database records in a particular way defined by you.

Filtering is the process of narrowing down the amount of information displayed by Access, either by showing fewer fields in each record, or by showing only those records that match certain criteria. To view all your records again, remove the filter.

You can filter a table by clicking on a particular field, or by dragging the mouse over the word (or part of word) that you want to match, and then clicking on the Filter by Selection button on the toolbar.

Note that if you are filtering based on a Yes/No field, you need to click on the field *twice* before you click on the Filter by Selection button. A single click on a Yes/No field will change the information in that field!

You can further filter the result of a filter operation to focus in greater detail on records of particular interest.

Section 5.4: Working With Forms

In This Section

Until now, you have been looking at your database records in a *datasheet* – they have been shown in rows, with a column for each field, perhaps extending beyond the edges of your screen, so that you have to scroll left and right and up and down to see the records and fields of interest. This may make reading the information difficult, and sometimes it's annoying. What you really want to do is see all the information relating to a single record on the screen at the same time, laid out in an eye-pleasing manner.

Or perhaps you want to restrict the amount of information displayed: you just want to see the name of the bird, along with the date and place you spotted it, for example.

You need to learn how to use forms.

New Activities

At the end of this Section, you should be able to:

- Create a form to display records, in whole or in part, one at a time

- Use a form to create new records

- Use a form to search for and modify a record

- Modify a form that you have previously created

New Words

You can relax: there are no new words in this Section.

What Are Forms For?

Remember in Section 5.1, we said that Access enables you to view and manipulate information in two ways: *Datasheet View* shows the information for many records, arranged in columns and rows; *Form View* presents information for one record at a time. You can arrange the layout of a form so that the information is easier to read, or so that it looks like a paper form. You can create a form that presents only some of the fields in each record.

Datasheets and forms are both ways of looking *at the same things* – the information in the database table.

Everything you can do in a datasheet, you can also do in a form: you can input new records and change existing records; you can sort the records into a different order; and you can filter the records so that only ones that match your criteria are displayed.

The added advantage is that forms can be much easier to read, and you can design different forms for different purposes.

Creating a Form

Forms are based on tables: a form is essentially a way of looking at a specific table. Therefore, you can create a form only after you have created a table. We have – Birds.

1) Open the Birds database, and click on the Forms tab.

Click **New**.

2) Once again, Access offers a number of semi-automated options. Explore, for example, the **AutoForm: Columnar** option, specifying the **Birds** table, and have a look at (but don't save) the result. Close it and you are returned to this screen.

```
Design View
Form Wizard
AutoForm: Columnar
AutoForm: Tabular
AutoForm: Datasheet
Chart Wizard
PivotTable Wizard
```

Choose the Form Wizard. Specify the table on which the form is based – **Birds**. Click **OK**.

3) You've seen something like this before, when you were using the Wizard to design the table. The screen shows two list boxes. The one on the left shows all the fields in the table; the one on the right shows the fields that you have chosen to include in the form. Initially, the one on the right is empty. To move a field from the left-hand box to the right-hand box, select it and click the > button. If you change your mind, select the field in the right-hand box and click the < button. You can move all the fields from one box to the other by clicking >> or << .

Move fields from the left-hand box to the right-hand box as shown below:

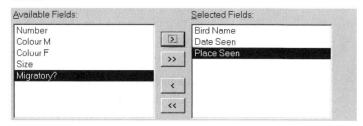

Click **Next**.

4) The Access Wizard then presents you with three possible layouts for the form. You can get an idea what each is like by selecting them in turn. The best for your purposes is **Columnar**. Select this one, and click **Next**.

5) The Wizard then offers you a choice of style for the Form. Again, you can preview them by selecting them in turn. For Birds, there can be no contest: the most appropriate has got to be **Clouds**. Select this one, and click **Next**.

6) Access suggests a name for the Form: change this to 'Birds Spotted' to make it easier to identify later. You can then either use the form immediately, or go back and modify it.

Choose the **Open** option, and click **Finish**.

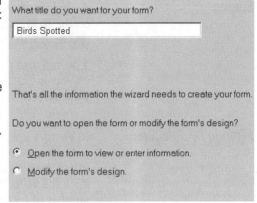

What title do you want for your form?

Birds Spotted

That's all the information the wizard needs to create your form.

Do you want to open the form or modify the form's design?

○ Open the form to view or enter information.

○ Modify the form's design.

Using a Form to View Existing Records

When you finish the exercise above, you are immediately presented with a Forms View of the database table.

At other times, to get to the same point, you start from the Database screen, click on the Forms tab, select the form (Birds Spotted), and click **Open**.

Bird Name   Gannet
Date Seen   12/06/98
Place Seen   Ireland's Eye

The form shows the selected fields from the first record in the table.

You can step through the different records one at a time by using the navigation buttons at the foot of the screen.

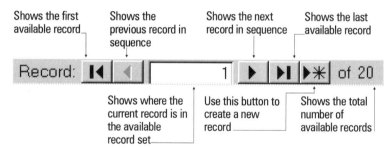

Shows the first available record

Shows the previous record in sequence

Shows the next record in sequence

Shows the last available record

Shows where the current record is in the available record set

Use this button to create a new record

Shows the total number of available records

Sorting

As in Datasheet View, you can sort the records by selection: click on the field that you want to use as the basis for the sort, and click ⬆ or ⬇ in the toolbar.

You can also perform a multiple criteria sort, in exactly the same way as in Datasheet View: choose **Records | Filter | Advanced Filter/Sort**.

Filtering by Selection

In Form View, you can filter records by selection, exactly as you did in Datasheet View: find a record that meets your criterion, select the relevant field (or the part of it that is of interest), and click the Filter by Selection button. You will see that the number of records shown beside the navigation buttons reflects the smaller number of records that satisfy your criterion.

Again as in Datasheet View, you can filter these records again to further narrow down the search for the records you are interested in.

Filtering by Form

Another option is to *Filter by Form*. Let's say, for example, that you only want birds that you have actually spotted to be shown. Click the Filter by Form button in the button bar, or choose **Records | Filter | Filter by Form**. A blank form is presented, into which you can enter your filter criteria. In this case, the date is the criterion of interest. Click on the Date Seen field. Note that the drop-down list shows all the dates on which you recorded sightings. If you wanted to find all the birds you spotted on a given date, you'd simply pick the date from the list. However, you want to find the birds you spotted on *any* date, that is, any record for which the date is not blank (or greater than zero). So enter the following in the date field: >0

Then click the Apply Filter button  : the first record with the date filled in is shown, and the record count shows the number of such records in the table. Click the Remove Filter button  (as it is now), and the full table is viewable.

Wildcards

You don't have to be precise when you are entering your filter criteria: you can use so-called *wildcards* to tell Access 'Give me everyone whose name includes Donnel', and it will get the Donnellys, McDonnells, MacDonnells, O'Donnells, and so on. The most important wildcards are * and ?. When you are specifying the criteria for a query or a filter, '*' means 'anything or nothing', and '?' means any single character.

Say, for example, you want to find all the birds that have 'sparrow' in their names: House Sparrow, Tree Sparrow, Sparrowhawk. In the Bird Name field in the form, enter the following:

sparrow

When you apply the filter, you will be presented only with the records that include 'sparrow'.

Or if you wanted to find birds that were coloured black or brown, you could construct a filter with the colour specified as:

b????

When you apply this filter, you will be presented only with records that have the colour specified as five characters beginning with 'b' – you would not, for example, get blue birds.

Using a Form to Create New Records

The easiest way to enter information into your database is to use a form. However, if you are adding new records to the database, the form you created in the previous exercise is not sufficiently detailed. You need a new form – one that enables you to fill in all the details for each bird. Let's do it the quick way.

From the Database screen, click the **Forms** tab. Choose **New**. Choose **AutoForm: Columnar**, and specify the **Birds** table.

Save as Birds: All Fields Form. And that's it. A new form is now ready for use.

In the navigation bar at the bottom of the form is the Create New Record button  . Click on this and Access presents a new, blank form. Fill this in. You can complete the fields in any order by clicking in the field and entering the information. However, the easiest way to complete the form is to fill in the first field (the cursor is automatically positioned there when you open the form), and then proceed in order through the fields *either* by pressing TAB *or* by pressing ENTER. When you have filled in the last field in the form, TAB or ENTER will open up a new, blank form.

Using a Form to Modify Existing Records

Any changes you make to the information in a form is immediately reflected in the table. Remember that the Datasheet and the Form are just two ways of looking at the same information. To use the form to modify the information in your table, locate the record you are interested in (by paging through the records, one at a time, or by sorting or filtering), click on the field you want to change, and delete, overwrite, or add information as you wish.

Modifying a Form

For the moment, and for most purposes, the Form Wizard does a fine job. However, Access enables you to design forms from scratch, and to redesign ones that have already been designed. To see some of the possibilities (and there is no need to go into this too deeply), try this:

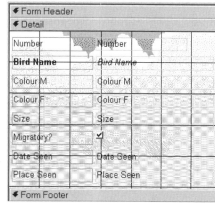

1) Open in Design View the form you created in the previous exercise. (At the Database screen, click the **Forms** tab, then select the form you previously created, and click **Design**.)

2) In Design View, you see the different elements in your form set against a grid. Notice how each field has a *title* and a *text box*.

You can change the formatting of either: click on the **Bird Name** title; click the **Bold** button in the button bar. Click on the **Bird Name** text box; click the **Italics** button in the button bar. Note that the button bar offers a variety of formatting options:

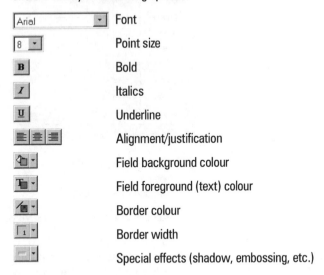

Arial	Font
8	Point size
B	Bold
I	Italics
U	Underline
≡ ≡ ≡	Alignment/justification
	Field background colour
	Field foreground (text) colour
	Border colour
	Border width
	Special effects (shadow, embossing, etc.)

Experiment with these to see the possibilities. Remember, however, that the best forms are simple, clearly laid out, and use colour and other graphic devices sparingly.

3) In Design View, you can change the shape and size of a field on the form. When you select a field, a number of 'sizing handles' appear around it: click on any of these, and use the mouse to drag the border to the new position.

You can also change the position of a field: click on the border anywhere *except* on one of the handles. The cursor changes to an 'open hand' shape. You can then drag the field to its new location; note that the label and the text box move together, and maintain their position relative to one another.

To move the label or text box independently, click on the large 'move handle' at the top left of the field. The cursor changes to a 'pointing hand'. You can then drag the field to its new location.

Change the size and position of the fields and labels as shown on the next page. Note that we have deleted the Bird Name label.

4) To add a new field to a form, choose **View | Field List**. Find the field you want to add in the list displayed, and use the mouse to drag it from the list to the approximate location you want it to appear in the form. Then adjust the size and location as described in Step 3.

Before   **After**

5)   Click the Close button
     -or-
     Choose **File | Close**.

     Access will prompt you to save your work.

Although you don't need it for the ECDL, it is worthwhile noting that if your database has a number of tables, you can create a form that includes fields from more than one table.

Section Summary: So Now You Know

Forms enable you to view your database records one at a time, with the fields laid out in an attractive way. Forms can also be used to display selected parts of each record, so that you can present different views of the database for particular users, or for particular purposes. You can have many forms associated with a given table (and a form can contain fields from a number of tables).

You can *sort* and *filter* forms in exactly the same way that you sort and filter records in a datasheet.

And you can use forms to change existing records, or to add new records. The important thing to remember is that it is the *same* information: any change you make to data in a form is reflected immediately in the datasheet, and any change you make in a datasheet is reflected in any associated forms.

Section 5.5: Reports

In This Section

In the earlier parts of this module, you have been learning how to put information *in* to your database, and how to manipulate it and view it on screen. In this Section, you will learn how to get information *out*, and how to present it in a useful and accessible way.

New Activities

At the end of this Section, you should be able to:

- Present information you have extracted from the database on screen

- Print out a report of information from the database

New Words

At the end of this Section, you should be able to explain the following term:

- Report

Your First Report

Generally speaking, a report is a way of presenting information in printed form. However, the word is increasingly used to describe information in a form *suitable* for printing – even if it is displayed on screen.

> **Report**
>
> *A document (printed or on screen) that presents information in a structured way.*

You have already seen how Access allows you to structure and organise your data, by filtering and sorting records, by using forms to choose the fields you want to display, and so on. You can, of course, print out any of these screens, and this may be quite adequate for your purposes: simply click the Print button on the button bar 🖨 , or choose **File | Print**.

However, Access gives you a great deal of control over how your information is presented: you can lay it out so that important information is highlighted, data can be grouped into categories, and you can give totals and count information for each category, subcategory, and for the entire report. Some of this is beyond the scope of this book, but you will find that Access provides automated solutions that will satisfy most of your requirements, most of the time.

For example, try the AutoReports. From the Database screen, click the **Reports** tab. **Choose AutoReports: Columnar**, and specify the **Birds** table. Voilà! Print that out and hang it on the wall.

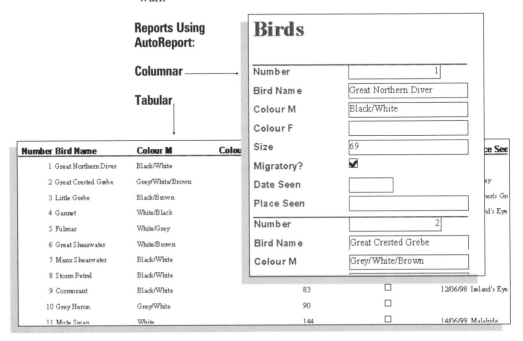

Reports Using AutoReport:

Columnar

Tabular

Birds

Number	1
Bird Name	Great Northern Diver
Colour M	Black/White
Colour F	
Size	69
Migratory?	☑
Date Seen	
Place Seen	
Number	2
Bird Name	Great Crested Grebe
Colour M	Grey/White/Brown

Number	Bird Name	Colour M	Colou
1	Great Northern Diver	Black/White	
2	Great Crested Grebe	Grey/White/Brown	
3	Little Grebe	Black/Brown	
4	Gannet	White/Black	
5	Fulmar	White/Grey	
6	Great Shearwater	White/Brown	
7	Manx Shearwater	Black/White	
8	Storm Petrel	Black/White	
9	Cormorant	Black/White	83
10	Grey Heron	Grey/White	90
11	Mute Swan	White	144

Now let's use the Wizard.

1) From the Database screen, click the **Reports** tab. Click **New**. Choose the Report Wizard. Specify that you want to produce a report based on the Birds table. Click **OK**.

Design View
Report Wizard
AutoReport: Columnar
AutoReport: Tabular
Chart Wizard
Label Wizard

2) You are presented with a familiar-looking screen. Choose the fields you want to include in the report from the list on the left and move them into the list on the right. For this exercise, include the fields shown below, and click **Next**.

3) The next step relates to *grouping*. You can, for example, produce a report for each *bird*, showing when and where you saw it: this report would group together all the sightings of a given bird. For the exercise, we'll produce a report by *date*: this will group together all sightings made on the same date. Select **Date Seen**. Have a look at the options: you can group the sightings by year, quarter, month, week, day, etc. Month seems most useful. Click **Next**.

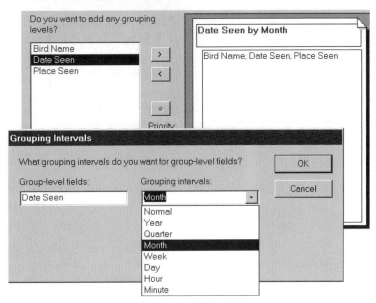

4) You are already familiar with the idea of sorting: in this step you specify the *sort order* of the report. Select **Date Seen** as the first sort criterion, and click the **Sort** button. Note that it switches between Ascending and Descending. Make it **Descending**. Select **Bird Name** as the second sort criterion, and make it **Ascending**. This means that the report will show the most recent sightings first, and on any given day, it will show the birds sighted in alphabetical order. Click **Next**.

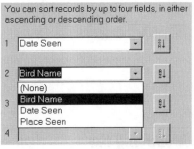

5) You are then offered a number of *layout options*. As in previous Wizard exercise, you can get a good idea of what the final result will look like by selecting each in turn. The best for our purposes is **Outline 2**, and, because we do not have very many fields in our report, **Portrait**. Choose these, and click **Next**.

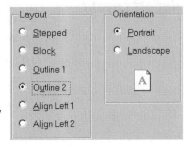

6) You are then offered a range of *typographic styles* for the report. Again, see what they look like by selecting them in turn. For the exercise, choose **Bold**, and click **Next**.

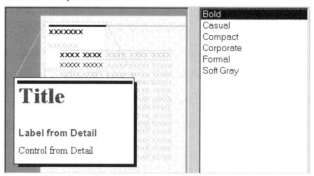

7) Give the report a title: Spotting Record ...

Choose the **Preview** option ...

and click **Finish**.

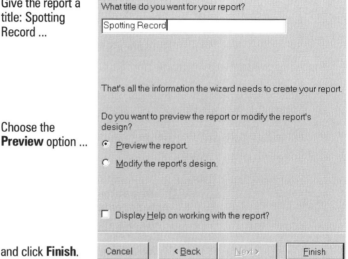

You then see the report on screen. If it is exactly what you want, click the Print button on the button bar 🖨 , or choose **File | Print**.

Modifying the Report Layout

It's unlikely that the Wizard grants your every wish. (This is real life, after all, and this is a computer.) You probably have to fine-tune the report. You can do all sorts of things with Access: we'll confine ourselves to a few.

The report you created in the exercise above needs to be tidied up a little.

1) Open in Design View the report you created in the previous exercise. (At the Database screen, click the **Reports** tab, then select the report you previously created, and click **Design**.)

2) As in the Forms exercise, Design View shows you the different elements in your report set against a grid. Each field has a *title* and a *text box*. You can change the content or formatting of these in the same way as you did in Forms. Make the text box for Month Name bold. Double-click in the label boxes listed below, and change them as follows:

Before	After
Before	**After**
Date Seen by Month	Month
Date Seen	Date

Then adjust the size of each label box: click on the box. The sizing and move handles are shown around it. (If you have already selected the box for editing, the handles do not appear: first click away from the box, anywhere else on the screen, and then click once on the box.) Use the handles to change the shape and size of the box, or the hand pointer to change the position of the box, just like you did when you were designing forms.

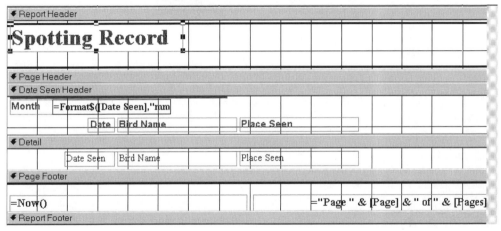

3) Click the Close button
-or-
Choose **File | Close**.

Access will prompt you to save your work.

4) Use the **Preview** button to open the report again, and print it out to see the effect of your changes.

Section Summary: So Now You Know

A database *report* is a document (printed or on screen) that presents information in a structured way. Access provides two automated solutions, *AutoReports* and the *Report Wizard*, that will satisfy most reporting requirements.

To use the Report Wizard, choose the relevant table, select the fields you want to include, and specify the *grouping*, the *sort order*, the *layout options* and the *typographic styles*.

You can modify a report by changing the content of each field's title and text box, and by adjusting the size of each field's label.

Hopefully, this Module gave you a glimpse of the power of Access, and enough confidence to explore that power further by yourself. If you want to use more advanced features, the Help features included with Access provide you with plenty of guidance.

6

Tomorrow you have two appointments. A visit to the dentist and a presentation in front of an audience. Which one fills you with greater terror?

Whether it's to a group of potential customers, a national conference of fellow workers or a local community group, delivering an address can be an intimidating prospect.

Faced with these situations, you'll want to hear and learn about any tools that can help you feel less pressurised and speak more persuasively. This is where presentation software comes in.

In this Module you will discover how to create support materials that will reinforce your message, both textually and graphically. You will also find out how to design your materials – both on-screen slides and paper hand-outs – so as to maximise their audience impact.

Software won't turn a bad presentation into a good one. But it can help a good presentation succeed in its aims: more money, more status, or a happy combination of the two.

Think of this Module as your chance to speak rather than be spoken to. Good luck with it.

Section 6.1: Creating Your First Slides

In This Section

Slides are the building blocks of a visual presentation. In this Section, you will learn how to use a computer to create simple slides, enter text in them, and control the appearance and positioning of text on a slide.

New Activities

At the end of this Section you should be able to:

- Start and quit PowerPoint

- Create a new presentation

- Enter text and edit text on a slide

- Format and align text, change font size and type, and control inter-line and inter-paragraph spacing

- Create text boxes to enter text

- Add and remove slides in a presentation

- Move, change the size and shape, and rotate and flip objects

- Use tabs to position columns of text and numbers

- Save, name, open, close and print PowerPoint presentations

New Words

At the end of this Section you should be able to explain the following terms:

- Slide

- Title Slide

- Placeholder

- AutoLayout

- Slide Sorter view

- Speaker Notes

Starting PowerPoint

PowerPoint

Double-click on the PowerPoint icon or choose **Start | Programs | PowerPoint**.

In this Section, you will learn how to create a new presentation in PowerPoint, and how to save it. Your presentation will consist of a number of slides.

Slides
A slide is the equivalent of a page in a printed document; it can contain text and/or graphics.

Creating a Presentation

PowerPoint does not create a new, blank presentation when you start the program. Instead it presents a screen that offers a number of options, one of which is to create a new presentation from scratch.

Title Slide

The first slide in a PowerPoint presentation is called the title slide. It introduces your presentation to the audience. Like the first page of a book, it usually has a different layout from the rest of the presentation.

Title Slide
The first slide in a presentation. Typically, it has a different layout from the remaining slides.

Exercise 6.1: Creating a Title Slide for Your Presentation

1) Select Blank presentation, and click **OK**.

2) PowerPoint displays a dialog box that offers a choice of ready-made layouts (called AutoLayouts) for your slides. As you click on a layout, PowerPoint shows the name of that layout in an area at the right of the dialog box.

3) Select the first layout, which PowerPoint calls Title Slide, and click **OK**. You are now shown a screen that contains two boxes surrounded by dotted lines. PowerPoint calls these boxes *placeholders*.

4) Click on the top placeholder. The border of the placeholder changes and blinking text cursor appears inside it. You can now type text in the placeholder.

Click to add title ⟶

5) Enter the following text in the first placeholder: Learning PowerPoint

6) Click on the second placeholder and enter the following text: Getting to grips with the basics

> ### Placeholder
> *A frame or box within a slide for holding text or graphics.*

Your screen should now look like that on the right.

Congratulations. You have created the first slide of your first presentation in PowerPoint.

Remember: Click on a placeholder to select it so that you can type or edit text. Click outside the placeholder to deselect it.

> ### AutoLayout
> *One of 24 ready-made slide layouts that include two or more placeholders for text and other items such as images and charts.*

Adding Slides to Your Presentation

After the title slide, you will want to create further slides to hold the main body of your presentation. Exercise 6.2 shows you how.

Exercise 6.2: Adding Slides to a Presentation

1) Choose **Insert | New Slide** by clicking the New Slide button on the Standard Toolbar.

2) Select the slide layout you want to use. This time, select the Bulleted List.

3) Click on the first placeholder and type: Sample Bulleted List

4) Click on the second placeholder and type: Open

5) Press ENTER. PowerPoint creates a second bullet point on a new line. Type: add

6) Press ENTER and type: amend

7) Press ENTER and type: close

8) Choose **Insert | New Slide**.

9) Select the layout called 2 Column Text and type the following text in the top placeholder: Days of the week

10) In the columns' placeholders, type the week days in the first column, and
type the days of the weekend in the second column.

Well done! A second Exercise completed.

Formatting and Aligning Text

As with other Microsoft programs, formatting or aligning text in PowerPoint is a two step process: first select, then format or align.

- Use the **Format | Font** command to change the font size, type, colour or effects.

- Use the **Format | Alignment** command to change the alignment of the text.

Alternatively, click on the formatting (bold, italic, underline and shadow) or alignment (left, centre, right) buttons on the Formatting Toolbar.

Line and Paragraph Spacing

On some slides you may have very few lines of text. On others, you may have quite a lot.

By controlling the inter-line and inter-paragraph spacing with the **Format | Line Spacing** command, you can 'space out' or 'squeeze' lines of text so that they fit the area of a single slide.

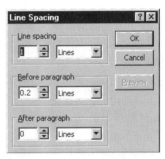

Exercise 6.3: Formatting and Aligning Text

1) Using the PAGE UP key, display the title slide on your presentation. Click anywhere on the second placeholder to select it. Then drag the mouse across the text to select the text.

2) Choose **Format | Font** and change the font to Arial, 24 point, bold. With the text still selected, click on the right-align button on the Formatting Toolbar.

3) Place the cursor before the word 'with', and press SHIFT+ENTER to insert a line break. The placeholder should look as below.

The Slide Sorter View

When you have more than one slide in your presentation, you will want to display different slides at different times on your screen. You have two main options:

- Press the PAGE DOWN key to move forward through your presentation, one slide at a time. And press the PAGE UP key to move backward.

- Use the **View | Slide Sorter** command to view all your slides at once, and then double-click on the one that you want to display.

       1   2   3

In Slide Sorter view you can also check that your formatting is consistent and that text placeholders are aligned.

By default, PowerPoint displays only one slide at a time on your screen. This view is called 'Slide view'.

Slide Sorter View
A view where you can see all the slides in your presentation at once.

Reordering Slides

When you look at your slides in Slide Sorter view, you may decide to change the order in which they appear. You can do this in two ways: by dragging them with the mouse (better for small presentations), or using the cut-and-paste commands on the **Edit** menu (better for large presentations).

Reordering with the Slide Sorter

In Slide Sorter view, select the slide, drag it with the mouse so that a vertical line appears to the *right* of where you want to position the slide, and release the mouse button.

Reordering with Cut and Paste

You can cut, copy and paste slides in PowerPoint as you would text in a word processor.

In Slide Sorter view, select the slide, choose **Edit | Cut** (or press CTRL+x). Click on another slide to select it, and choose **Edit | Paste** (or press CTRL+v). The pasted slide appears *after* (to the right or beneath) the slide that you selected before choosing **Edit | Paste**.

Practise reordering the three slides in your presentation by first dragging them to new positions, and then cutting and pasting them back to their original locations.

Formatting Bullets

Bullets are a popular way of presenting information, but they don't have to be boring! You can change the bullet size and colour, and select a different bullet character, with the **Format | Bullet** command. You can also unbullet text that is currently formatted as bullets.

Exercise 6.4: Formatting Bullets

1) Display the slide with the title: Days of the week

2) Insert a new slide and select the slide layout called Bulleted List.

3) Click on the first placeholder and type: Rainbow Bullets

4) In the second placeholder type the following:

Red
Orange
Yellow
Green
Blue
Indigo
Violet

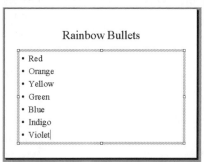

5) Select all the bulleted text and choose **Format | Bullet**.

In the Bullets from: drop-down box, select the font called Wingdings.

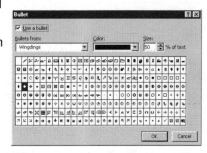

Next, click on the diamond bullet character.

In the Size % of text: box, select 50%. Click **OK**.

6) Select each of the rainbow colours individually, choose **Format | Bullet**, and from the Colour: list, select a colour appropriate for the text.

Speaker Notes Pages

For each slide you insert in your presentation, PowerPoint creates what it calls a speaker notes page. You can ignore or use these pages as you wish. PowerPoint does not display them on screen as part of your presentation.

You can type text to your speaker notes pages at any stage when creating or editing your presentation, and then print out the pages to help you remember key points or additional background information when you are delivering your presentation.

Speaker Notes
A page created by PowerPoint to accompany each slide. You can use
it to record key points or extra details about your presentation.

Notes View

Use the **View | Notes Page** command to type and edit speaker notes for the currently selected slide. Each notes page contains:

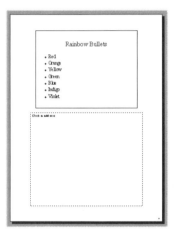

- A miniature of the slide

- An area for typing text

To type or edit, click on the text placeholder. By default, PowerPoint displays a notes page at 40% of its full size. You may wish to increase this to nearer 100% when typing or editing.

Handout Pages

You can create and print handouts of slides to give to your audience. Choose **View | Master | Handout Master** to select your preferred format: two, three or six slides per printed handout page.

Three slides per page option is a popular choice: the slides are printed large enough to be easily read, and there is space on onc sidc of the page for your

audience to write their own notes or comments. You can override any choice you make here when printing the handouts.

Entering Text Using the Drawing Toolbar

You have learned how to enter text by selecting a placeholder and then typing text in it. You can also enter text by drawing a text box – in effect, a text-only placeholder – and then typing text in that.

If not already displayed, choose **View | Toolbars | Drawing** to display the Drawing Toolbar at the bottom of the PowerPoint window.

Text Box button

Click the Text Box button. Next, click on the slide and drag the mouse to create the text box. Type your text in the new text box. To deselect the text box, click outside it.

Working With Objects

Placeholders and text boxes are examples of what PowerPoint calls objects. In Section 6.2 you will meet some other examples, such as rectangles, ovals and AutoShapes. There are a number of common operations that you can perform on objects, regardless of their type.

Moving Objects

To move an object within the same slide, first select it by clicking anywhere inside it. Next, position the cursor over any edge of the placeholder until the cross appears at the tip of the cursor arrow. Then drag the object to its new location.

To move an object between slides, use the **Cut** and **Paste** commands on the **Edit** menu.

Changing the Shape and Size of an Object

You can change the shape and size of an object by selecting it and clicking on any of its eight handles. Hold down the mouse button and drag the edge of the object to change its shape. As you drag the object, PowerPoint changes its border to a dashed line.

Rotating and Flipping Objects

You can rotate a selected object at any angle to the left or right up to 90 degrees. You can only rotate objects created in PowerPoint, and not graphics or other files imported from other applications.

Free Rotate button

To rotate a selected object, click the Free Rotate button on the Drawing Toolbar. The border of the selected object disappears, and is replaced by four green dots, one at each corner.

Drag a corner of the object in the direction you want to rotate it. Click outside the object to deselect it. You can limit the object's rotation to 15-degree steps by holding down the SHIFT key as you drag with the mouse.

Draw button

To flip (turn over by 180 degrees) a selected object, click the Draw button on the Drawing Toolbar, choose **Rotate or Flip**, and then **Flip Horizontal** or **Flip Vertical**.

Exercise 6.5: Creating and Rotating a Text Box

1) Display the slide with the title: Rainbow Bullets

2) Choose **Insert | New Slide** or click the New Slide button on the Standard Toolbar.

3) Select the slide layout called Title Slide.

4) Select, and then using the DEL key, delete the first and second placeholders.

5) Click the Text Box icon on the Drawing Toolbar and draw a text box in the centre of the slide.

6) Type the following words in the text box: This is a text box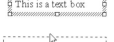

7) Click on any edge of the of the text box and move it to a new location on the slide.

As you drag it with the mouse, its border changes to a dashed line and its contents are not displayed.

8) Click the Free Rotate button on the Drawing Toolbar, and then on the text box. Its border disappears, and is replaced by four green dots, one at each corner.

Click on the bottom-right green dot and drag downwards to rotate the text box.

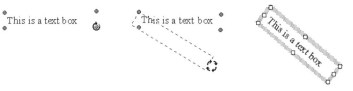

That completes the Exercise.

Deleting a Slide

Want to remove a slide from your presentation? Display the slide and choose **Edit | Delete Slide**.

Practise this command by deleting the slide containing the text box that you created in Exercise 6.5.

Using Tabs Stops on a Slide

You can insert tabs to create side-by-side columns of text and numbers on a slide. The following Exercise shows you how.

Exercise 6.6: Using Tabs with PowerPoint

1) Open your presentation and display the last slide, the one with the rainbow bullets.

2) Insert a new slide and select the layout called Title Slide. This allows you to enter non-bulleted text. Click on the title placeholder and type: Sales Figures

3) Click on the second placeholder and type the following four months, pressing the TAB key (but not the SPACEBAR) after each of the first three: Sep Oct Nov Dec

4) Press ENTER to create a new line.

5) Type the following numbers, pressing the TAB key (but not the SPACEBAR) after each of the first three: 34 56 68 84

Sales Figures

| Sep | Oct | Nov | Dec |

Sales Figures

| Sep | Oct | Nov | Dec |
| 34 | 56 | 68 | 84 |

The Tab Ruler

You can display and amend PowerPoint's default tab stops by choosing **View | Ruler**. The tab ruler appears along the top of the slide window. You can see the default tab stops at evenly-spaced positions along the base of the ruler.

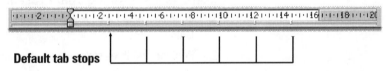

Default tab stops

You can change the position of a tab stop by dragging it left or rightwards to a new location on the ruler. The space between all default tab stops changes proportionately. As you drag a tab stop, PowerPoint displays a vertical, dashed line stretching down from the tab ruler to the slide itself.

∟	**Left**
⊥	**Centre**
⌐	**Right**
⊥	**Decimal point**

At the top left of the slide window you can see the tab button. As you click on this, it cycles through four values: left-aligned (default), centre-aligned, right-aligned, and decimal point-aligned.

To add a new tab stop, click the tab button to display the type of tab you want, and then click the ruler where you want to place the tab.

To remove a tab stop, drag it off the tab ruler.

PowerPoint's Undo Feature

Enter the wrong text? Press the wrong key? PowerPoint allows you undo your most recent text entry or action if it has produced unwanted results.

Choose **Edit | Undo** or Click the Undo 🔄 button on the Standard Toolbar.

Printing Your Presentation

PowerPoint's **File | Print** command gives you a wide range of options.

Print What Options

In the Print what: drop-down box you can choose to print slides, speaker notes or handouts. If you choose handouts, you can change the number of slides per handout previously selected with the **View | Master | Handout Master** command.

(Another option is Outline view. You will learn about Outline view in Section 6.2.)

Print Range Options

In the Print range area of the dialog box you can choose to print all slides, the current slide or a selected range of slides.

To print a continuous range of slides, type the beginning number, a hyphen and the ending number. To print non-continuous slides, type the individual slide numbers separated by commas.

Exercise 6.7: Printing Your Presentation

1) Print a handout for your entire presentation with three slides on each page.

2) Print the first three slides of your presentation.

3) Print the first and fourth slide of your presentation.

Saving Your Presentation for the First Time

Although your presentation contains only four slides, you should save it now. As in all programs, you must name your presentation when you save it for the first time. Exercise 6.8 shows you how.

Exercise 6.8: Saving and Naming Your Presentation

1) Choose **File | Save** or click the Save 💾 button on the Standard Toolbar.

The first time that you save a presentation, PowerPoint asks you to give the file a name. Enter a name that you will find easy to remember and recognise.

If your initials are KB, for example, call it KBpres1 and click the **Save** button.

Working With PowerPoint Presentations

The file names of PowerPoint presentations end in .ppt. This helps you to distinguish them from Word documents (.doc), Excel workbooks (.xls) and other file types.

Creating a New Presentation

To create a new presentation:

Choose **File | New** or click the New ⬜ button on the Standard Toolbar.

Opening an Existing Presentation

To open an existing presentation file:

Choose **File | Open** or click the Open 📂 button on the Standard Toolbar. Select the file you want from the dialog box.

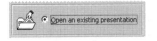

To open an existing presentation immediately after you start PowerPoint, select the Open an existing presentation option on the first dialog box displayed.

Closing a Presentation

Choose **File | Close** or click the Close button on the presentation window.

If you have made changes to your presentation since you last saved it, PowerPoint prompts you to save the changes before it closes the file.

Quitting PowerPoint

To leave PowerPoint, choose **File | Exit** or click the Close button on the PowerPoint window.

If you have left open any files containing unsaved work, PowerPoint prompts you to save them. You are then returned to the Windows desktop.

Section Summary: So Now You Know

You use PowerPoint to create the *slides* to form a presentation. PowerPoint file names end in *.ppt.*

When you create a new presentation, PowerPoint creates a single, new slide. You *add* further slides by inserting them individually. You can *delete* a slide at any stage.

When you create a new slide, you can choose from 24 ready-made slide layouts called *AutoLayouts*. One layout, called the title layout, is designed to be the first slide in a presentation, the *title slide*.

Each layout contains one or more boxes called *placeholders*, within which you enter and edit text. You can *format* and *align* text, and change the inter-line and inter-paragraph *vertical spacing*.

You can use PowerPoint's preset *tab stops* to create side-by-side columns of text and numbers. Using the tab ruler, you can add and remove left-aligned, centre-aligned, right-aligned, and decimal point-aligned tab stops, as required.

You can also enter text on a slide by drawing a *text box* – in effect, a text-only placeholder – and then typing text in that. The Text Box tool is one of the buttons available on the Drawing Toolbar.

Placeholders and text boxes are examples of what PowerPoint calls *objects*. You can move, change the size and shape, and rotate and flip objects.

Speaker notes are pages that PowerPoint creates to accompany each slide. Each notes page contains a miniature of the slide and an area for typing text. You can create and print *handouts* of slides to give to your audience.

Section 6.2: Transforming Your Slides into a Presentation

In This Section

In the previous Section you learnt how to enter, edit, format and align text on slides. Here you will discover how to inject visual flair into your presentation by adding colours, images, charts and multimedia clips, plus shapes such as lines, rectangles and ovals.

You will also learn how to transform your individual slides into a consistent presentation, and deliver your presentation so as to maximise its audience impact.

New Activities

At the end of this Section you should be able to:

- Apply a consistent colour scheme to your presentation
- Use the Slide Master to apply default text and graphics to all slides
- Insert clip art, other images, sound and video clips, and change image colours to suit your chosen colour scheme
- Create and insert statistical and organisation charts
- Insert geometric shapes using the AutoShapes feature or the Drawing Toolbar
- Group and ungroup objects
- Usc Outline view to inspect your presentation content
- Run your presentation, manually and automatically
- Create and insert transitions between slides
- Use builds to control the display of bulleted text

New Words

At the end of this Section you should be able to explain the following terms:

- Colour scheme
- Slide Master
- Clip art
- Organisation chart

- AutoShape
- Outline view
- Transition
- Build slide

Creating a Sample Presentation

You begin this Section by creating a new presentation.

Exercise 6.9: A New Presentation

1) Create a new presentation and insert two slides as shown below.

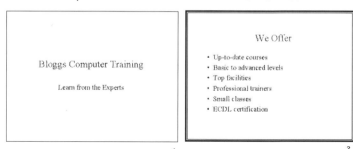

2) Save and name your presentation. If your initials are KB, for example, save it as KBtrain.ppt.

Consistent Colour Schemes

You can make your presentation look attractive – and consistent – by using one of PowerPoint's built-in colour schemes. Each scheme consists of a set of eight co-ordinated colours.

When you select a particular scheme, PowerPoint applies the different colours of the scheme to different slide elements, such as title text (the text in the title placeholder), non-title text, background, graphic fills, and so on. In Exercise 6.10, you will apply a colour scheme to your presentation.

Exercise 6.10: Applying a Colour Scheme

1) Choose **Format | Slide Colour Scheme**. (It does not matter which view of your presentation you have open when you choose this command.)

2) On the Standard tab, select one of the schemes, and click **Apply to All** (slides in the presentation).

   A common choice is the second colour scheme, the one with the blue background.

You can select a different colour scheme at a later stage, if you wish.

> **Colour Scheme**
>
> *A set of eight, preset co-ordinated colours you can apply to give your presentation an appearance that is both attractive and consistent.*

The Slide Master

Whether you know it or not, every slide you insert in a PowerPoint presentation is based on a template slide called the Slide Master.

It is from the Slide Master that all slides take their default text formatting and positioning. To view the Slide Master, choose **View | Master | Slide Master**. It consists of two placeholders:

- **Title Placeholder:** Determines the format and positioning of text in every title placeholder in your presentation.

- **Object Placeholder:** Determines the format and positioning of text in every non-title placeholder.

Your audience never sees the Slide Master; they see only its effects on the slides that you insert in your presentation.

You can override the defaults supplied by the Slide Master on any individual slide. You can also use the Slide Master to insert a graphic – such as a company logo – on every slide of your presentation.

Slide Master

A template slide that provides the default text format and text positioning for the slides in a presentation.

Exercise 6.11: Changing the Slide Master

In this Exercise, you change the text format of your presentation by changing the Slide Master.

1) Choose **View | Master | Slide Master** and select all the non-title text in the lower placeholder.

2) Change the font of the selected text from Times New Roman to Arial, and click Close.

PowerPoint changes the font of the text in the non-title placeholders of all the slides in your presentation.

Inserting Images

You can illustrate your slides by inserting images such as drawings created in other software applications or even scanned photographs.

PowerPoint contains hundreds of clip art images that you can use and reuse in different presentations. Sixteen clip art categories are available, ranging from Academic to Food and Travel.

Clip Art
Standard or 'stock' images that can be used and reused in different presentations.

Exercise 6.12: Inserting a Clip Art Image

1) Create a new, third slide and select the layout called Text & Clip Art.

2) In the title placeholder, type: Instructors

3) In the text placeholder, type the following bullet points:

Technically expert
Trained teachers
Friendly and helpful

3) Double-click on the clip art icon, select the category called Academic, and select the second clip art image.

4) PowerPoint inserts your selected image, and displays the Picture Toolbar. Click on the close box at the top right of the Picture Toolbar to remove it. Your slide should now look as shown on the right.

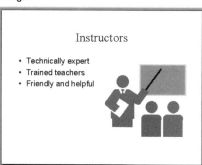

You are not restricted to inserting images on slides whose layout includes a graphic icon. You can insert a clip art image on any slide by choosing the **Insert | Picture | Clip Art** command.

To insert an image of your own – your company logo, for example – choose **Insert | Picture | From File**, and selected the required image file. PowerPoint accepts images in most common image file formats.

If you insert an image on the Slide Master, PowerPoint displays it by default on every slide in your presentation.

Changing Image Colours

If a colour in an inserted clip art image clashes with your chosen colour scheme, you can change the image's colours.

Click on the image and choose **Format | Picture**. Select the Picture tab and click the Recolour button to display the Recolour Picture dialog box.

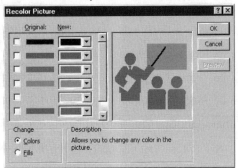

From the Original: list, select the colour you want to replace. From the New: list, select the replacement colour, and click **OK**.

Inserting Sound and Video Clips

You can include sound files (ending in .wav) and video files (ending in .avi) in your PowerPoint presentations.

To insert such multimedia objects in the current slide, choose **Insert | Movies and Sounds**, and then select the required file or files.

Inserting Charts

PowerPoint provides a variety of bar and other chart types. When you insert a chart, PowerPoint displays the following:

- **Datasheet:** A small spreadsheet that you can adapt by typing in your own text and numbers, over-writing those already present. You can add or delete rows and columns as you require.

- **Chart:** This changes according to the datasheet contents.

- **Chart Menus:** Excel-like menus of charting commands appear at the top of the PowerPoint window.

Datasheet ————→
Chart Area ————→

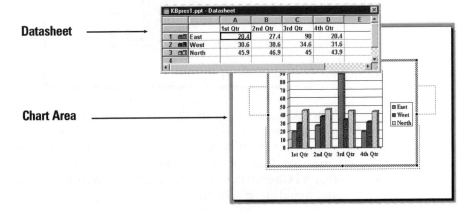

Text & Chart

Double click to add chart

Exercise 6.13: Inserting a Chart

1) Insert a new, fourth slide. Select the layout called Text & Chart.

2) In the title placeholder, type: Students: 1998-00. In the text placeholder, type the following bullet point: Steady growth in student numbers

3) Double-click on the chart icon. The following datasheet window appears. Notice that it contains sample numbers and text.

KBpres2 - Datasheet		A	B	C	D	E
		1st Qtr	2nd Qtr	3rd Qtr	4th Qtr	
1	East	20.4	27.4	90	20.4	
2	West	30.6	38.6	34.6	31.6	
3	North	45.9	46.9	45	43.9	
4						

4) Enter the following numbers and text to the datasheet, overtyping the sample data already present.

		A	B	C
		1998	1999	2000
1	Students	900	1200	1600

5) You do not need rows 2 and 3, and column D, of the datasheet. Click on the row 2 heading to select the entire row, and choose **Edit | Delete**.

Repeat this for row 3 and column D. Click the close box at the top right of the Datasheet to remove it. Your slide should now look as shown below.

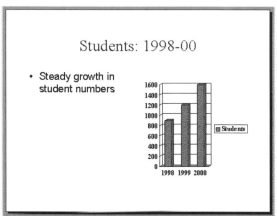

You can change the chart type – to a bar or pie chart, for example – by selecting it and choosing **Chart | Chart Type**. You are not restricted to inserting charts on slides whose layout includes a chart icon. You can insert a chart on any slide by choosing the **Insert | Chart** command. You can move and resize a chart as you would any other object.

Inserting Organisation Charts

These charts provide templates for you to display the people or units in an organisation (represented by boxes) and their relationships (represented by lines).

Although the boxes have text labels in them, such as 'Type name here', you can enter any type of information in any box. The labels are for your guidance only.

Right:
The default and simplest organisation chart template

When you insert and edit an organisation chart, PowerPoint opens a new window that displays the chart and offers new menus of commands. The **Styles** menu, for example, allows you to choose different chart types, while the **Text**, **Boxes** and **Lines** menus each allow you format the respective chart elements.

Exercise 6.14: Inserting an Organisation Chart

1) Insert a new, fifth slide. Select the layout called Organisation Chart.

2) In the title placeholder, type: Training Staff

3) Double-click on the org chart icon and enter the text as shown below.

   To select a box, click on it. When you have finished typing text in a box, deselect that box by clicking on another or by pressing ESC.

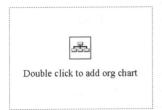

4) When you have finished working in the organisation chart window, return to your slide by choosing **File | Exit and Return to**, and then clicking **Yes** on the dialog box displayed.

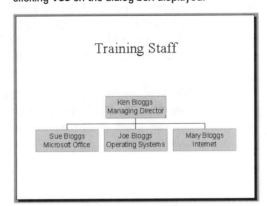

You are not restricted to inserting organisation charts on slides whose layout includes an organisation chart icon. You can insert such a chart on any slide by choosing the **Insert | Picture | Organisation Chart** command. You can move and resize a chart as you would any other object.

Organisation Chart
A template for displaying the people or units in an organisation (represented by boxes) and their relationships (represented by lines).

Inserting AutoShapes

AutoShapes are categories of ready-made shapes that you can insert in your presentations. They include lines, basic shapes, flowchart elements, stars and banners, and callouts.

When you insert an AutoShape on a slide, you can change its size and colour, and rotate it, as required.

To select an AutoShape, click the AutoShapes button on the Drawing Toolbar and choose from the options offered by the pop-up menu.

AutoShapes
Categories of ready-made shapes, including lines, geometric shapes and flowchart elements that you can use in your presentations.

Drawing Tools

On the Drawing Toolbar you can see a number of tools for drawing simple objects, including lines, lines with arrows, squares and rectangles, and circles and ovals.

Line and Arrow Tools

To draw a line, click on the Line button, place the cursor where you want the line to begin, click and drag to where you want the line to end, and release the mouse button. To draw an arrow, click on the Arrow button and draw it in the same way.

Line Colour

What colour do you want your line to be? You can click on the Line Colour button and select a colour before you draw a line. Or you can select an existing line and change its colour with the Line Colour button.

Rectangle Tool

To draw a rectangle, click on the Rectangle button, place the cursor where you want to position one corner of the rectangle, click and drag diagonally to where you want the opposite corner of the rectangle, and release the mouse button.

To draw a square, hold down the SHIFT key as you drag with the mouse.

Ellipse Tool

To draw an oval, click on the Ellipse button, place the cursor where you want the shape to begin, click and drag until the shape it is the size you want, and release the mouse button. To draw a circle, hold down the SHIFT key as you drag with the mouse.

Fill Colour

Use this button to fill a rectangle or oval with a colour other than the background colour of the slide. You can choose the fill colour before you draw the shape, or you can select an existing shape and then choose a fill colour.

Grouping and Ungrouping Objects

You can group objects so you can work with them as if they were a single object. You can format, move, rotate, flip and resize grouped objects in a single operation.

To group objects, hold down SHIFT and click the objects. Next, click the Draw button on the Drawing Toolbar and choose the **Group** command.

To ungroup a selected group of objects, click the Draw button on the Drawing Toolbar and choose the **Ungroup** command.

Outline View

You know that Slide View displays a single slide, Slide Sorter View displays miniatures of all slides, and Notes View displays the speaker notes page accompanying the current slide.

Another display option is Outline view. To apply Outline view, choose **View | Outline**.

While Slide Sorter view is best for looking at the *format* of your presentation, Outline view is best for reviewing its *content*.

1 □ **Bloggs Computer Training**
   Learn from the Experts
2 □ **We Offer**
   • Up-to-date courses
   • Basic to advanced levels
   • Top facilities
   • Professional trainers
   • Small classes
   • ECDL certification
3 ▣ **Instructors**
   • Technically expert
   • Trained teachers
   • Friendly and helpful
4 ▣ **Students: 1998-00**
   • Steady growth in student numbers
5 ▣ **Training Staff**

You can use the buttons on the Outlining Toolbar to move slides or text, show only slide titles, and change the indent level of titles and text.

Outline View
Shows the text of all your slides so that you can judge how well your ideas and text flow smoothly from one slide to the next.

Running Your Presentation

When you have created a number of slides, you can preview how they will look to your audience by choosing the **View | Slide Show** command or click the Slide Show button 💻 in the lower-left corner of the presentation window.

This shows the first slide – without any of the PowerPoint menus, toolbars or other screen elements that are displayed when you are creating or editing slides.

To advance from the current slide to the next one, press PAGE DOWN, or click on the Next button shown at the bottom-left of the screen. To move backwards, press PAGE UP or click the Previous button. To exit Slide Show view, press ESC.

You can also use Slide Show view to deliver your finished presentation to your audience.

Automating Your Presentation

You don't need to press PAGE DOWN or click with the mouse each time you want move on from the current slide. Here's another option: get PowerPoint run the show for you, so that your presentation proceeds automatically. You are then free to stand back from the computer and interact more directly with your audience.

Exercise 6.15: Automating Your Presentation

1) Choose **Slide Show | Slide Transition**.

2) Under Advance, click Automatically after, and then enter the number of seconds you want the slide to appear on the screen.

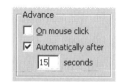

3) Click Apply All to apply the automated slide advance method to your entire presentation.

You can view your timings by choosing **View | Slide Show**.

If you want to advance to the next slide manually (by clicking the mouse or by pressing the SPACEBAR), select On mouse click. If you choose both options, the slide will advance either manually or after the specified interval, whichever comes first.

Slide Transitions

A transition is a graphic effect that determines how one slide replaces another – for example, the slide could drop down from the top of the screen, or dissolve out of the previous slide.

You can set two factors for a transition:

- *Effect Type:* The nature of the special effect with which PowerPoint introduces the current slide.

- *Effect Timing:* The speed with which PowerPoint runs the visual effect when introducing the current slide.

Optionally, for added impact, you can also link a sound to a transition.

Exercise 6.16: Applying a Transition to Your Presentation

1) Choose **Slide Show | Slide Transition**.

2) Select from the following options:

   Effect: Each time you click an option from the drop-down list, PowerPoint runs the effect in the sample picture. You can rerun the preview by clicking the picture.

   Select the effect called Checkerboard across.

   Timing: The options – Slow, Medium or Fast – set the speed at which the transition effect runs. Click an option and PowerPoint runs the effect with that timing in the sample picture.

   Select Medium Timing.

3) Select the option Apply to All to apply the transition effect and timing to your entire presentation.

   You can view your transition effect and timing by choosing **View | Slide Show**.

Advance Methods and Transition Effects

You select the slide advance method (manual, automated or both) and apply transitions from the same dialog box, called Slide Transitions. The two effects are independent, however.

- You can automate the running of your slide show without applying a transition, and apply a transition without automating your slide show.

- Transition timing specifies the duration of the transition effect. The automated advance time specifies how long a slide is displayed before being replaced.

Transition

A visual effect, such as a box-out, dissolve or fade, that determines how one slide in a presentation is replaced by another.

Build Slides

Build slides allow you to display bulleted text gradually to your audience. When you first show a build slide of bulleted text, the audience sees only the first bullet. You can then reveal the remaining bullets, one-by-one, as you talk to your audience.

Also, builds allow you to dim previously-presented points on the slide as new points appear, and create a special effect for the appearance of new bullet points – for example, bullet points can fly in from the right, left, top, or bottom.

Exercise 6.17: Applying a Build to a Slide

1) Display the second slide, called We Offer

2) Select the bulleted text.

3) Choose **Slide Show | Preset Animation** and select the option called Flying.

4) Choose **Slide Show | Custom Animation** to display the Custom Animation dialog box.

   On the Effects tab, select the settings shown on the right.

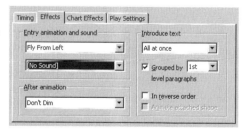

5) Click on the Timing tab, select the Automatically option, enter 12 seconds, and click **OK**.

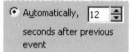

You can view your build slide by choosing **View | Slide Show**.

Build Slide

A slide of bulleted text where the bullets are introduced one-by-one to the audience.

Section Summary: So Now You Know

You can make your presentation more visually attractive by adding *images*. These may be your own or they may be from PowerPoint's collection of ready-made *clip art*. You can also add multimedia *sound* and *video clips*.

Two kinds of special diagrams that you can add are Excel-style *charts* for illustrating statistics, and *organisation charts* that show the people or units in an organisation (represented by boxes) and their relationships (represented by lines).

You can add lines, rectangles, ovals and other geometric shapes by selecting from the several categories of ready-made *AutoShapes*. Or you can draw such shapes yourself by using the tools on the Drawing Toolbar. You can apply line and fill colours to any shape.

You can *group objects* together and manipulate them in a single operation.

PowerPoint's *transitions* allow you add graphic effects to the way that one slide replaces another. *Builds* enable you to control the display of bulleted text on a slide.

Use *Outline view* to review the text of your entire presentation, and ensure that your ideas flow smoothly from one slide to the next. PowerPoint's *colour schemes* will give your slides a consistent and attractive appearance, while the *Slide Master* provides a template that controls the default text and graphics for all slides.

To run your presentation, use *Slide Show* view. You can even automate your presentation so that PowerPoint automatically displays the next slide a preset time after the current one.

7

Information Network Services

'The Internet is like a library'. You will hear this kind of statement a lot from people who know nothing about either.

If the Internet is a library, it's a strange one indeed. For starters, there is no indexing system. At any rate, the books are not arranged on numbered shelves but scattered on the floor. A lot of what is in the books is untrue, even in the non-fiction ones. There is no librarian, and no information desk. Did we mention also that the lights are turned off?

As you will learn in this Module, the Internet is in fact a collection of individual networks – groups of computers connected together. You will discover why networks are built the way they are, and what benefits they bring to their users.

Another myth: 'The Internet has no rules'. It has. There are not many, but they are important. You will find out about these too. Expect to meet a little jargon along the way – such as domain names, mail servers and TCP/IP – but by the end of the Module you will know exactly what terms like these mean.

One more thing about the Internet and libraries: you can make as much noise as you like when using the Internet.

Think of this Module as your chance to borrow knowledge and skills you won't ever be asked to return. They are yours to keep and use. Good luck with it.

Section 7.1: Computer Networking

In This Section

What do computers talk about when they connect to one another?

This Section introduces you to the basics of computer networks. You will discover the four benefits that come from connecting computers (and printers) together; learn the three questions to ask about any computer network; meet a device called a modem and find out what it does and how it got its name.

New Activities

At the end of this Section you should be able to:

- Explain the difference between stand-alone and network computing

- List and describe the four common network services: printer-sharing, file-sharing, e-mail and remote access

- List and describe the three defining features of any network: size, access type and protocol

- Explain why a modem is necessary when connecting a computer to the telephone system

- Explain the difference between a dial-up and a leased line

New Words

At the end of this Section you should be able to explain the following terms:

- Stand-alone computing
- Network
- LAN
- WAN
- Protocol

- Modem
- Dial-up connection
- Leased line connection
- Remote access
- Teleworking

Stand-alone Computing

You are working on your computer – perhaps typing a letter in Word or doing calculations in an Excel spreadsheet.

A cable trails from the back of your computer to the electricity socket. Possibly there is a second cable connecting your computer to a printer, and a third to a scanner. But your computer is not connected to any other computer. This we call stand-alone computing.

Stand-alone computer
A computer that is not connected to any other computer.

Network Computing: Three Good Things

Now imagine that your computer is in some way connected to other computers. Don't worry about how many others. Or whether they are in the same building or on the other side of the world.

The point is that your computer is no longer stand-alone. It is part of a computer network. You can still do your spreadsheets, word-processing, and so on – but now three other things are possible as well:

- **Printer-sharing:** In a stand-alone world, people can print only if a printer is attached directly to their computer.

  By connecting one or more printers to a computer network, everyone whose computer is also attached to the same network can print their documents.

  Printer-sharing means that everyone can print (although not at the same time) without everyone having an individual printer.

- **File-sharing:** On a stand-alone computer, you can work with all the files stored on your computer's hard disk. On a network-connected computer, you may be able to work with files stored on on other people's computers too.

  Rather than have network users rummaging through each other's hard disks, information that is needed by everyone in a particular department (in accounts, for example, or in a warehouse) is usually stored on a single, powerful, permanently switched-on computer called a *file server*.

- **E-mail:** Meetings, telephone conversations, letters and memos – typically, these are the ways in which people in an organisation communicate with one another.

  Computer networks make possible another form of communication called electronic mail, or e-mail for short. This is the exchange of (usually plain-text) messages between users of computers that are connected to a common network.

You will meet a fourth possible benefit of computer networking – remote access – later in this Section.

Computer Network

Two or more computers that are connected together by some means to provide their users with such services as printer-sharing, file-sharing and electronic mail.

Networks: Three Things You Need to Know

Now that you have learnt three benefits of computer networks, let's look at the main features of a network. There are really only three questions you need ask about any computer network. The answers tell just about everything worth knowing about it:

- What size is it?
- Who is allowed join?
- What 'language' (protocol) does it speak?

What Size Is It?

Networks come in two sizes: big and small. A Local Area Network or LAN is the kind that connects the computers in a single office, building or group of adjoining buildings.

Local Area Network (LAN)

A network that connects computers located within a small area.

Large corporations operate computer networks that connect offices at locations within the same or different countries. Such Wide Area Networks or WANs can enable, for example:

- The Frankfurt office to exchange e-mails with the Sydney office

- The Tokyo office to read files that are stored on a computer in the New Orleans office

- The Cape Town office to print a report on a printer that is located in the Bombay office.

Wide Area Network (WAN)

A network that connects computers over a wide area, typically across international boundaries.

In reality, most networks are bigger than LANs but smaller than WANs. But, for some reason, no one has thought up a name for them.

Who Is Allowed Join?

Like clubs, computer networks can be open to everyone or restricted to the chosen few. An example of a *private access* network is one operated by a company or government agency for its own personnel only.

Alternatively, a network can be public, allowing anyone to join and use it (usually for a fee!). A good example of a *public access* network is the Internet.

What Language (Protocol) Does It Speak?

In international diplomacy, the word *protocol* describes an agreed way for people from different cultures to meet and communicate. In networking, protocol means the rules and etiquette governing communications between computers.

TCP/IP (you don't need to know what the letters stand for) is the world's most popular network protocol. Hundreds of thousands of networks 'speak' TCP/IP, including the biggest network of them all, the Internet. (Actually, the 'I' in TCP/IP stands for Internet.)

Regardless of its make, model, type, power, size or age, any computer that 'speaks' TCP/IP can communicate over a TCP/IP-based network with any other computer that also speaks TCP/IP.

Network Protocol
A set of rules governing how computers communicate over a network. TCP/IP is the most popular protocol, and is used in the Internet.

Network Connections: The Modem

What have you learnt so far? That networks bring three benefits (printer-sharing, file-sharing and e-mail), and have three defining characteristics (size, access type, and protocol).

A question we have not yet asked is: how do the computers in a network actually connect with one another?

Connecting computers (and printers) to create an office LAN is a relatively simple matter of running cables from one device to the next.

But what about WAN connections? How do computers, located at opposite sides of a country or different parts of the globe, connect with one another?

The answer is that they use the cables of the national and international telephone system. This has advantages, and one major disadvantage too.

- **Advantages**:
  It's already in place (so there is no need to run WAN cables across rivers and over mountains), and its connection points are never far away (the phone system reaches into every workplace and virtually every home).

- **Disadvantage**:
  Computer signals (the ones that travel around inside a computer) are a different 'shape' to the signals accepted by the phone system (ones resulting from the sound of the human voice).

Above:
A sample computer (digital) signal

We therefore have a problem: a *signal shape* problem. To connect a computer to a phone line, we need a device than can do two jobs. Which job it does at any particular time depends on the direction of information transfer:

- **Outgoing Information:** When your computer sends data (such as an e-mail) down the phone line, the device must 'shape' the signal – convert it from computer-shape to phone-shape.

- **Incoming Information:** When you receive data (such as a file from a distant computer), the device must 'deshape' the signal – reconvert it back from phone-shape to its original computer-shape.

Above:
A sample phone system (analog) signal

Another, rather poetic, word for the act of shaping anything in this way is *modulation*. A device that shapes (<u>mo</u>dulates) and deshapes (<u>dem</u>odulates) a signal is – guess what? – called a modem.

Modem

A device that enables computers to communicate over the telephone system. At the sending computer, the modem converts the outgoing data to the format acceptable to the phone system. At the receiving computer, another modem reconverts the data back to its original computer format.

Right:
Two computers, each with an external modem, communicating over the telephone system.

Think of this as a two-computer WAN.

Many modern computers now contain built-in modems. To connect such a computer to the telephone system, you plug the phone line into the back of the computer, just as if you were attaching a printer. (Of course, the phone line and printer cable go into different slots!)

Network Connections: Temporary and Permanent

Telephone conversations cost money, whether they occur between people or between computers. Using the telephone system extends the geographic range of a network – and also to its operating cost.

There are two ways to connect a computer and modem to the telephone system: dial-up and leased line. You need to understand what these two terms mean.

Dial-up Lines

One way to connect computers over the telephone system is to use the phone line only when absolutely necessary. This type of occasional and temporary network connection is called a dial-up line.

Suppose you are a travelling sales representative, for example, and you are equipped with a portable computer and a modem. At the end of the day you might dial a computer located at your company's headquarters, send a file containing your sales figures down the line, and then close the connection.

Dial-up Line
A telephone-based connection to a distant computer or computer network that you use only when you need it.

Leased Line Connection

If people in an organisation need to use e-mail and file-sharing around-the-clock, seven days a week, the organisation can lease (rent) a permanent line from a telecommunications company.

Leased Line
A connection between two locations that is permanently 'open'. Leased lines are generally faster and more reliable that dial-up ones.

Remote Access Computing

At the beginning of this Section you were introduced to the three main network services: printer-sharing, file-sharing and e-mail. You are now ready to learn about a fourth service: remote access.

The computers on a LAN are called *local computers*; they are 'here' – in the same room, building or group of buildings. Computers that are anywhere but 'here' are called *remote computers*.

Using a modem and the telephone system, a person with a remote computer can connect to an office LAN – even though they may be hundreds or thousands of miles away.

When connected, they can read and send e-mail, view files on a computer in the office – perhaps even print on an office printer.

Remote Access

The ability to connect to a computer or computer network from a distant location. Generally, you need a computer, modem, and the phone number at which the computer or network can be dialled.

Remote computer access makes possible *teleworking* arrangements, whereby people can work, at least in part, from their homes.

Teleworking can help people who might not otherwise be able to take up a full-time, onsite job – perhaps because of caring responsibilities, or because commuting to work every day would be too time-consuming or expensive.

EU and international research shows that teleworking can increase productivity by 15–40%, and that teleworkers are:

- More reliable and loyal

- More likely to produce better quality work

- Less likely to take time off

- More likely to stay with the organisation for longer

Teleworking

Taking advantage of network technology to do a job at a distance from the employer.

Section Summary: So Now You Know

A *network* is two or more computers (and perhaps printers, scanners and other devices) connected together by some means to provide useful services.

Networks bring four main benefits: *printer-sharing*, *file-sharing*, *e-mail* and *remote access*. The last makes possible *teleworking* arrangements, whereby people can work from their homes.

Three characteristics define a network: size (*LAN* or *WAN*), access type (*private access* or *public access*) and *protocol*.

A protocol is a set of rules governing how computers communicate over a network. The most popular protocol, and the one used by the Internet, is *TCP/IP*.

Computers on a WAN generally connect via the telephone system, either by a *dial-up* (temporary) or *leased line* (permanent) connection. An intermediary device, called a *modem,* is necessary when connecting a computer to a phone line.

Section 7.2: Servers and Clients

In This Section

There was time when networking meant a few computers, a printer or two, and some cabling to join the lot together. Not any more.

Modern networks include special-purpose computers to handle network administration and security, and e-mail storage.

This Section builds on the networking basics you covered in Section 7.1. After this, you will be ready to move on to bigger things: inter-networks, and particularly the biggest inter-network of all, the Internet.

New Activities

At the end of this Section you should be able to:

- Explain the roles of user name and password in a login procedure, and the need for a network server

- Explain how the presence of a mail server with personal mail boxes affects the way that users send and receive e-mail on a network

- Explain why an e-mail address has two components, and state the purpose of each

- Explain what is meant by client-server computing, and state the roles of the server and client components

- Distinguish between networks and network services

New Words

At the end of this Section you should be able to explain the following terms:

- Accessing/Logging in
- Network server
- E-mail
- Mail server

- Server software
- Client software
- E-mail protocol

Logging In to a Network

To connect to most networks, you need more than just a physical cable – or, if you are a remote user, a modem and a telephone line. You also need to pass a test that presents you with two questions: 'Who are you?', and 'Are you really who you say you are?'.

- **Who Are You?**
  You answer this by typing in your *user name* (sometimes called user ID). The network needs this information to track who uses it and for how long.

- **Are You Really?**
  You answer this by entering your confidential *password*. It is your guarantee that no one else can join and use the network in your name.

The procedure for joining a network is called accessing or logging in A login dialog box typically looks like that below.

| User name: | kbloggs |
| Password: | ****** |

Notice how your user name is displayed on screen after you type it. As you type your password, however, the screen masks the characters beneath a line of asterisks – just in case some inquisitive person is looking over your shoulder.

Accessing or Logging In

The procedure for joining a network. It typically involves entering your user name (for network administration) and confidential password (for network security).

The Network Server

Confusion Corner:
The term 'network server' is sometimes used to describe not just the software program, but both the program and the (usually) dedicated computer on which the program runs.

Where does a login procedure come from? It is provided by a software program called a network server. This program:

- Presents the login dialog box to anyone asking to join the network

- Checks the entered user name and password, and

- Grants ("Welcome to Bloggs Computer Network") or denies ("ILLEGAL ACCESS: Please Leave Immediately") access accordingly.

Network Server

A software program that administers and protects the security of that network.

Let's look at the difference that adding a network server makes to the operation of a network.

- **Without a Network Server**
  No network access procedure. No central record exists of who accessed it or when.

- **With a Network Server**
  Only authorised persons have access. A central record exists of who logged in and when.

The opposite of logging in is logging out, where the network user signs off the network.

More About E-mail

E-mail is like the postal system – only that the messages are electronic rather than on paper.

E-mail

The exchange of (usually plain-text) messages between users of computers that are connected to a common network.

Mail Boxes and the Mail Server

A mail server is a software program that provides mail boxes, one for every user connected to the network. Mail boxes are files on the mail server's hard disk that store incoming and outgoing e-mails.

Let's see what difference adding a mail server makes:

- **Without a Mail Server:**
  E-mails are sent directly to the recipient's computer. If the recipient's computer happens to be switched off, then the message is 'lost'.

  E-mails pop up on their recipients' screens immediately after they are sent, interrupting the recipients' normal work routine.

- **With a Mail Server:**
  E-mails are sent to the appropriate mail box on the mail server. Like the network server, this is switched on permanently.

  Users read their e-mail when they choose. They look in their mail box, view a list of waiting e-mails, and read them in order of priority.

Confusion Corner:
As with 'network server', the term 'mail server' is sometimes used to describe not just the software program, but both the program and the (usually) dedicated computer on which the program runs.

Mail Server

A computer running software that makes e-mail more convenient by providing personal mail boxes for each user. Users send e-mails to each other's mail boxes on the mail server, and e-mail is held in the mail boxes until the users are ready to read it.

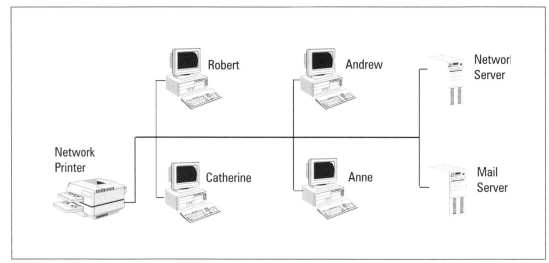

Above: A four-user LAN with a networked printer, a network server and a mail server. On some networks, the network server and mail server software programs may run on the same computer.

Putting the @ in E-mail Addresses

To work properly, e-mail, like the traditional postal system, needs some kind of addressing system. E-mail addresses have two parts:

- **The name of the person's mail box**:
  Typically, the person's first name (such as robert), or the initial of their first name, followed by their second name (such as rbloggs). Sometimes you will see names containing a full stop (robert.bloggs) or an underscore (r_bloggs).

  Mail box names are usually written in lower-case letters, and *never* contain spaces.

- **The address of the mail server:**
  A mail server has a network address too – just as does a post office in the traditional postal system.

In a simple office LAN with four users – Robert, Andrew, Catherine and Anne – and a mail server called 'mailserver', the e-mail addresses might be as follows:

robert@mailserver   catherine@mailserver
andrew@mailserver   anne@mailserver

The 'at' symbol (@) separates the mail box name from the name of the mail server. If a fifth person, who is also named Robert, later joins the network, he cannot claim the address robert@mailserver, as it is already taken. He would have to settle for robert1@mailserver, robbie@mailserver, or some other such variation.

E-mail Address

A mail box name, the @ symbol, and the network address of the mail server on which the mail box is stored. Spaces are not permitted. Typically, e-mail addresses are in lower-case characters.

E-mail addresses can also be assigned to departments or functions within the organisation. For example: sales@mailserver, help.desk@mailserver and complaints@mailserver.

Right:
Mail server holds users' mail boxes as files on its hard disk

robert@mailserver
andrew@mailserver
catherine@mailserver
anne@mailserver
sales@mailserver
help.desk@mailserver
complaints@mailserver

E-mail Clients and Servers

If you install a software application such as Microsoft Word, you can say "I have word processing on my computer". If you install e-mail software, however, you cannot (or should not) say: "I have e-mail on my computer". You don't.

What you have is *half* the software needed to exchange e-mail. The other half of the software runs on your network's mail server.

Server Software

Software that runs on servers is, naturally enough, called s*erver software*. Server software typically does two things:

- Stores information

- Accepts (or rejects!) requests from network users to access that information

Server Software

Software that typically stores information on a server, and handles requests from network users to obtain that information.

Client Software

The other, non-server half of e-mail software – the part that runs on the computers of the ordinary network users – is called *client software*.

E-mail client software should allow a network user to:

- Type text into a new e-mail message

- Put an e-mail address at the top of the message, so that it travels to the correct recipient

- Access their mail box and copy received e-mails to their computer

- Display received e-mails on their computer and, perhaps, organise e-mails into folders

Client Software

Software that typically requests information from a server, and controls how that information is displayed on the user's computer.

E-mail software, as you can see, is not like Word or Excel: it is not something that you install and run on a single computer. Instead, different parts of what adds up to an e-mail service are split across two different types of computers: the server, and the clients.

Client-server Computing

The splitting of functions between networked computers: one (the server) stores and manages the information; all the others (the clients) request and display that information.

So: if you do install e-mail software, what you say is: "I have an e-mail client on my computer."

Networks and Network Services

Don't confuse what a network is (a group of connected computers) with the kinds of services you can operate over a network.

A network makes lots of things possible; but on its own it does nothing at all. A network is like a railway track: it is not much use without trains (such as e-mail) running over it.

When we talk about an e-mail network, for example, we mean a network running client-server software that provides an e-mail service. E-mail is not the network: take away the e-mail software and the network is still there.

SMTP: The E-mail Protocol

TCP/IP, as your learnt in Section 7.1, is the world's most popular network protocol: the common 'language' computers must speak if they wish to communicate over most networks. A computer speaking TCP/IP to another computer, however, does not say very much, other than:

'Hello, this is me, and that seems to be you. Let's keep this connection open in case some information needs to travel from me to you, or you to me.'

Here, in summary, is what TCP/IP does and does not do:

- **What TCP/IP Does**
  Provides the the basis for computer-to-computer conversations.

- **What TCP/IP Does *Not* Do**
  Provide any rules for what type of conversations can take place.

To operate an e-mail service, another set of rules is needed: a protocol just for e-mail. An e-mail protocol sets out standards for:

- Addressing (to avoid messages going astray)

- Message formatting (so that you can read what I type), and

- Client-server interaction (so that e-mail client software made by one company, say, Microsoft, can communicate with mail server software made by another, different company, say, Netscape).

The e-mail protocol used on the Internet is called SMTP (Simple Mail Transfer Protocol).

E-mail Protocol
A set of rules stating how e-mails may be addressed, how their contents may be formatted, and how e-mail client software on users' computers interacts with mail servers. The Internet's e-mail protocol is SMTP.

Section Summary:
So Now You Know

Most networks present a *login* or *access procedure* that asks users to enter a valid *user name* (for network administration) and confidential password (for network security). The login procedure is provided by a software program called a *network server*.

A *mail server* is a software program that provides *personal mail boxes* for each user. Users send e-mails to each other's mail boxes, and e-mail is held in mail boxes until the recipients are ready to read it.

E-mail addresses must be unique and consist of the mail box name, the @ symbol, and the mail server name. Spaces are not permitted.

Client-server computing is the splitting of functions between networked computers: one (the *server*) stores and manages information; all the others (the *clients*) request and display that information.

Networks make possible useful *network services* such as e-mail. Each service has its own protocol, which typically includes standards for addressing and formatting, and rules for server and client interaction. The Internet's e-mail protocol is *SMTP*.

Section 7.3: E-mail and the Internet

In This Section

If a group of connected computers is a network, what do you call a group of connected networks? Answer: An inter-network.

In this Section you will discover how e-mail messages are exchanged on an inter-network, and find how Internet e-mails are addressed.

You will also learn how ISPs enable just about everyone (who can afford it) to share the benefits of Internet e-mail.

After reading this Section, you will be ready to use Internet e-mail, as described in Section 7.4.

New Activities

At the end of this Section you should be able to:

- Explain how an inter-network can enable anyone on any attached network to send and receive e-mail

- Describe the e-mail address standards in the US, France, Germany the UK and Ireland

- Explain how an ISP enables individuals and small companies to exchange e-mail over the Internet

New Words

At the end of this Section you should be able to explain the following terms:

- Inter-network

- Domain Name

- Internet Service Provider (ISP)

An E-mail Inter-network

In the diagram below you can see a very basic inter-network that offers an e-mail service to all connected users. The components are:

- Three LANs, each one with a network server and mail server. The mail servers are named white, blue and red.

- Three leased lines connecting the LANs to a common point, thereby forming an inter-network.

A user on one LAN can exchange e-mails with a user on any other LAN.

Right:
A three-LAN,
12-user
inter-network

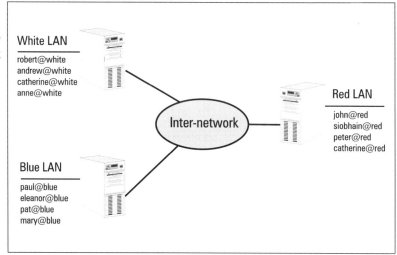

You can see that two people on the inter-network are named Catherine. Does this matter? No: one is catherine@white and the second is catherine@red. That is, the mail server parts of their e-mail addresses are different, with the result that each address is unique.

Imagine not three but hundreds of thousands of individual networks, all inter-connected in a way that their users can exchange e-mails with one another. The system you have just created in your mind exists in reality: it is the e-mail service provided by a global inter-network called the Internet.

Inter-network
Two or more networks connected together by some means to provide their users with such services as inter-network e-mail. The Internet is an example of an inter-network.

Internet Domain Names

On the Internet, the following terms are used:

- The term *site* describes an individual network.

- The term *domain name* describes the unique address of a site.

- Each domain name consists of at least two parts, separated by full stops. The full stops are called *dots*.

In the US, where the Internet was developed, the right-most part of a domain name (the suffix) indicates the nature of the organisation that operates the site. The three main suffixes are:

.com: A commercial organisation.
For example, sales@microsoft.com

.edu: An educational institution.
For example, provost@harvard.edu

.gov: a governmental organisation.
For example, president@whitehouse.gov

Look again at the basic inter-network on the page opposite. If this follows US naming conventions, and White is a business, Blue is a college and Red is a government department, the e-mail addresses become:

robert@white.com	paul@blue.edu	john@red.gov
andrew@white.com	judy@blue.edu	siobhain@red.gov
catherine@white.com	pat@blue.edu	peter@red.gov
anne@white.com	mary@blue.edu	catherine@red.gov

You pronounce an e-mail address like this:

robert at white dot com

Non-US Domain Names

As the Internet spread outside the US, different countries adopted different conventions for domain names.

Ireland does not categorise sites by type. It adds just the single suffix of .ie (pronounced dot ie). Examples of Irish Internet e-mail addresses are:

nutrition@superquinn.ie
infodesk@dcu.ie
webmaster@rte.ie

France (.fr) and Germany (.de) are two other countries that apply just a country identifier. Another is Austria (.at), where, allegedly, there is an e-mail address of at.at@at.at.

In the UK, sites have two identifiers: one for site type and a second for country.

> **.co.uk**: A commercial site. For example, the sports editor of the *Belfast Telegraph* is at sportseditor@belfasttelegraph.co.uk
>
> **.ac.uk**: An academic site. For example, you can e-mail the Computing Services Helpdesk of Queen's University Belfast at advisory@qub.ac.uk
>
> **.gov.uk**: A governmental site. For example, you can e-mail the Northern Ireland Information Service at press.nio@nics.gov.uk.

Domain Name

The unique name of an Internet site at which there is typically a network of computers and devices that are administered as a single unit. A domain name has at least two parts, separated by a dot.

ISPs: Now Everyone Can Join

In its early years, only people who worked in large companies, universities and government agencies had access to Internet e-mail. No other organisations could afford to operate the type of network of which the Internet is composed.

How can a single individual gain access to the Internet? Let's look at this not as a problem but as a business opportunity. Why? Because there are lots of other individuals and small companies, equipped with no more than personal computers and modems, who also want Internet access.

Here is what you do. Go on a shopping spree and:

- Buy a network server, mail server, a few personal computers, and some cables to connect them all together in a LAN.

- Lease a line from the telephone company to open a permanent connection between your LAN and the Internet.

- Register your LAN with an Internet domain name.

Congratulations. You now have an Internet site. But how are you going to pay for all this equipment?

You go shopping again and you:

- Rent (say) one hundred phone lines from the telephone company, and set them up so that a single phone number will dial any one of them.

  For example, if twenty-six of your phone lines are busy at one time, the next incoming call is switched through to the twenty-seventh phone line.

- Buy one hundred modems, and use them to connect your one hundred phone lines to your LAN.

  Now, up to one hundred people, equipped with personal computers and modems, can simultaneously dial up your LAN, and through your LAN, access Internet e-mail.

- Advertise in your local newspaper, saying: 'Dial-up Internet Access Now Available. Just £10 per month.'

You are now in business as an *Internet Service Provider* or ISP. As customers join your ISP, you give them a user name and password (so that they can log in to your LAN), and a mail box on your mail server (so that they can exchange e-mail over the Internet).

Internet Service Provider (ISP)
A company that operates a network of the type that can connect to the Internet. An ISP charges its customers for dial-up or leased line access, via its network, to the Internet.

Consider the difference between networks operated by ISPs and those run by organisations such as large companies, colleges and government agencies.

- **Organisational Network:** Exists for reasons other than just Internet access. They typically provide internal e-mail, file-sharing and printer-sharing.

  Most users of the network are local users, working inside the organisation's premises.

- **ISP Network:** Has no purpose other than to provide its users (that is, paying customers) with access to the Internet.

  Except for a few help desk and maintenance staff, all network users are remote users.

Irish ISPs include Ireland On-line, Tinet, Indigo and Esat.

If the users in the simple example at the start of this Section subscribed to ISPs, their e-mail address might read as follows.

robert@iol.ie	paul@tinet.ie	john@indigo.ie
andrew@iol.ie	judy@tinet.ie	siobhain@indigo.ie
catherine@iol.ie	pat@tinet.ie	peter@indigo.ie
anne@iol.ie	mary@tinet.ie	catherine@indigo.ie

Section Summary: So Now You Know

An *inter-network* is a group of networks connected together, the largest of which is the Internet. *Inter-network e-mail* enables a user on one network to exchange e-mail with a user on any other connected network.

Each network of which the Internet is composed is called a *site*, and has a unique *domain name*. An Internet *e-mail address* consists of the user's mail box name, the @ symbol, and *domain name* of the site at which the mail server is located.

Domain names have at least two parts, separated by a dot (.). In the US, the first part is the organisation's name; the second indicates its type. Commercial sites end in *.com*, educational sites in *.edu* and government sites in *.gov*.

Irish, German and French sites are not categorised by type. Their domain names consist of just the organisation name and a suffix indicating their nationality (*.ie*, *.fr*, and *.de*). In the UK, commercial sites end in *.co.uk*, academic sites in *.ac.uk* and government sites in *.gov.uk*.

An *Internet Service Provider (ISP)* is a company that operates a LAN of the type that can connect to the Internet, and charges its customers for Internet access, via that LAN. It assigns user names and passwords (so that customers can log in to the ISP's LAN), and mail boxes on its mail server (so that customers can exchange e-mail over the Internet).

Section 7.4: Using Internet E-mail

In This Section

Ever wanted to send an e-mail? This Section takes you through the steps of performing various e-mail activities, explains the main components of every e-mail message, and shows you how to use the features of a popular e-mail client.

New Activities

At the end of this Section you should be able to:

- List and explain the three components of an e-mail message: header, message area, and signature file

- Use a popular e-mail client to receive, read, reply, forward, write and send an e-mail

- Attach a file to an outgoing e-mail

- Create and edit a signature file

New Words

At the end of this Section you should be able to explain the following terms:

- E-mail client software

- E-mail header

- E-mail file attachment

- E-mail signature file

The Three Parts of an E-mail

An e-mail is made up of three parts: header, message area, and signature file:

- **Header:** Think of this as the e-mail's *envelope* – it contains the name and address of the recipient(s). Your e-mail software automatically 'date stamps' each e-mail you send, so there is no need for you to type the date anywhere on the e-mail.

  As a matter of courtesy to your recipient(s), you should also type the subject of your e-mail in the box called Subject: in the e-mail header.

  When you receive an e-mail, the header tells you where it came from, when it was sent, and (ideally) its subject.

- **Message Area:** This is where you write or read the text of the message.

- **Signature File:** You don't need to type such details as your name, job title and postal address into every e-mail you send.

  Your e-mail software lets you create what is called a signature file (or sig file) to hold such contact information, and it will add this file to all your outgoing messages.

E-mail Client Software

Here is a definition of e-mail client software.

> ### E-mail Client Software
> *A software application that enables the user to send, receive and organise e-mail. E-mail client software, or e-mail client for short, works in co-operation with the network's mail server.*

A number of excellent e-mail clients are available, such as Eudora Lite, which you can obtain without charge from http://eudora.qualcomm.com/eudoralight/. (Section 7.6 shows you how to download software from the Web.)

In this Section, however, we will use the e-mail client called Microsoft Internet Mail that is supplied with Microsoft's Internet Explorer Web browser. A broadly similar e-mail client, called Netscape Messenger, is available with Netscape's Navigator Web browser.

Most e-mail clients share the same features and functions. If you can use one, you should be able to use any of the others without difficulty.

Starting Microsoft Internet Mail

Choose **Start | Programs | Microsoft Internet Mail** to display the program's opening screen.

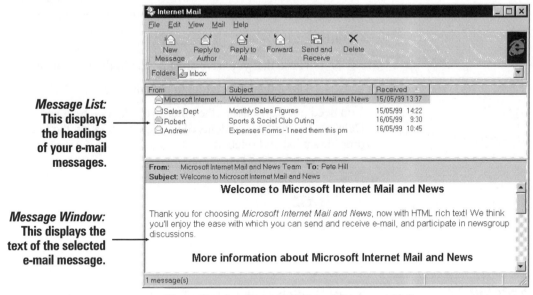

Message List: This displays the headings of your e-mail messages.

Message Window: This displays the text of the selected e-mail message.

Above: Opening Screen of Microsoft Internet Mail

The Incoming Message List

Internet Mail's message list provides details about the e-mails in your mailbox:

A *read* message. The header is displayed in light type.

An *unread* message. The header is displayed in bold type.

A message with one or more files *attached*. You will learn about e-mail attachments later in this Section.

Sorting Your Message List

By default, Microsoft Internet Mail sorts your message list in ascending order of receipt date and time (most recently received e-mails are listed first).

You can change the sort method (to Subject or Sender Name) and sort order (ascending or descending) by choosing the **View | Sort By** command, or simply by clicking on the relevant word in the title bar. Other e-mail clients offer similar sort options.

Your E-mail Folders

Microsoft Internet Mail organises your messages into two main folders:

- **Inbox:** Lists your received e-mails, both read and unread.

- **Outbox:** Lists e-mails of two kinds:

    - Those that you have already sent to their recipients.

    - Those that are waiting to be sent.

You need not worry about the other two folders – Sent and Deleted. To view the contents of any folder, click on the Folders drop-down list and select it.

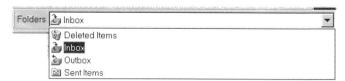

Reading Your E-mail

To read a received message, click on the message header in the Inbox message list. Internet Mail displays the text of the selected message in the lower half of the screen.

Alternatively, double-click on a message header to view its text in a separate, larger window.

Replying to an E-mail

You can reply to a received E-mail that is open on your screen by choosing **Mail | Reply to Author** or by clicking the button of the same name on the toolbar.

The e-mail becomes 'live', allowing you to scroll down through the text of the e-mail to add your comments where appropriate. Alternatively, you can just type your reply above the text of the old message. Internet Mail automatically inserts the address of the original sender in the To: field of the e-mail header.

Replying to All Recipients

When your choose the **Mail | Reply to All** command, or click the button of the same name on the toolbar, Internet Mail sends your reply to all the recipients of the original e-mail – and not just to the person who sent the e-mail to you.

This feature is particularly useful for setting up meetings.

Forwarding an E-mail

Forward

If you receive an e-mail that you think may be of interest to someone else, you can pass that e-mail on to them. With the e-mail open, choose **Mail | Forward** or click the button of the same name on the toolbar, and type the address of the person(s) to whom you want to send the e-mail in the To: field of the e-mail header.

Composing an E-mail

New Message

To write a new e-mail, choose **Mail | New Message** or click the button of the same name on the toolbar. This displays a new header and a blank message area.

Complete the following fields in the header:

- **To:** The e-mail address of the person you want to send the e-mail to. You can send an e-mail to multiple recipients by separating their addresses with a comma.

- **cc:** An abbreviation for carbon copy. Enter the e-mail address of other recipient(s) you think should see this e-mail as a matter of courtesy or organisational procedure.

- **Subject:** You do not need to enter anything here, but it is good manners to type a word or phrase that describes the contents of your e-mail.

E-mail Header
This contains the sender or recipient address(es), the message subject, and the automatically inserted date and time.

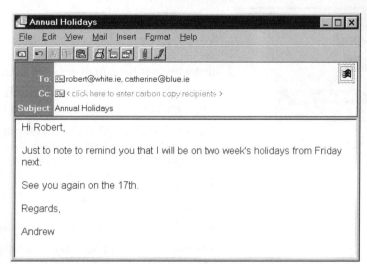

Right:
A sample new e-mail message

Next, type your e-mail text in the message area.

Sending an E-mail

When you have finished typing your message, choose **File | Send Message** or click on the toolbar button called Send and Receive. This sends your e-mail – *but only as far as the Outbox folder*. What happens to your outgoing message then? The answer depends on your type of Internet connection:

- **Permanent Internet Connection:** Microsoft Internet Mail sends the e-mail immediately to your mail server. At the next pre-timed interval (typically every 5 to 30 minutes), the mail server delivers it to its recipient(s).

- **Dial-up ISP Connection:** The e-mail remains in your Outbox folder until you next log in to your ISP and choose the **Mail | Send and Receive** command.

  Microsoft Internet Mail then sends the e-mail to your ISP's mail server, which in turn delivers it to the mail box(es) of its recipient(s).

  You do not need to be connected to an ISP to write (or read) e-mail. It is cheaper to compose your messages *before* dialling your ISP. Internet Mail stores them in the Outbox folder, and then sends them in a single operation the next time that you connect.

'Bounced' E-mail

If you attempt to send an E-mail to a non-existent E-mail address, your mail server will send it back to you. This is called bouncing. It's the electronic version of 'Return to Sender, Address Unknown'.

Attachments and E-mail

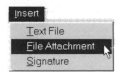

You can use Internet e-mail to send formatted files (such as a Word documents, Excel spreadsheets and PowerPoint presentations). How? By attaching them to an e-mail message, so that wherever the e-mail goes, the attached file goes too.

To attach a file to an e-mail, choose **Insert | File Attachment**, select the file you want to attach, and click **OK**.

Microsoft Internet Mail displays the attached file as an icon in a new window at the bottom of the e-mail message area.

eul305.exe   Pete's second   CLM stuff
(4486K)   test doc   (6).doc (54K)
           (slides).ppt
             (83K)

The e-mail recipient has only to double-click on the icon or name of the attached file for it to open up in the relevant application, for example, in Word, Excel or PowerPoint.

Before sending an attachment to someone, you may want to check that they have the software application needed to open and read that formatted file.

E-mail File Attachment

A file, typically a formatted file such as Word document, that is attached to and sent with an e-mail message.

Saving an E-mail as a File

Microsoft Internet Mail saves all your outgoing messages in the Outbox folder, and all incoming messages in the Inbox folder. Messages are not stored as single files, however, but are combined with all other messages in a single file in the relevant folder.

To save an e-mail as an individual file, choose **File | Save**, select the location you want to save the e-mail to, name the e-mail, and click **Save**.

Deleting E-mails

To delete an e-mail from any Microsoft Internet Mail folder, click the message you want to delete, and choose **File | Delete**. Is the message really message deleted? No. Microsoft Internet Mail moves it to the Deleted Items folder. The message is deleted only when you quit the program. Other e-mail clients may work differently.

Your Signature File

To create a signature file for appending to every message that you write and send, choose **Mail | Options** and click the Signature tab.

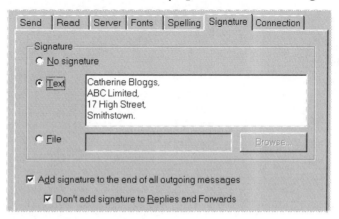

Select the Text option, enter your name and contact details, and click **OK**.

Signature File
A short text file you create for use as a standard appendage at the end of e-mails. Typical contents include full name, occupation or position, phone and fax numbers, and e-mail and web site addresses. Some people also include a favourite quote, company slogan or short personal statement.

Section Summary: So Now You Know

An e-mail is made up of three parts: the *header* (containing the recipient address(es), the message subject, and the automatically inserted date), the *message area* (containing the message text), and the *signature file* (containing such details as your name, job title and postal address).

An *e-mail client* presents your incoming messages, sorts them (the default sort order is by date and time), and indicates which are read, which are unread, and which have a file attached.

The e-mail client also enables you to *reply* to a received e-mail, or *forward* it to others, and to *compose* an e-mail. To compose an e-mail, complete the header, enter the message text, and send it to your mail server.

If you connect via an ISP, you do not need to go online to write e-mail messages. It is cheaper to compose your messages before dialling your ISP, and then send them in a single operation.

You can *attach a formatted file* to an e-mail, and send it with the e-mail to its recipient. You can save e-mails as individual files, and delete e-mails that you no longer need.

Section 7.5: File-sharing and the World Wide Web

In This Section

Beginning with a simple file server on a network, this Section leads you step-by-step to an understanding of that part of the Internet that catches most public attention – the World Wide Web.

You will learn about web servers and web clients, URLs (web addresses), HTML and HTTP, and discover the difference between the Internet and private intranets.

New Activities

At the end of this Section you should be able to:

- Distinguish between one-to-one and one-to-many communications and explain why a file server is an information publisher

- Explain how an inter-network can enable anyone on any attached network to request and view files on a file server

- Describe the URL (web address) standards in the US, France, Germany, the UK, and Ireland

- Explain the twin roles played by HTML in formatting and linking web pages

- Name the file-sharing protocol of the Internet

- Distinguish between intranets and the Internet

New Words

At the end of this Section you should be able to explain the following terms:

• File server	• Web server
• Web browser	• URL (web address)
• Markup language	• Hypertext
• HTTP	• Internet
• World Wide Web	• Intranet

File Servers: Publishing Information

As you learnt in Section 7.1, file-sharing is one of the four main benefits than can come from connecting computers in a network. (Do you remember the other three? That's right: printer-sharing, e-mail and remote access.)

Files that are needed by various people in a department, or by different departments, are usually stored on a single computer called a *file server*. Using the organisation's network, anyone who needs information from files can display it on their personal computer.

E-mail versus File-sharing

One-to-one communication

One-to-many communication

Let's look at the difference between e-mail and file-sharing.

- *E-mail and one-to-one communication:*
  Like telephone calls, e-mail messages are good ways for individuals to hold one-to-one conversations. E-mail has the added advantage (or disadvantage!) of providing both persons with a written record of what was said.

- *File-sharing and one-to-many communication:*
  Company announcements, management directives, and social and recreational news – these are all examples of information that comes from a single, central source, and that needs to be distributed to a wide audience.

A file server is rather like a notice board, newspaper or television station (other instances of one-to-many communication) as it distributes or 'broadcasts' information.

For this reason, you can think of a file server as a computer that *publishes* information to network users.

> **File Server**
>
> *A computer that stores information which can be requested and viewed by users of the network.*

File Servers and Inter-networks

On an inter-network, information published on one file server can be available to users of all attached networks.

Consider a simple inter-network of three LANs, each LAN having a file server. The file servers are named Yellow, Magenta and Purple.

- **Yellow:** This is operated by a university, and holds information on courses offered, lecturer profiles, and a catalogue of books available in the university library.

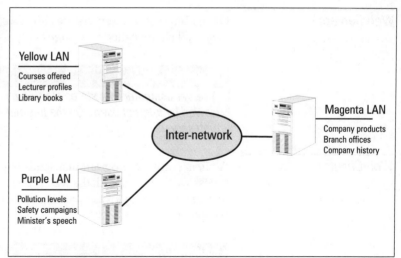

Yellow LAN

Courses offered
Lecturer profiles
Library books

Inter-network

Magenta LAN

Company products
Branch offices
Company history

Purple LAN

Pollution levels
Safety campaigns
Minister's speech

- **Magenta:** This belongs to a company. Its fileserver lists details of the company's products, the addresses of its branch offices, and a company history.

- **Purple:** This is operated by a government agency responsible for protecting the environment. On its fileserver you will find information on pollution levels, safety campaigns, and the text of a recent speech by a government minister.

None of the information on the file servers is confidential, and each LAN administrator is happy to share their files with network users on the other two LANs.

Imagine an inter-network of not three but many hundreds of thousands of LANs, each with file servers, and each willing to share its information with all the others. The picture you have just imagined is the World Wide Web – the file-sharing service on the Internet.

(You will discover the meaning of the term 'web' later on in this Section.)

File Server and Client Software

As with e-mail software, file server software follows the client-server model of computing. The server software stores the information, and handles requests from the clients to access that information.

Web Servers

On the Internet, file servers are called *web servers*, and the files they publish are called *web pages*.

Web Server
A server computer that stores files which can be requested and viewed by Internet users. On the Internet, file servers are called web servers.

Web Clients

A client software program that sends requests to a web server to access web pages is called a *web browser*. Web browsers also manage the display of the requested information on the user's computer.

Web Browser
A client software program that enables a user to request a web page from a web server, and displays the requested page on the user's computer.

Right:
Web browser clients from Microsoft (Internet Explorer) and Netscape (Navigator)

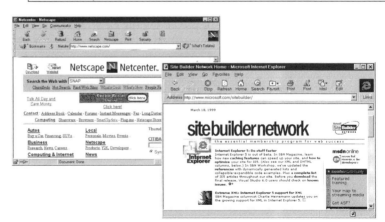

URLs and Web Addresses

To request a web page with your web browser, you need to know two things:

- The name of the *web server* (that is, the file server)
- The name of the *web page* (that is, the file) on the web server

Add these two items together and you get what is called a *web address*. Another, more technical, term for a web address is a URL (Uniform Resource Locator).

URL (web address)
The unique address of a web page. It contains the name of the web server and includes (or implies) the name of the particular web page.

Sample URLs

The best way to learn about web addresses is to look at a few examples and discover why they are written the way they are. Here are the URLs of three American web sites:

www.latimes.com   www.princeton.edu   www.cia.gov

URL Suffixes

As you can see, US web addresses end in the same way as US e-mail addresses: the last part of the addresses indicates the type of organisation.

For a commercial business (such as the *Los Angeles Times* newspaper), the suffix is .com; for an educational institution (such as Princeton University), it's .edu; and for a government agency (such as the CIA), it's .gov.

Here are some Irish (.ie), French (.fr) and German (.de) URLs.

www.irlgov.ie	www.yahoo.fr	www.infoseek.de
www.rte.ie	www.lemonde.fr	www.bmw.de
www.dcu.ie	www.louvre.fr	www.berlinonline.de

As with Irish, French and German e-mail addresses, the suffix indicates only the country. Addresses are not categorised by type.

UK web addresses end in .uk, but they also include a component to identity the organisation type: .co for commercial, .ac for academic, and .gov for government. Here are a few examples:

www.belfasttelegraph.co.uk	www.cam.ac.uk
www.armagh-planetarium.co.uk	www.ox.ac.uk
www.thisislondon.co.uk	www.nio.gov.uk
www.bbc.co.uk	www.scotland.gov.uk
www.chelseafc.co.uk	www.royal.gov.uk

URLs and Files

A URL specifies *two things*: the name of the web server and the name of a particular web page on that server. So: where is the web page name in this URL?

www.dcu.ie

Answer: when you enter just the web server name, the server displays the default web page. This is the front or main page of the web site, and is usually called index.html (or index.htm).

The web address of www.dcu.ie, therefore, is really:

www.dcu.ie/index.html

Here are some other URLs with the name of the default web page included as part of the web address:

www.wit.ie/index.html   www.ucd.ie/index.html   www.ucg.ie/index.html

Notice how a forward slash (/) separates the web page name from the the web server name.

When you to view a web page that is *not* the front or main page, enter a URL that includes the page name. For example:

www.ucg.ie/departments.html   www.refdesk.com/paper.html
www.botany.com/narcissi.html   www.surfnetkids.com/pocahontas.htm

---

URLs and Folders

On web servers, as on other computers, files are organised into folders. In the four examples above, the web pages are in the main folders of the web servers. But web servers can also store pages in sub-folders or sub-sub-folders. Here are some examples of URLs that include sub-folder names.

www.irlgov.ie/aras/hist.htm
www.lastampa.it/sport/datasport/risa.htm
www.fieldandstream.com/bookstore/fishbooks.html
www.ozsports.com.au/cricket/commentary.html

A forward slash (/) separates folder names and page names.

Sometimes a URL contains just the web server and folder name – but not the name of the page within the folder. In such cases, your web browser displays the default web page within *that* folder. Again, this is typically called index.html (or index.htm). For example:

www.tcd.ie/drama/

is really:

www.tcd.ie/drama/index.html

All About HTML

If you read magazines or books about the World Wide Web, sooner or later you will come across the four-letter term HTML. In the next two topics we will explain what the term means, two letters at a time.

Formatting:
The ML in HTML

In the publishing industry before the coming of computers, *marking-up* was something done by designers to pages of plain text that had been produced on typewriters.

Rather than scribbling long instructions such as 'Put this word in italics', 'Make this text 16 point Times' or 'Insert a photograph above this paragraph', they developed a set of shorthand codes to indicate how the text should look when it was printed in its final form.

Examples of such quick codes would be <B> for bold and <I> for italics. A complete set of mark-up codes is called a markup language.

Markup Language

A collection of shorthand codes that indicate how a document should look when it is printed or displayed. It covers such properties as font, font size, alignment, image positioning and page margins.

There are lots of different MLs, each one with different codes. The ML used in web pages is set by an international standards organisation called W3C (World Wide Web Consortium).

Here are three things you need to know about the ML in HTML:

- It's a list of shorthand codes representing formatting instructions. (In fact, it is not really a 'language' at all.)

- Web page designers insert HTML codes in a page to control the page's format and layout.

- Web browsers such as Internet Explorer and Netscape Navigator recognise HTML codes, and display web pages accordingly.

The HT part of HTML stands for *hypertext.* Like text on a printed page, hypertext documents contain words, but they also contain 'hot spots' or *hyperlinks* that, when clicked on, take the reader to further information regarding the selected word or phrase.

You can recognise hyperlinked words as they highlighted in some way, generally by underlining.

Hyperlinks

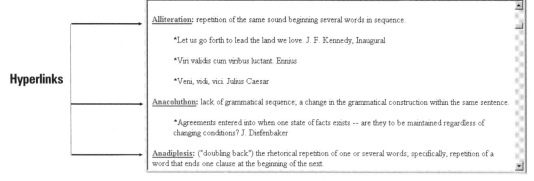

Alliteration: repetition of the same sound beginning several words in sequence.

    *Let us go forth to lead the land we love. J. F. Kennedy, Inaugural

    *Viri validis cum viribus luctant. Ennius

    *Veni, vidi, vici. Julius Caesar

Anacoluthon: lack of grammatical sequence; a change in the grammatical construction within the same sentence.

    *Agreements entered into when one state of facts exists -- are they to be maintained regardless of changing conditions? J. Diefenbaker

Anadiplosis: ("doubling back") the rhetorical repetition of one or several words; specifically, repetition of a word that ends one clause at the beginning of the next.

Above: A sample hypertext document

When you click on a hyperlink, where are you taken? Three destinations are possible:

- **Another Part of the Same Web Page:** It is so much easier to move around long web pages by clicking on hyperlinks rather than by scrolling.

  Long web pages that fill several screens often begin with a hyperlinked table of contents, so that clicking on a particular link takes you to the relevant section of the page. At the bottom of long pages, you will frequently see a hyperlink called <u>Back to Top</u>.

- **Another Web Page on the Same Web Server:** As long web pages can take a while to display, longer documents are more commonly split into series of smaller ones that you can move between by clicking on the relevant hyperlinks.

- **Another Web Page on Another Web Server:** Many web pages offer links to other pages that cover the same subject matter – but which are located in another country or continent.

  For example, the Newslinx web site (www.newslinx.com) consists almost entirely of links to external sites operated by newspapers, television stations and technology magazines.

Right:
Web site consisting almost entirely of links to web pages on external web servers

The term 'World Wide' comes from the Internet's international reach; the term 'Web'' comes from the ability, by clicking hyperlinks, of web users to move within and between pages on the same or different servers.

Hypertext was around long before the Web. The idea was pioneered in the early 1960s by American Ted Nelson as a way of presenting a document that allowed computer users "to read in all the directions (they) wish to pursue...(with) alternate pathways for people who think in different ways".

In 1990, Tim Berners-Lee, a British scientist then working in Switzerland, applied Nelson's concept to the Internet file-sharing by writing the first hypertext-based file server and client software.

Hypertext

A way of linking documents (such as web pages) so that a user can, by selecting links, navigate between different parts of the same document and between different documents.

HTTP: The Web Protocol

TCP/IP, the Internet's network protocol provides the basis for computer-to-computer communications. To provide a useful service that transfers information over the Internet, additional sets of rules (protocols) are needed.

Internet e-mail, for example, is governed by the SMTP protocol, which sets out standards for message addressing and formatting, and for the interaction between e-mail clients and mail servers.

The protocol of the World Wide Web is called HTTP, for Hypertext Transfer Protocol.

HTTP Protocol

The set of rules stating how hypertext files are accessed across the Internet between web servers and web clients.

If you have gotten this far, you are ready for definitions of the Internet and the World Wide Web.

The Internet

A public access, TCP/IP based inter-network that offers e-mail based on the SMTP protocol and file-sharing of HTML documents based on the HTTP protocol.

World Wide Web

The vast array of interlinked documents (and program, video and sound files) that can be accessed over the Internet using the HTTP protocol – typically with a browser, such as Internet Explorer or Netscape Navigator.

Intranets

It looks like a misspelling, but it's not. There are things called intranets (note the lower-case 'i'). An intranet is similar to the Internet in all but two respects:

- **Private Access:** Intranets are run by companies and other organisations as private networks for the benefit of their own personnel. In contrast, the Internet is open to the public to join.

- **Network not Inter-network:** A few intranets may run on inter- networks, but the vast majority run on simple networks, and most of those are humble LANs. The Internet is an inter-network, and a huge one at that.

An intranet takes its name from the fact that it uses the same protocols as the public-access Internet (TCP/IP, SMTP and HTTP), and, therefore, the same type of server and client software can be used as on the Internet.

Section Summary: So Now You Know

A *file server* publishes information on a network or inter-network. It provides a form of *one-to-many communication*: a single, central source broadcasting to a wide, passive audience.

On the Internet, file servers are called *web servers*, the files they publish are called *web pages*, and the clients that request and display the pages are *web browsers*.

A *URL* is the unique web address that contains the name of the web server and includes (or implies) the name of the particular web page. Where no page is specified in a URL, the browser displays the default page, usually *index.html* or *index.htm*.

URLs have at least two parts, separated by a dot (.). In the US, the first part is the organisation's name; the second indicates its type. Commercial sites end in *.com*, educational sites in *.edu* and government sites in *.gov*.

Irish, German and French sites are not categorised by type. Their domain names consist of just the organisation name and a suffix indicating their nationality (*.ie*, *.fr*, and *.de*). In the UK, commercial sites end in *.co.uk*, academic sites in *.ac.uk* and government sites in *.gov.uk*.

A *markup language* is a collection of shorthand codes that indicate how a document should look when it is printed or displayed. *Hypertext* is a way of linking web pages so that a user can, by selecting links, navigate between different parts of the same document and between different documents. Web pages combine formatting with navigation in a set of codes called *HTML*.

The *World Wide Web* is a vast array of interlinked documents and other files that can be accessed over the Internet using the HTTP protocol – typically with a browser, such as Internet Explorer or Netscape Navigator.

An *intranet* is a private-access, TCP/IP-based network or inter-network that uses the SMTP protocol for e-mail and the HTTP protocol for file-sharing. Accordingly, the same type of server and client software that is used on the Internet can be used on intranets.

Section 7.6: Browsing, Downloading and Searching

In This Section

Browsing – also called surfing – the Web can be either a rewarding or an infuriating experience. Sometimes you find treasure troves of useful information. On other occasions, you find only irrelevant, or, worse, distracting material.

This Section takes you through the basics of using the Web, from starting your browser, to copying information and using search techniques to find what you are looking for.

New Activities

At the end of this Section you should be able to:

- Dial-up an ISP and start a web browser
- Enter URLs and click on hyperlinks
- Use the toolbar buttons on a web browser
- Use a web browser's Favourites or Bookmarks facility
- Save web pages on your computer, and selected images and text from web pages
- Download software programs or other files from the Web to your computer
- Locate information on the Web by navigating through the categories of a directory site
- Locate information on the Web by entering words and phrases to search engine and meta search engine sites

New Words

At the end of this Section you should be able to explain the following terms:

- Home page
- Favourites/Bookmarks
- Downloading
- Web directory site
- Web search engine site

Starting Your Web Browser

Microsoft Internet Explorer

Netscape Navigator

Choose **Start | Programs | Microsoft Internet Explorer** (or **Netscape Navigator**), or click on the program's icon. What happens next depends on your type of Net connection:

- **Permanent:** You are ready to explore the Web with your web browser.

- **Dial-up:** You must first log in to your ISP. Your web browser may be set up so that, when you start it, it automatically dials your ISP. Alternatively, you may need to dial your ISP separately.

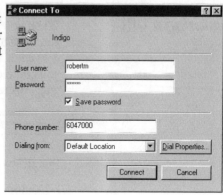

To log in to your ISP, enter your user name and password, and click **Connect**.

Your Browser's Start Page

Typically, a web browser is set up so that it always takes you to a particular web page whenever you start browsing.

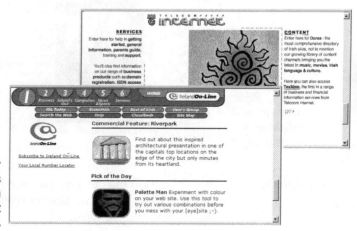

Right:
Home pages of two Irish ISPs, Tinet and IOL

If you obtained your web browser from your ISP, this starting page is probably the front page of the ISP's web site. Such a front page is called a home page.

Home Page
The first or front page of a web site. Typically, it presents a series of hyperlinks that you can follow to view the site's other pages.

Entering a URL

When you have logged in to the Net and started your browser, you have the World Wide Web at your fingertips. Your next step is to enter a URL (web address) of a particular site. For starters, you could enter your company or school Web address. Or try this one, Australia's *Melbourne Age* newspaper at:

Address www.theage.com.au

Practice your Web browsing skills by:

- Double-clicking on hyperlinks to display new web pages
- Scrolling up and down each web page.

Right:
Home page of Melbourne Age newspaper

Browser Toolbar Buttons

Both Microsoft Internet Explorer and Netscape Navigator display a toolbar along the top of their browser window. Here are the buttons you will use most:

- **Back:** Returns you to the previously displayed web page (assuming this is not the first you have browsed).

- **Forward:** Takes you to the next web page (assuming you have previously clicked the Back button).

- **Stop:** Halts the browser's request to the web server. Click this button if a web page is taking a very long time to display.

- **Refresh:** Re-requests the current Web page from the Web server. Click this button if a web page displays incorrectly or incompletely.

- **Print:** Prints the currently displayed web page.

- **Home:** Returns you to your browser's start page (assuming one has been set up).

Internet Explorer Toolbar

Netscape Navigator Toolbar

Favourites and Bookmarks

As you browse the Web, you will find pages that you would like to return to at a later stage. You can tell your browser to store a page's URL by using the Favourites (Internet Explorer) or Bookmarks (Navigator) feature.

- **Adding a web page:** To add the currently displayed web page to your list of stored URLs, click on the Favourites or Bookmarks button on the toolbar. This saves you having to remember (or write down) the page's URL.

- **Revisiting a web page**: To revisit a web page you have previously added to your URL list, click on the Favourites or Bookmarks menu and select the name of the relevant page. This saves you needing to retype the page's URL.

Favourites and Bookmarks store just web page addresses on your computer, and not the actual pages themselves. As your list of stored URLs increases over time, you can create folders to organise them according to subject matter.

> **Favourites/Bookmarks**
> *A list, stored on your Web browser, of web site addresses. This feature removes the need to remember or retype the URLs of frequently-visited web sites.*

Saving from the Web

If you see something on the Web that you like – such as an entire web page, some text, a graphic or a file – can you copy it from the web server to your hard disk? Yes.

Saving a Web Page

To copy the currently displayed web page, choose **File | Save As File**, select the folder you want to save to, name the page, and click **Save**. The web page is still on the web server. You have saved only a *copy* of that page on your computer.

Saving a web page saves:

- The general layout of the page

- Any page background colours

- The text of the page

- The formatting of the text, such as text colours, headings, bold, italics and bullets

Saving a Web page *does not* save any images that the page may contain. You need to save images separately.

Saving an Image

To save an image from the currently displayed Web page, right-click on the image to display a short-cut menu.

Click **Save Picture As**, select the folder you want to save to, name the image, and click **Save**.

Saving Text

To save the text from the currently displayed Web page, place the cursor at the point where you want to start from, click with the mouse, and then and drag down the page until you have selected the text you want.

> I shall begin my case history by telling you about some experiments that tested how accurately people can assign numbers to the magnitudes of various aspects of a stimulus. In the traditional language of psychology these would be called experiments in absolute judgment. Historical accident, however, has decreed that they should have another name. We now call them experiments on the capacity of people to transmit information. Since those experiments would not have been done without the appearance of information theory on the psychological scene, and since the results are analyzed in terms of the concepts of information theory, I shall have to preface my discussion with a few remarks about this theory.

***Above:* Text selected from http://www.well.com/user/smalin/miller.html**

Next, choose **Edit | Copy** to copy the selected text to the clipboard. You can then paste the text to a word processor or other application. Text copied in this way loses any formatting it may have had on the web page.

As you can see, it's not difficult to copy text and images from the Web. But it may not always be legal. If you intend reproducing copyright material that you obtained from the Web, ask for permission first.

Saving a File: Downloading

The Web offers not only information – but software too. Here are just four web sites from which you copy freeware and shareware software, plus test versions (called betas) and demonstration versions (called demos) of commercial software applications:

www.download.com
www.winfiles.com
www.hotfiles.com
www.newapps.com

Saving a copy of a file from the Web is called *downloading*. Files that are available for download are displayed as hyperlinks, so that clicking on the file's name displays the Save As dialog box. Select the folder you want to save the file to, name the file, and click **Save**.

Downloading
Copying a file from a web server to your computer.

Finding Information on the Web

If you are browsing the Web for information on a particular topic, two types of web sites can help you find what you are looking for:

- **Index sites:** These are web sites that catalogue information on the Web according to subject matter.

- **Search engines:** These are web sites that search the Web for occurrences of a specified word or phrase.

Web Directory Sites

A directory web site organises information in an easy-to-follow, top-down structure. They tend to be selective, so that only the better sources of information are listed. Unfortunately, the Web changes so quickly that directory sites may not always be up-to-date.

The original and biggest directory site is www.yahoo.com, at which you can browse information by category, sub-category, and, more often than not, sub-sub-category.

Right:
**Yahoo's index
site categorises
information
according to
subject matter**

Arts & Humanities
Literature, Photography...

News & Media
Full Coverage, Newspapers, TV...

Business & Economy
Companies, Finance, Jobs...

Recreation & Sports
Sports, Travel, Autos, Outdoors...

Computers & Internet
Internet, WWW, Software, Games...

Reference
Libraries, Dictionaries, Quotations...

Education
Universities, K-12, College Entrance...

Regional
Countries, Regions, US States...

Entertainment
Cool Links, Movies, Humor, Music...

Science
Biology, Astronomy, Engineering...

Government
Military, Politics, Law, Taxes...

Social Science
Archaeology, Economics, Languages...

Health
Medicine, Diseases, Drugs, Fitness...

Society & Culture
People, Environment, Religion...

For example, on the www.yahoo.com home page, part of which is shown above, click on the Astronomy link under the Science heading.

Science
Biology, Astronomy, Engineering... →

- Ask an Expert *(8)*
- Astronomers *(82)*
- Astronomical Calendars *(17)*
- Astronomy Humor@
- Astrophotography *(52)*
- Astrophysics *(207)* NEW!
- Comets, Meteors, and Asteroids@
- Companies@
- Conferences@
- Deep Sky *(7)*
- Eclipses@
- Education *(180)*
- Extrasolar Planets *(16)*
- FITS (Flexible Image Transport System) *(4)*
- Galaxies *(14)*
- History *(21)*

- Magazines *(21)*
- Newsletters *(12)*
- Northern Lights@
- Organizations *(249)*
- Pictures *(87)*
- Planetaria *(62)*
- Radio Astronomy *(48)*
- Research *(254)*
- Scientific Constants@
- SETI (Search for Extraterrestrial Intelligence)@
- Software *(13)*
- Solar System *(612)* NEW!
- Space@
- Stellar Cartography *(10)*
- Telescopes *(36)*
- Web Directories *(20)*

This displays a page of astronomy sub-categories, part of which is shown above. Click on the link named Planetaria, to view yet another page. This one lists the web sites of some fifty planetaria, including Armagh (at www.armagh-planetarium.co.uk).

- Pictures *(87)*
- Planetaria *(62)*
- Radio Astronomy *(48)* →

- Adler Planetarium & Astronomy Museum - interprets the exploration of the Universe for the broadest possible audience and hosts one of the finest collections of early astronomical instruments in the world.
- Albert Einstein Planetarium - National Air and Space Museum - 70-foot diameter domed planetarium.
- Allentown School District Planetarium
- Armagh Planetarium (United Kingdom)
- Astronaut Memorial Planetarium and Observatory - Brevard Community College
- Canberra Planetarium & Observatory (Australia)
- Cernan Earth and Space Center - features public and group planetarium shows and a space hall with exhibits on space exploration and astronomy.
- Christa McAuliffe Planetarium
- Cook Center - a 60-foot domed planetarium and an observatory containing a 14-inch Celestron computer operated telescope.
- Drake Planetarium - features online educational activities, gift shop, and information about the Cincinnati facility.
- Dreyfuss Planetarium - Newark Museum - utilizes the latest technologies in an elegant and intimate atmosphere. Educational and entertaining planetarium programs are offered to both

This simple exercise demonstrates both the range and depth of information available on the Web – and the usefulness of index sites such as Yahoo. A version of Yahoo, that catalogues UK and Irish web sites, is www.yahoo.co.uk. Another good directory site is www.about.com.

Three Irish directory sites are:

www.niceone.com
doras.tinet.ie/doras
www.browseireland.com

Most directory sites also offer a search engine facility.

> ### Web Directory Site
>
> *A web site that lists and categorises other sites on the Web according to their subject matter. Typically, it offers several hierarchical layers, with a listing of web site addresses at its lowest level.*

Web Search Engines

A search engine allows you to enter a word or phrase, searches for instances of it, and then displays ('returns') a list of web sites that match your entered word or phrase, with a summary of each. You can then click on the one that seems most appropriate to you.

Search engines *do not* search the entire Web, but their own smaller, regularly-updated list of web sites, which typically accounts for about 10–15% of the total number of sites on the Web.

Right:
A search
on the
word 'ECDL' at
www.altavista.com
returns 2987
matching
web pages

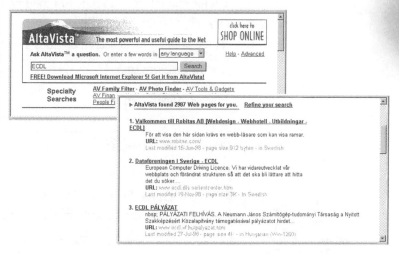

Search engines frequently find individual pages from web sites that have nothing to do with what you are looking for. You can often discover unexpected gems of information this way – but be prepared to wade through a lot of irrelevant information too!

Your Browser's Search Button

The Search button on your web browser's toolbar typically takes you to one particular search engine site. But you should explore the various alternatives and choose the search engine that best suits your needs.

Here are some of the better search engine web sites:

www.altavista.com   www.infoseek.com
www.hotbot.com   www.lycos.com
www.webcrawler.com   www.mckinley.com

The following Irish sites offer a search engine:

www.niceone.com
www.iesearch.ie

Web Search Engine Site

A web site that enables users to search for material on the Web by entering a word or phrase. The search engine returns a list of sites where the specified word(s) were found.

Meta Search Engines

A meta search engine is a search engine that searches search engines. Just enter your word or phrase and the meta search engine submits it to a range of individual search engines, and returns the matching results.

Three popular meta search engines are:

www.askjeeves.com
www.dogpile.com
www.mamma.com

Right:
The result of entering the word 'Waterford' in www.askjeeves.com.

ASK! Where is/are Waterford, Ireland ▾ ?

ASK! 8 matches by Yahoo! Waterford Gardens - Saddle River, NJ ▾

ASK! 9 matches by WebCrawler The Charter Township of Waterford, Michigan ▾

ASK! 8 matches by AltaVista Voyager Internet Cafe Cybercafe Waterford City Waterford Ireland ▾

ASK! 10 matches by InfoSeek hotels in Waterford, Ireland, Eire - Waterford Castle, Waterford, Ireland ▾

ASK! 6 matches by Lycos MOVIE FINDER: MJR WATERFORD CINEMA 11 ▾

A few last words of advice about searching for information on the Web:

- The Web may not be the best place to find certain information. While it abounds with computer-related subjects, it is not so good for historical information.

- Information on the Web is published by individual users with varying degrees of experience and knowledge. Do not treat information you read on the Web as unfailingly accurate.

Section Summary: So Now You Know

A web browser typically takes you to a particular web page whenever you start the program. If you obtained your web browser from your ISP, the starting page is probably the *home page* of the ISP's web site.

Along the top of the web browser window is a *toolbar* that gives you one-click access to commonly-used browsing actions such as moving back and forwards, and halting and repeating web page requests.

You can use your web browser's *Favourites* or *Bookmarks* feature to store URLs, so that you can revisit them later without needing to remember or retype their addresses.

Your browser enables you to *save* web pages on your computer, or selected images and text from web pages. You can also download *files* such as software applications from the Web to your computer.

A *web directory site*, which categorises other web sites by subject matter, offers one method of locating material on the Web. An alternative is to enter a word or phrase to a *search engine*, which then returns a list of sites containing the word or phrase.